Writing Responsibly

Communities in Conversation

Loyola University Chicago

General Editor: Victoria Anderson

Second Edition

FOUNTAINHEAD
PRESS

Our "green" initiatives include:

Electronic Products
We deliver products in non-paper form whenever possible. This includes pdf down-loadables, flash drives, & CDs.

X Electronic Samples
We use Xample, a new electronic sampling system. Instructor samples are sent via a personalized web page that links to pdf downloads.

FSC Certified Printers
All of our printers are certified by the Forest Service Council which promotes environ-
FSC mentally and socially responsible management of the world's forests. This program allows consumer groups, individual consumers, and businesses to work together hand-in-hand to promote responsible use of the world's forests as a renewable and sustainable resource.

Recycled Paper
Most of our products are printed on a minimum of 30% post-consumer waste recycled paper.

Support of Green Causes
When we do print, we donate a portion of our revenue to green causes. Listed below are a few of the organizations that have received donations from Fountainhead Press. We welcome your feedback and suggestions for contributions, as we are always search-ing for worthy initiatives.
Rainforest 2 Reef
Environmental Working Group

For information, please call or write:
1-800-586-0330 Fountainhead Press Southlake, TX. 76092

Web site: www.fountainheadpress.com
Email: customerservice@fountainheadpress.com

ISBN 978-1-59871-267-4

Second Edition

Printed in the United States of America

TABLE OF CONTENTS

V.   Language

VI.   Challenges

I

WRITING RESPONSIBLY

WRITING RESPONSIBLY

◈

F. Scott Fitzgerald once quipped that "the test of a first-rate intelligence is the ability to hold two opposed ideas in mind at the same time and still retain the ability to function" (41). As an author, Fitzgerald understood that the ability to navigate contradictory viewpoints – to summarize, analyze, synthesize, and develop arguments about a variety of texts – is an essential part of the manner in which writing asks us to interact with a topic from multiple perspectives. As you enter the first phase of your higher education, you'll need to practice and sharpen those analytical and argumentative writing skills you have already developed and begin to understand their importance in dealing with diverse points of view both in and outside the classroom

The single most misleading myth about writing is that it is an inherent skill: that some have it, others don't, and while the former pursue a life of novel-writing, letters, and memoirs, the rest of us are left with nothing but text messages and tweets of 140 characters or less. Yes, writing comes more intuitively to some students, but it is also a process with identifiable patterns, elements, and stages. The four genres of writing mentioned above – **summary, analysis, synthesis, and researched argument** – can all be broken down into manageable steps, and with practice, those steps help to create a better and more persuasive piece of writing. In your high school classes, you no doubt studied summary, analysis, synthesis, and argumentation to some degree, but your college classes (and your life beyond that) will require more complexity and sophistication than have been asked of your writing in the past. A thorough understanding of the writing process will allow you to expand your writing capabilities on multiple fronts – from the topics you discuss to the complexity with which you approach them.

And as the range of your writing increases, so will the breadth of what you study. In college, the definition of the term "text" expands exponentially. In addition to the works of classic literature, poetry, history, and the heavy textbooks you are probably accustomed to, your courses at Loyola University Chicago will ask you to analyze graphic novels, newspaper articles, advertisements, political campaigns, speeches, film, music, art, and research studies in psychology, economics, mathematics, science, and medicine. University courses view nearly any document that conveys information or a position about a topic as having intellectual and sociological value, and college-level writing asks you to adeptly compose and respond to this diverse array of texts.

This writing guide is designed to help you anticipate and navigate the sophistication and diversity of writing you will engage in at Loyola. It is organized around the four forms we have already briefly discussed – summary, analysis, synthesis, and argument – and encourages you to view these elements as foundations upon which you can build and develop the skills you already possess. We view college writing as a contribution to ongoing academic discussions; the topics and texts you will study belong to a long history of conversation and debate among scholars, intellectuals, and professionals, and the writing techniques you hone here will allow you to enter those conversations with confidence and complexity.

Summary

As you probably already know, a summary is a sentence, paragraph, or paper that gives an overview of another text. A summary is significantly shorter than its source text, but it still covers the source text's main ideas. The idea behind a summary is that it allows a reader to understand the point or "gist" of the source text without actually reading it.

According to linguists and educators, summary writing is a sophisticated cognitive task. First of all, it demands that the writer reads and fully understands the source text. Then, it requires the writer to select information based on its importance in the source text, to condense details by incorporating them into more general statements, and to integrate all of the selected, condensed materials into an organized structure. In other words, summary writing is more than just deleting insignificant material from the source text; it transforms the source text's details and ideas into a new, more condensed piece (Hidi and Anderson). Research has also shown that knowing how to summarize is crucial for students. Not only is summary writing a common assignment at all levels of education, but it also improves reading comprehension, content-area learning, and information retention (Maclellan; Hidi and Anderson 473; Yu 116-7).

No doubt you have already written a summary at some point in your schooling, and the situations in which you will need to write a summary will only become more frequent at the university level. Across disciplines, university instructors assign summaries in many ways. In class, they might ask for an "overview" of a reading or the "point" of a particular argument. They might require that you write a summary of a text as an introduction to a paper that **analyzes** that text or **synthesizes** it with another text. Also, summary questions often appear on final exams because they not only effectively test reading comprehension but they also require students to identify and prioritize important ideas within a reading. Furthermore, as you progress to upper-division classes, you will be asked to write **research papers** in which you will want to summarize the work of another scholar in order to use it as evidence. In that case, a summary of another person's research will function as part of your own argument.

The Basics of Summary Writing

Summaries share certain basic characteristics or *conventions*. Most importantly, a summary re-presents or reproduces the content of a source text. A summary is always written in the writer's own words and is shorter than the source text. The following summary of Malcolm X's "A Homemade Education" was written by student Teyana Morgan and conforms to these conventions of summary writing:

> *In Malcolm X's "A Homemade Education," he details how creating a self-educational system while in prison allowed him to gain a love for education and new knowledge. While in prison, he explains how he felt incapable of expressing his thoughts and emotions through writing due to his limited vocabulary. This limitation compelled Malcolm X to begin teaching himself. He tells how after teaching himself how to read and write, he began spending a vast amount of time consumed in his newfound literature. Malcolm X describes how studying mostly history and philosophical readings gave him fresh feelings about the knowledge and action of the black race in America. In closing he tells how his homemade education system was more valuable than if he had chosen or had the fate of being anywhere else. Malcolm X gained a freedom in the captivity of prison through immersing himself in new knowledge.*

Notice how this summary of "A Homemade Education" demonstrates some of the key characteristics of a well-written summary. To begin with, it does not include any of the student writer's ideas; it focuses on the material in "A Homemade Education." In addition, it is composed entirely in the writer's own words; none of the phrases or sentence structures is taken from Malcolm X's piece. Also, it is much shorter than the source text; Malcolm X's essay is forty-four paragraphs long whereas the summary is only around 150 words. Note as well that the student's summary is a well-constructed paragraph: it contains a topic sentence, in this case, the paragraph's first sentence, that identifies the main idea of "A Homemade Education" and supporting sentences that cover the source text's main points.

The first step in writing a strong summary is knowing when a summary is being asked for by an assignment. The following are essay prompts from various disciplines that ask for some kind of summary:

- What is Vaida's opinion about the importance of water cluster mediated atmospheric chemistry?

- Give an overview of Hanson's and Mohn's discussion on educational assessment trends.

- Summarize Piaget's stages of cognitive development.

- What is Caroline Bird's argument concerning college education?

When looking for key words or phrases that indicate that a prompt is asking for a summary, look for instructions that somehow ask you to re-state what you read in a source. You might see words like "overview," "point," "identify," or "describe." These words, and words like them, ask you to re-encapsulate, but not interpret or analyze, what is in a source text. When this happens, you should examine the prompt more carefully to see if you are being asked to summarize a source. Be aware, too, that sometimes an instructor will ask for a summary and then ask for an interpretation in the same prompt; summaries are frequently used as introductions to arguments and response essays.

In order to write a strong, efficient summary, you will need to understand your source text hierarchically. In other words, you will need to identify the text's main idea, or the idea that encapsulates all the other ideas in the text. Then, you will need to prioritize the main points that support or explain the main idea, understanding that all of the details in the text can be generalized into these main points. In source texts that are already well structured by the author, this task will be relatively easy. However, not all source texts are well organized; often, you will need to analyze the text and infer the hierarchy of ideas. It might help for you to think of a source text in terms of a tree diagram like the one below. Each level encapsulates the levels that are underneath it.

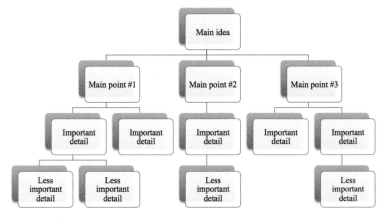

Thinking about a text in this way and ordering information according to importance will help you with many aspects of summary writing. Most importantly, it will help you to eliminate unnecessary information from your summary, and it will help you group details under more general main points. For example, in the summary above, the writer does not, like Malcolm X, list the books from the prison library that he checked out and read, nor does she tell us exactly what information these books contained. These are details that are generalized in the statement that Malcolm X studied "history and philosophical readings."

Although brevity is a defining feature of a summary, different assignments require different lengths for summaries. Again, thinking of your source text in terms of a tree diagram can help you decide how much information to include in your summary. If you are asked for a single-sentence summary, you will only want to include the first, broadest level of the diagram, the source text's main idea. If you are asked to write a paragraph-length summary (and this is the most common kind of summary), you will probably include only the first two levels of the diagram, the source's main ideas and main points. Although it is rare, you might be asked to summarize a text over several pages; in this case, you might (if there are not too many main points to cover) include the third level of information, some important details.

As you compose your summary, you should be aware that conventions of strong academic writing are still relevant. In other words, your paragraphs should be well organized with a main idea and corresponding topic sentence. Fortunately, your tree chart will provide you with a ready-made structure. For paragraph-length summaries, simply turn the main idea identified in your chart into a topic sentence, and use the main points to fill in the paragraph. If your summary is longer than a single paragraph, decide how to logically divide the main points into several paragraphs, each with its own topic sentence. Usually, you will still state the main idea of the source text at the beginning of the first paragraph.

As we have discussed, a lot of cognitive work goes into writing a strong summary. When students do not fully understand how to write a summary or do not want to do the cognitive work, they often make two crucial mistakes. The first should be obvious from the discussion above: it is the mistake of including too much detail or unimportant information. The second is what is called "patchwriting" or "copy-delete" summarizing. This happens when students copy chunks of the source text, possibly changing some grammar or vocabulary, and stitch these chunks into a single paragraph (Howard 264; Maclellan). Not only does patchwriting fail to accomplish the goals of summarizing, but also, when quotation marks are not used to indicate original phrasing and word choice, it is a form of plagiarism. Below is a summary that exemplifies patchwriting:

> *While Malcolm X was in prison, he was jealous of Bimbi and other inmates who could take charge of conversations. He decided to get hold of a dictionary. He copied the first page and read it aloud to himself over and over again. Once his word-base broadened, Malcolm X checked out books from the prison library and joined weekly debates between inmate teams. He loved to read so much that he read at night in his prison cell in the glow from the hallway. Not even Elijah Muhammad could have guessed what a new world opened up to Malcolm X as he learned that the collective white man had acted like the devil by oppressing black people. When people asked Malcolm X where he went to college, he said that prison enabled him to study more than college where there are too many distractions.*

If you refer back to Malcolm X's essay, you will see that the writer of this summary has copied much phrasing and vocabulary, not to mention sentence structure, from the source text. In addition, this summary does not generalize details but instead includes an unbalanced sampling of them (with a few misreadings) from different parts of "A Homemade Education." This summary does not show that the writer has understood the source text, processed and prioritized the information in it, and reproduced it in an organized way for her readers.

Strategies for Writing Strong Summaries

It is important to reflect the source text's genre in your summary. If you don't, your reader will not get a full understanding of your source text. Your job as the summary writer is to give your reader an understanding of not only the content of the source text but also the source text's form – its purpose and structure. For example, if you summarized Malcolm X's essay, which is a narrative, by emphasizing his argument about the "whitening" of history, you would not be giving your readers an accurate idea of what the source text is. "A Homemade Education" tells the story of Malcolm X's education, and it is important that your summary offers a shortened, condensed version of that story, not an analysis of his ideas or an outline of his underlying argument.

Although, in your university classes, you will encounter and be asked to summarize many different kinds of source texts, three of the most common genres you will see are narrative, expository, and argument. These three genres not only have very different structures, but the hierarchies of ideas are different as well. In a source text that is an argument, the main idea is – predictably – the author's thesis or position. Usually, the main points are the author's major reasons that support his or her thesis. Concrete evidence makes up the details that correspond to the author's major reasons. A tree diagram for an argument, then, would look something like this:

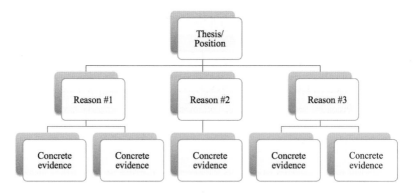

Here, the tree diagram reflects the structure of an argument, which is the source text's genre. A tree diagram for another genre would likely look very different. For example, if we constructed a tree diagram for a narrative, the main idea would not be the thesis of an argument, but a statement of the main action in the narrative. The second level of the diagram, the main points, would be the main plot points in the narrative. On the other hand, an expository text, which is a text that explains something and the purpose of which is to inform the reader, would have as its main idea an overview of the information provided in the source text and more specific statements of fact as the main points. Understanding a source text hierarchically means understanding what kind of hierarchy is in place. That way, your summary will accurately represent the source text's content and form.

At the beginning of this section, you read a summary of a narrative, Malcolm X's "A Homemade Education." Below are a few more examples. Consider, first, this summary of an argument, Caroline Bird's "The Case Against College," which was written by a student in a first-year composition course. As with the other summaries you have read in this section, the first sentence states the main idea of the source text, in this case, the source text's thesis or position, and the following sentences explain the source text's main points, in this case, the argument that supports the thesis:

> *Evaluating higher education in "The Case Against College," Caroline Bird questions the effectiveness of such an institution. She argues that the expectations of the value of college may not actually be assessed in college. For example, some expectations people have of what they will derive from college are supposed to be acquired during earlier stages in life. Caroline Bird also discusses how education can be learned elsewhere, such as through books or television, and does not need to be learned in a school setting. Another point that Bird asserts in her argument is that putting the weight of the future of mankind on university students is quite unrealistic. She explains that most students do not know or are too young to have determined their wants for the future. Caroline Bird closes by suggesting that college be closely critiqued by potential students for its possible worth before they make the decision to attend (Morgan).*

Following the structure of Bird's own argument, this student begins and closes by stating Bird's position. In the middle of the paragraph, she lists some of the main reasons that Bird uses to justify her position.

The next example is a summary written of an expository text, "On the Breeds of Cattle – Historic and Current Classifications." Notice the differences between this summary and those of "A Homemade Education" and "The Case Against College":

> *In "On the Breeds of Cattle – Historic and Current Classifications," the authors list, sort, and discuss the various systems used to classify cattle breeds over the last several hundred years. In doing so, they report the difficulties scientists have faced in classifying cattle because of the long, largely undocumented history of cross-breeding. However, they also detail the reasons why classifying cattle is important and why many scientists over the years have attempted to establish a classification system. According to this article, classification systems of the past were based on head/ horn shape and size, coat color, or geographic origin. More modern classification systems have been founded upon modern scientific advances; these systems use biochemical traits – often in conjunction with previous systems – to classify cattle. The most recent developments in cattle classification are DNA-based; the article implies that scientists believe that the DNA-based classification system is the most accurate and useful.*

You can see that, in this summary, the writer focuses on what information is provided by the source text and how that information is presented. The topic sentence, which states the source text's main idea, gives an overview of the information covered in the source. The following sentences break that information down into parts; these sentences discuss exactly how the authors list, sort, and discuss cattle classification systems. Notice that, unlike a summary of an argument, which reproduces the logical framework of an argument, a summary of an expository text reports a set of facts.

Once you have an idea of *what* you want to say in your summary – that is, once you have identified the main idea and main points – you will move on to thinking about *how* you want to say it. There are specific writing strategies, or composition "moves," that effective summary writers use in order to indicate to their readers that the piece they are reading is a summary. Below are some of the common moves summary writers make in their summaries:

- They introduce a written summary by orienting their readers to the author and title of the source text. Here are two different ways of introducing the source text at the beginning of a summary:

  a. "In Malcolm X's 'A Homemade Education,' he tells the story . . ."

  b. "Malcolm X's 'A Homemade Education' tells the story of . . ."

- They refer often to their source as a way of reminding their readers that the information is coming from a source text. Notice below how the writer intentionally refers back to the source text in the phrases, "the narrative" and "Malcolm X":

  a. "The narrative begins by describing his frustration."

  b. "Malcolm X details the many books he encountered in prison."

- They use verbs that are appropriate to the genre of the source text. Below are examples and lists of verbs that correspond to narrative, expository, and argument source texts:

  a. Narrative

     - Example: "Malcolm X *recounts* his experiences learning to read and write."

     - Verbs: *recounts, tells, narrates, describes, remembers*

  b. Expository

     - Example: "The authors *detail* the many classification systems used over the last 100 years."

     - Verbs: *explains, lists, reports, expands upon, details*

  c. Argument

     - Example: "Bird *defends* her position by providing specific examples as evidence."

     - Verbs: *asserts, argues, affirms, reasons, defends, justifies*

To see how these moves work to produce a coherent, clear summary, see the examples provided earlier in this section.

Other Kinds of Summaries

Before concluding, there are a few variations on the standard form of summary, which you should know about. The first is the directed summary, which is a summary of a particular aspect of a text rather than the whole text (Strahan, Moore, and Heumann 19-20). So, for example, in a literature class, you might be asked to summarize Jay Gatsby's long romance with Daisy Buchanan in *The Great Gatsby* instead of summarizing the entire novel. Or, on a psychology exam, you might be asked to summarize the censoring function of the conscious mind rather than the entire text of Freud's *Interpretation of Dreams*. A directed summary is written just like a standard summary, but the hierarchy of main ideas and main points is more specific. This is why it is important to carefully read the prompt or question before you begin writing your summary.

Another variation on the standard form of summary is the annotated bibliography entry. Typically, an annotated bibliography is formatted like a normal bibliography, but it also includes a brief summary-like entry, or annotation, after each source's information. Below is an excerpt from an annotated bibliography:

> Bird, Caroline. "The Case Against College." *Writing Responsibly: Communities in Conversation.* Southlake, TX: Fountainhead Press, 2012. 80-84. Print.
>
> *In "The Case Against College," Caroline Bird argues that potential college students should consider options other than attending college. She provides many reasons that suggest that college has been overvalued in American culture. While Bird's argument is compelling, much of her evidence is anecdotal and undermines the strength of her position. However, the essay is helpful in that it gathers many of the most reasonable arguments offered against attending college. For my paper, which is an academic essay on why attending college is the best option for high school seniors, I can use Bird's essay when constructing my counterarguments.*

What you include in an annotation always depends on what your instructor asks for. However, usually, the annotation includes at least one, but sometimes all three, of the following elements:

1. A one- to two-sentence summary of the source text;

2. An evaluation of the credibility or general usefulness of the source text and/or how it compares to other sources on the list; and/or,

3. A reflection on the source as to its relevance to or usefulness for your specific project (Bisignani and Brizee).

While, technically speaking, an annotated bibliography entry is not a summary, it almost always includes a summary of the source text. As you can see in the example above, the annotation opens with a summary of Caroline Bird's essay and then continues on to evaluate it and reflect on its usefulness.

Analysis

Simply put, analysis is a detailed examination and investigation of the elements of a text, often a piece of writing, literature, art, film, or music. As students, you engage in analysis in nearly every facet of your daily academic lives: in classroom discussions about economic policy, literary theory, or history; in biology labs; in law practicums or in pre-med study groups. Analysis occurs in the form of engaged study, discussion, and dissection that leads to a deep understanding of a subject and its importance, effects, and implications for the future.

In the previous section, we discussed how an effective **summary** condenses a text to its core elements and arguments and re-presents them in a way that is concise and clear. While summarizing, writers need to search for the main points that comprise a text and then separate important details that support these core points from the other secondary elements in the text. In a way, the process of summarizing a text involves analysis: determining the main arguments of a text and prioritizing the evidence and detail that an author gives in support of these points requires a writer to think critically about which elements are most important to a novel, film, essay, or work of art. More than a rote memorization of facts, analysis is the ability to critically evaluate a work and come to a conclusion about it.

As we've said, analysis is a central part of a student's academic work, and it is a requirement in essays, discussions, and assignments in most (if not all) classes you will take in college. It is also important to grasp that analysis can be applied to any imaginable text. You are probably accustomed to being asked to analyze written stories in your high school English classes, but consider how in film studies courses, students analyze the themes, lighting, plot, shot construction, cinematography, and dozens of other components of a movie. In history courses, professors ask students to evaluate the factors that lead to and surround an event and perhaps to analyze the outcomes or the solutions proposed by historical figures. In nursing and pre-med courses, the patients are the texts, and the students determine the best course of treatment using facts or inferences gleaned from a patient's condition and the student's own knowledge of medical treatment. Advertisements, cartoons, news stories, business meetings, works of music, or political speeches are all texts that you can analyze.

While analysis relies on some of the same skills that you use when summarizing, remember that analysis extends beyond summarization. Good analysis implicitly *makes an argument* about the text – for example, its subject matter, its format, its rhetorical strategies, its origin – and so the most effective analyses do not simply restate what the original text says. A compelling piece of analysis examines specific elements of a text and then evaluates them for meaning or effectiveness. The following example of analysis is a paragraph drawn from an actual student's response to Alan Moore's graphic novel *Watchmen*. In it, this student analyzes the nature of the character Rorschach:

> *The character Rorschach elicits varied, yet strong, responses from readers. Throughout the novel, Rorschach reacts to events with an absolute, black-and-white manner. He is guided by a conservative, fundamental set of morals from which he never wavers. For example, when Rorschach and Nite Owl II learn about Veidt's scheme, and the deceit and murder involved, Rorschach reacts by saying, "No. Not even in the face of Armageddon. Never Compromise" (20). Although Veidt argues he is acting for the greater good, Rorschach cannot see past the use of Veidt's amoral means to an end. This scene in particular is an instance where the reader identifies with Rorschach; we are just as surprised and disgusted at the turn of events as he is, and therefore, we identify with him. Rorschach is perhaps attractive to the reader because he is a concrete viewpoint in a story where right and wrong are hazy.*

This student's analysis is effective for a number of reasons. To start, the student begins with a claim about the role of the character Rorschach in *Watchmen*, suggesting that he is an uncompromising character with a clear moral code (that he "reacts to events with an absolute, black-and-white manner"). Then, the student supports that claim with a quote from the text as evidence of how Rorschach responds to a complex situation with unwavering certainty. The last portion of the paragraph is the most significant; in it, the student contends that the Rorschach character, despite holding some extreme views, is nonetheless appealing to the reader because his "concrete viewpoint" represents moral certitude in a story where good and bad always seem to be in flux. This student's analysis is stylish and perceptive and attempts to draw larger conclusions about the text from the smaller element being analyzed in this particular paragraph.

Approaching Analysis Assignments

Instructors approach analysis in a variety of ways. While many will ask you to analyze the work and ideas of others, you also will be asked to turn the lens of analysis back on yourself and your own work. In the following sample assignment, drawn from an actual course, the instructor asks students to analyze the impact of their disciplinary background on a difficult or controversial issue.

> **Assignment:** *This project asks you to analyze an issue of public importance from the context of your disciplinary background or interests. The project will have two parts, detailed below:*
>
> *You will choose a single issue of public significance and produce an analysis of the issue, its current stakes, and its importance or future implications. For example, you might explore how the current public debate about the balance between government spending and the need to reduce the deficits affects public employees in Chicago. Or, you might examine issues of environmental awareness, public health, or union funding. Whichever issue you choose, you need to analyze its parameters, stakes, and implications.*
>
> *You will then turn to an analysis of your topic from the perspective of your disciplinary field (if you have not declared a major, simply pick a subject area that you might like to study in the future). What does your field of study/interest have to contribute to the larger public debate about the issue? Are there specific concerns for your field in regards to this topic? Are there certain elements, theories, or practices from your field that will help illuminate the issue or more effectively work toward a solution?*

Through the assignment, the instructor is encouraging students to draw numerous connections between their class and a real-world issue and between that issue and their disciplinary background. Requiring a disciplinary reflection means the student must analyze their own work and begin to think critically about the ways in which their individual studies will intersect with the world outside the classroom. Below is a brief excerpt from a student response to this assignment:

> *The English discipline plays a huge role in the issue of immigration and immigration laws, not only when it comes to the immigrants and aspiring US citizens, but the people who are trying to change and rectify this issue through rhetoric, argumentation, and persuasion. These are all skills learned in the English discipline and can be used when trying to sway a certain group a certain way. Many news stations such as FOX News and MSNBC constantly talk about the issue of immigration and what it means to this country, but both networks have very different viewpoints when it comes to this issue.*

This student is attempting to connect the discipline of English to the issue of immigration reform. In this paragraph, she notes that English is important not only because literacy and language fluency is a central component of the immigration debate, but also because the skills that English students practice are needed to navigate the public debate over immigration reform. Processing the arguments made in different outlets – from FoxNews, MSNBC, and many places elsewhere – and determining their persuasiveness requires critical thinking. In essence, she is suggesting that navigating a public debate demands analysis skills. In connecting the skills of English majors to a contemporary public controversy, this student uses the same skills of analysis that she suggests the discipline of English provides.

A Methodology for Analysis

Though there are many ways to approach analysis – and we encourage you to develop your own, specific to your preferences, the context of your writing, and your discipline – here are a few critical steps to get started with analysis:

1. **Begin with the text.** Strong analysis begins by being exceptionally familiar with the text. You can't analyze a text successfully unless you have identified its main points and clarified for yourself any moments of confusion. For example, are there any vocabulary terms that you do not understand? Look them up. Are there any references to outside events and information that you do not know – for example, historical figures or movements? Again, research these things until you are comfortable with the ins-and-outs of the text. Not only

will this research make you more familiar with the text, it will give you more insightful things to say in your analysis and ensure your credibility as an informed authority on the topic.

2. **Start small.** Because analysis requires that you define and defend an arguable claim, the best way to find this claim is by using the text(s). Think of yourself as a lawyer in a courtroom, and the text is your best and most persuasive piece of evidence! Identify the pieces of the text(s) you are interested in and then ask yourself these questions: What do these things tell me? What is the effect these pieces of evidence have on the text overall, or in comparison to other texts, or on how I understand the subject matter? Are there any pieces of evidence available that contradict each other or my assumptions?

   Notice that we are advocating that you start with your evidence and only then build a claim. You are more likely to achieve a defendable claim when you *work from* the text than if you *look for* specific moments to defend a pre-existing assumption. Why? Because you end up plundering the text for only those facts or moments that support your idea, which makes it easy to overlook evidence that doesn't fit or may even overrule your claim.

3. **Define your claim.** Analytical claims can be as big as the whole thesis for a dissertation or as small as a simple, conversational declarative sentence like, "Brian Urlacher is the most consistent middle linebacker in the NFL." Regardless of whether they require ten pages or ten seconds to defend, claims need to be **specific**. Spend time identifying just what you want to argue and how. In the same way that summary requires that you to make clear all the parameters of another person's argument, analysis requires that you make clear all the parameters of your own argument.

   Be incredibly intentional with your word choice; generalizations always hurt an argument and make it harder for your reader to anticipate the steps you will take to defend your claim. For example, in the statement made above, it matters whether the writer argues that Brian Urlacher is the *best* middle linebacker or the *most consistent*. A reader can anticipate how the writer will defend the claim that Urlacher is the "most consistent" middle linebacker by using statistics and comparisons with other middle linebackers in the NFL. It would be much harder to anticipate, and to argue, that he is simply the "best" without relying too much on opinion. If you are thoughtful about the words you choose to define your claim, it should provide you with a blueprint for the rest of your analysis.

4. **Quote, summarize, and paraphrase selectively to guide your interpretation.** As we mentioned above, the text is your best piece of evidence. Use it carefully and constructively to advance your claim. Remember, though, that evidence – particularly quotations – don't speak for themselves; your analysis should indicate *how* you want your reader to understand the textual evidence. It is your responsibility as a writer to drive the conversation with your insights. Phrases such as "this demonstrates," "which results in," or "revealing that" can provide helpful clues to your reader and will force you to make strong choices about how the evidence should be interpreted.

5. **Work outward.** The most effective pieces of analysis consider a range of implications beyond the specific text being analyzed. It's not enough to simply make a claim when analyzing for the sake of making a claim; your audience should understand why your claim matters, and you should be to answer the age-old question, "So what?" There are a number of different ways to work outward when analyzing. In the immigration and disciplinary reflection example we looked at before, the student considers the impact of the field of English on the public debate over immigration. While her narrow conclusion is that the skills of analysis taught in an English classroom will help a person navigate the contentious arguments related to immigration reform, her work also implies that those analytical skills can serve a person in processing nearly any controversial public debate. Your analysis does not necessarily need to be connected to national or international issues like immigration reform, but working outward from the text can be valuable.

Once you have made an argument about a text, consider how your conclusions relate to other texts you have read or watched. Are there parallels or differences? You should also consider the larger themes or discussions that you have studied in your course. Does this particular text have something new or significant to say about a topic of interest to your class? Does it bring you any closer to fully understanding a subject? Knowledge is found in the fissures and overlaps of ideas, and you can illuminate yourself (and your fellow students and instructor) as to how the thoughts and arguments in one text relate to the bigger picture.

Consider the following example of student work as a model of the methodology we proposed. The student was asked to write a brief analysis of a play, Henrik Ibsen's *The Wild Duck*, specifically examining its themes of illness and blindness:

> *Ibsen's The Wild Duck connects Gregers's inability to understand what is really happening within himself to blindness and physical sickness. Gregers is driven by guilt from not helping his friend Hjalmar Ekdal's family at a critical time in the past. By revealing the lies within Hjalmar's marriage, Gregers convinces himself that he has saved his friend from living a life that is not his own. However, his help actually is very poisonous to the Ekdal family, because Gregers himself, according to the doctor Relling, is "a sick man, too," whose main problem is that he is "forever going around in a delirium of adoration—forever butting in where [he doesn't] belong, looking for something to admire" (5.54-57). Relling wants Gregers to realize that because he is "blind" to his own motivations, he cannot possibly help Hjalmar and in fact is making everything much worse for the Ekdal family.*

You'll notice that the student begins by identifying the text in question and then proceeds to state her claim (that the play connects the character "Gregers's inability to understand what is really happening within himself to blindness and physical sickness"). She demonstrates her familiarity with the text by summarizing concisely and quoting intelligently; as an audience, we have the sense that the author is guiding the analysis and not simply dropping in quotes to fill space. Finally, she works outward from claim, not merely proving that Gregers is physically ill but suggesting that Ibsen, the play's author, is using Gregers's physical illness to symbolize his "blind[ness]" to his internal inadequacies. This analysis is effective, then, because it is concise, demonstrates the author's familiarity with the text, and uses the evidence from the text to advance her thoughts and perceptions.

Synthesis

The term "synthesis" has a number of specific meanings, depending on the disciplinary context of the term. In chemistry, synthesis is the process of combining two or more simple substances to make a more complex one. In psychology, synthesis is the integration of attitudes, traits, and responses into a personality. In philosophy, synthesis reconciles two propositions, the thesis and the antithesis, into a new configuration of meaning. In college writing, synthesis involves combining and integrating ideas from two or more sources to develop a new idea. Synthesis writing is sometimes called *discourse synthesis* or *dialectical thinking*, because the task is to put source texts into dialogue, or conversation, with one another (McGinley 227). In a synthesis paper, the writer discusses how two or more texts can be viewed in the light of an organizing theme, structure, or idea and integrates these perspectives to form a complex conclusion or develop a starting point for further inquiry. Synthesis is one of the most effective operations of learning because it requires a constructive thought process. Through synthesis, new ideas are generated; not only our thoughts but also our thought processes are transformed (McGinley 234).

As a university student, you will be required to synthesize in a variety of assignments. For example, in a paper prompt or an exam question, your instructor might ask you to consider the position of theorist C in relation to the views of theorists A and B. In a research paper, you might discuss several arguments about possible causes of the 2008 financial meltdown and use the evidence and viewpoints in these papers to come to your own conclusions about the cause. You might be asked to consider how two authors from the same literary period exemplify the characteristics of that period and how their works have influenced each other. You could be expected to consolidate and explain data from several experiment results. Here are some prompts that ask for a synthesis response:

- Discuss Martin Luther King's notion of an "unjust law" in the light of the Dalai Lama's criteria for "great compassion."

- Compare and contrast what Helen Keller, Malcolm X, and Richard Rodriguez have to say about education and identity.

- How do Robert Reich, Gregory Mantsios, and Fatema Mernissi affect your thinking about class and choice?

Successful synthesis requires mastery of two other writing/ thinking processes that we have already described in this chapter: **summary** and **analysis**. First, the writer must be able to demonstrate an understanding of the source texts by objectively restating those ideas in her own words (summary). The writer must also demonstrate an understanding of the component parts of the source text arguments and how these components work together as a whole (analysis). Synthesis completes the process of transformation begun by summary (transforming another's ideas into one's own words) and analysis (selecting, organizing, and interpreting the components of another's ideas) by connecting and integrating the ideas of several texts under a common structure to create a new set of ideas. If the synthesis writer does not have a clear sense of the source texts' meaning, structure, and context, she will have difficulty relating those texts to each other or to her own ideas and experience. The synthesis will fail, and no complex understanding will emerge, if the writer lacks the ability to think *about* and to think *with* source texts.

The Process of Synthesis

We might consider the process of synthesis as a journey, a thought excursion on which we lead our readers. Think of Dorothy and her journey through the Land of Oz. She begins with a question that is of interest to her (How can I get home?) and a hypothesis (The Wizard can get me home.). Her experiences in Kansas give her a certain perspective about how to address her problem. Along the way to the Emerald City, Dorothy encounters a variety of characters, each with a different perspective. She learns the story of the Scarecrow and alters the goal of her journey to include his point of view. Together, they meet the Tin Man and connect his knowledge, experience, and goals to their own. The Cowardly Lion's take adds a new dimension. The integration of these perspectives alters the hypothesis about the Wizard's capabilities as the journey moves forward. Just as every argument meets with opposition, Dorothy and company must deal with the counter-objectives of the Wicked Witch of the West as well as those of the Wizard. The travelers take unexpected detours. Each character has a talent or skill that responds to these challenges, just as each text in a synthesis can provide elements of a counterargument or different strategies for pursuing a question. Dorothy's journey culminates in a new thought configuration, one quite different from the original hypothesis (There's no place like home – I was home all along).

Synthesis writing is a complex process, and research and experience tell us that students struggle with this kind of writing. While synthesis may seem to be the result of a linear procedure (reading → summarizing → analyzing → synthesis), such an understanding of synthesizing would be misleading. Research has shown that writers who think of synthesis as the last step in a linear process tend to produce papers that are strung-together summaries and analyses rather than true integrations and connections of ideas (Mateos and Solé 448; McGinley 235).

In order to put texts into conversation with each other, the synthesis writer plays several roles. First, she is a careful reader of texts, placing herself in the position of each text's ideas in order to fully comprehend them. Next, she is a careful summarizer and analyzer, selecting significant ideas from the texts, integrating and connecting them in accordance with an overarching idea that begins as a hypothesis and emerges as a thesis from interaction with the texts. This second role requires note-taking and draft writing, as well as revisiting the texts in order to develop and support a thesis. Then she must become the reader of her own draft, ensuring that she leads the reader clearly through the thought processes that connect the texts she is synthesizing. Successful synthesis writers engage in a recursive process, moving back and forth between reading and writing. Likewise, the structure of the synthesis reflects this recursive process, considering each text in light of both the controlling idea (thesis) and the texts that have already been discussed so far.

Strategies for Synthesis Writing

When you write a synthesis, much of your thought journeying will take place before you begin to write the paper that will be the final product – in reading, note-taking, pre-writing, drafting, and especially *thinking* about the texts you are synthesizing. Careful reading (or viewing, if it is a visual text) and annotation of each source text is a good way to begin. You may find it useful to write a brief summary of each text to consolidate the main and subordinate points of the argument or information firmly in your mind. In note-taking or free-writing, analyze elements of each text such as context, structure, strategy, and tone. As you progress through your note-taking and annotations, you will already be comparing sources in your mind, revisiting the first text in the light of subsequent texts.

A synthesis paper can begin with a question to be explored through multiple source texts. An instructor may ask you to generate your own *issue question* about the texts, or you may be asked to respond to a prompt question. Working with source texts through summary and analysis will lead to the refinement of a controlling idea: the thesis. The synthesis writer will bring the texts into dialogue with each other by asking questions: What do these texts have in common? In what ways do they disagree? Do they differ in the presentation or interpretation of evidence? Do they disagree about underlying beliefs or important assumptions? How do I, as the writer, respond to these texts and the subject or issue under discussion? How do the texts bring my own knowledge and assumptions into question? What insights come out of this interaction among source texts and my own ideas? After considering such questions, you should be able to formulate a tentative thesis or at least an issue question (Ramage, Bean, and Johnson 44-45).

This writer, student Lisa Regganie, begins an exploratory argument by introducing an issue question that she will use as a controlling idea in the synthesis of three texts:

> *Growing up in a small farming town, I have witnessed many of the townspeople not continue on to college after high school. They instead go into trades and work blue collar jobs. I am the daughter of parents who did not go to college. My father just did not want to go; he wanted to be a blue collar worker. My mother, on the other hand wanted to go, but her parents could not afford it. My father does not regret not going to college, but my mother regrets it every day that she steps into her dead end job. Both of my parents did not even question sending me to college, and I knew that going to college would be the only way out of the tentative lifestyle I grew up in. Luckily my parents knew this from the day I was born, so they started a college fund early and told me I could go wherever I wanted to go, be whatever I want to be, and they would bask in the glow of my success. My background leads me to the question: Does education really open up a whole new world to students? I explored this idea in three essays by Helen Keller, Richard Rodriguez, and Malcolm X.*

The author develops her argument by exploring the three essays with the aim of answering her question. She arrives at her conclusion by considering how each text relates to her issue question:

> *Helen Keller, Richard Rodriguez, and Malcolm X experience the awakening of different kinds of opportunity through very different modes of education.* In all three cases, opportunity lies within the learner; the opportunity of education is not something I passively receive, but is mine to take, as these students did. *The new outlook on the world I will gain after college will be worth the hard classes, homework, and stress.*

In the example above, the author began with a question and answered it in her conclusion. In the following introduction, writer Gabrielle Caputo answers a prompt question (What do Robert Reich and Colin Beavan say about the relationship between happiness and material success, and how do these authors affect your view of this relationship?) in a thesis that synthesizes the views of two authors and her own view:

> *People are distracted from what is truly important in life because they fixate on making decisions concerning insignificant things and believing that possessions will bring happiness. Robert B. Reich in his article "The Choice Fetish: Blessings and Curses of a Market Idol," and Colin Bevan in his book* No Impact Man *insist upon this, and while they are right, each fails to address how the lack of popular examples of people who are successful without money makes us think having money and items is the sole way to achieve success.*

Refer to the department website for the complete essays.

Methods of Organization

There are two common methods for organizing a synthesis: around the source texts (*block method*) or around the points of connection (*alternating method*).

1. **Block Method:**
   - » **Introduction** with claim or issue question.
   - » **Text 1**
     - – Introduce this source with a brief summary of its ideas, providing its rhetorical context. (Some relevant points for context might include the following: Who is the author(s)? Why should the reader pay attention to what the author(s) has to say about this

subject? What is the source's place in the conversation about the claim or issue?) Apply the methods and conventions of good **summary** writing.

- **Analyze** this source's ideas in relation to the points of connection you have discovered among the source texts and the controlling idea that has emerged from these connections. Respond with your own ideas about the source's position on these points. For example, if your main idea is that knowledge of language opens the door to human relationship and you are discussing Helen Keller's "Everything Has a Name," you will consider how her account of acquiring language demonstrates a new connection to the people in her life.

» **Text 2**

- Introduce this source as well, by giving a summary of its main ideas and putting it in context. The difference between this introduction and the first one is that you will transition from the first text to this one by pointing out some similarity or dissimilarity (or both) between the first source text and this one. This connection you establish between texts is crucial and should be discussed in clear, specific fashion. Don't expect your reader to see or make the connection herself. For example, let's say you are introducing Richard Rodriguez's "Private and Public Language" into a conversation about language and human relationship. You might open the summary by pointing out that while Keller's account tells of how language leads to a discovery of relationships in her immediate family circle, Rodriguez's knowledge of language opens the possibility of public relationships.

- Analyze this source's ideas in relation to the controlling idea, but do so by putting this source in conversation with the previous text as well as your own ideas. How is Rodriguez's experience similar to Keller's, and how is it different?

» **Text 3**

    – Repeat this process with the third text and with any subsequent texts you discuss. Avoid isolating the texts into a string of separate summaries/analyses. Keep the texts in conversation with each other by discussing points of connection.

» **Conclude** by telling the reader how the conversation among these texts has changed our understanding of the subject under discussion.

2. **Alternating Method:**

» **Introduction** with claim or issue question. Let's say that in your essay you want to discuss three components of happiness: choice, wealth, and community. You will be considering these ideas in the light of essays by Robert Reich ("The Choice Fetish,") and Gregory Mantsios ("Class in America – 2006") and Colin Beavan's book *No Impact Man.*

» **First point of connection** among the source texts. Describe one of the ideas that these texts have in common. The texts may agree or disagree or take differently nuanced positions on this point.

    – Introduce Text 1 by briefly placing it in its rhetorical context (see questions relevant to rhetorical context in "Text 1" above). Discuss this text's position on this point of connection. For example, Robert Reich sees the overabundance of trivial choices as a nuisance that distracts us from issues that are more important to our ultimate happiness.

    – Add Text 2 to the conversation, also briefly placing it in context. Colin Beavan would agree with Reich, in that he believes that most of the choices we make concerning material objects are unnecessary and even destructive.

    – Add Text 3 and any subsequent texts in the same way. Include your own ideas in the conversation. Gregory Mantsios would point out that many Americans are too poor to have *enough* choice and would appreciate having some of the choices that Reich and Beavan are complaining about.

> » **Second point of connection.** Repeat the process described above, putting the texts in conversation about this point. In the discussion of this and subsequent points, you obviously will not need to introduce the texts and put them in context.

> » **Continue discussion with connecting point 3.**

> » **Conclude** by telling the reader how the conversation among these texts has changed our understanding of the subject under discussion.

You can combine these methods by beginning with the block method and then putting sources in conversation with each other using the alternating method. Notice that decisions about the order in which you discuss texts or connecting points will be very important to your argument. You may decide, during the drafting process, to change the order of these elements to enhance the effectiveness of your argument.

Dorothy and friends follow the yellow brick road and signs along the way of the journey. In synthesis writing, you must use *transitional language* to guide readers on the thought journey, helping readers identify the various "speakers" in the conversation and their positions. Use words and phrases to introduce a new perspective and to signal a shift in thought. To introduce the ideas of one text, use active verbs. Don't merely tell us that an author or work "says" something. Try:

- Jones *demonstrates, argues, asserts,* or *reminds . . .*

- This film *portrays, represents,* or *tells the story of . . .*

Use transitions to signal the relations of source ideas to each other:

- While Jones believes _____, Smith takes the opposite view.

- Jones and Smith hold similar positions in all but_____. (Graff, Birkenstein, and Durst 71-75)

Note in the following paragraphs how student writer Judith Howard uses transitional language to put the ideas of her sources in a conversation about the individual and community responsibility:

Both Beavan and the Dalai Lama *see individual action as having a powerful impact on more than just the individual. At various places in No Impact Man,* **Beavan expresses** *the idea that individual actions are what constitute collective action. He values the influence of small, individual actions as being critical to the formation of larger movements.* **The Dalai Lama speaks** *about the impact of one person's actions on another person. He calls for compassion in action, arguing that if our actions lack compassion, they can become dangerous. He makes the point that if we are not considerate of how our individual actions affect the welfare of other people, "inevitably we end up hurting them" (261).* **Beavan makes a similar point** *concerning the environment: that if we are careless about our impact on the environment, we will cause great harm to it and all other people as a result.*

When discussing the individual, **Reich maintains** *a position that supports the value of individual choice for the individual's sake* **while the Dalai Lama, in contrast,** *considers individuals almost entirely as part of a collective.* **Reich, despite supporting community**, *puts more emphasis on personal desires. After dismissing the smaller, less significant choices that people are able to make, he calls for us to make the more relevant choices, "Such as what we stand for, to what and whom we're going to commit our lives, and what we want by way of a community and a society" (Reich 66). The focus in this sentence is on the important aspects of life from an individual's perspective.* **When the Dalai Lama focuses** *on the desires of people, he uses the same phrase various times to describe the most basic desire of humanity: "to be happy and not to suffer" (258). He uses this shared wish to connect all of mankind and to therefore emphasize the responsibility that we have toward each and every other human being.*

Remember that the conventions of acknowledging sources apply in this kind of writing. Cite sources in text whenever you summarize, paraphrase, or quote another author's ideas. Provide a Works Cited page that fully and accurately cites all your sources.

Researched Argument

Types of Research Assignments

A Research-Based Argument vs. An Informational Research Project
In UCWR 110, you will be required to compose a research paper that makes an argument. This requirement may be different from research projects that you have done in the past.

In high school, students are often asked to do research projects for the purpose of gathering information and presenting that information to the reader. This type of project is akin to creating an encyclopedia entry or Wikipedia page.

However, the purpose of the research assignment is different in UCWR 110. Most often, the main purpose is to develop an argument based on the research you have done. While the project will of course require you to do substantial information gathering, in your paper you will be expected to develop an argument and shape the paper around a thesis. Students sometimes struggle with this argumentative aspect of the assignment because they see research as strictly collecting information about a topic. As you conduct your research, you should therefore not only gather information but also identify the different debates your sources are engaged in. These debates can point you toward a more specific issue around which you can structure your argument.

Here is an illustration of the difference between an informational project and a research-based argument: Suppose you are interested in the protest movement against the Vietnam War in the 1960s and 1970s. For an informational project you would gather material about the leading anti-war figures and the major anti-war organizations, their reasons for opposing the war, and the methods of protest they employed. Indeed, your paper itself might be organized around these sub-topics. However, for a research-based argument, you would gather the same information but would also investigate the various debates among historians about the antiwar movement. There are a number of these, but one prominent debate focuses on the effectiveness of the movement in helping bring the war to an end.

As a researcher, you could enter this conversation about the movement by researching and analyzing the different interpretations of its effectiveness. In your paper, you would frame the debate in your introduction, present your broad stance on the issue of the movement's effectiveness, and then structure your paper around the reasons that support your argument. Be sure to make your argument throughout the paper. Each paragraph should advance your argument in some way. Beware of the misguided perception that a research-based argument is just an informational paper with your personal opinion tacked on in the introduction and conclusion.

Writing as Inquiry or Exploratory Research
While some instructors may require a researched argument, others require a paper in which you conduct research as a means to explore or inquire into an issue you find compelling. As discussed above, in order to produce a research-based argument, you need to gather information, identify key questions related to your issue, and consider different views on the subject. Then you structure your paper around a thesis on the issue. But in an exploratory essay the focus and content of your paper will be the very type of research and thinking you do *before* writing a thesis-driven research paper. Rather than making an argument about a specific issue and developing that argument throughout your paper as you would in a researched-based argument, an exploratory essay offers a sort of analytical overview of your process of discovery.

Although it does not present an overarching argument, an exploratory essay does nevertheless involve a great deal of **analysis**, **synthesis**, and evaluation of the sources and their views on the topic. This is the major distinction between an exploratory essay and an informational one. Informational essays tend to focus primarily on summary and contain only minimal analysis, synthesis, and evaluation. An exploratory essay on the antiwar movement of the 1960s, for example, would not only summarize the information you have gathered but would also lay out the main debates or differences in interpretation that historians have offered on the issue. In addition, and perhaps most importantly, it would offer some analysis of the strengths and weaknesses of different views and point the reader toward the more convincing ones, even though it might not necessarily come to definitive conclusions about the debates it has reviewed.

Planning and Time-Management

One of the greatest challenges of writing a successful research paper involves planning the various stages of your project and setting aside sufficient time for each. One reason a research paper can seem so daunting is that we tend to see it as one huge task. This can make us feel overwhelmed and lead to a deadly pattern of procrastination. However, effective planning and time-management can reduce the stress of a big project and help you produce a more successful research paper.

Your instructor will likely break down parts of the project into various stages. Typically, an instructor may require you to submit a proposal, do an annotated bibliography, write a draft for peer review, and revise that draft for submission. However, you should break those tasks down as well. Instead of seeing the project as a series of deadlines and assignments (a sort of "teacher-centered" or "assignment-centered" view), approach it from a writer's point of view. This means trying to see it as a set of discrete yet related tasks that can be tackled at various stages and even re-visited as you proceed.

As a writer, in order to meet the deadlines and do the assignments, you are faced with the following: choosing a topic, finding sources, making notes, drafting a thesis, planning and organizing your paper, writing a draft, revising, and editing. This is quite a bit, but by tackling the various tasks in stages and seeing how they relate to one another, you can keep the project manageable.

Here are some suggestions for planning and time-management:

- Start exploring topics soon after you've received the assignment. You will likely have to narrow, refine, and even discard topics before you settle on one. This takes time, so don't put it off.

- Set aside ample time to find sources. Plan for multiple research sessions, and consider asking for help from your instructor or a research librarian.

- Avoid doing your research in one big push before a deadline. You should regularly re-examine the sources you have in order to consider what kinds of sources you still need to find.

- Adopt an effective and organized note-taking system. There's nothing worse than scrambling to find that great quotation you want to plug in but have lost track of.

- Develop a tentative thesis early on. Your argument will likely change, but having a thesis will help you focus and manage your research more efficiently.

- Create an outline before drafting, ideally one organized around your argument, i.e., its thesis, the reasons supporting that thesis, and/or the major counter-arguments you will be addressing. Elaborating on your argument is crucial to your success, so structuring your outline around its key components, rather than broad topics or sources, will streamline the drafting process and help you produce a draft that is focused and convincing.

- Set aside extensive time for drafting. Unlike other assignments, with a research paper you are juggling large amounts of material. Even with a strong outline, synthesizing this material on the page can be challenging and time-consuming.

- Draft in stages. Consider beginning with a section you feel comfortable with. We often assume that drafting is a linear process. It rarely is. Starting with the parts you find easier to write can build confidence and momentum for those more challenging aspects of the project.

- Revise in stages as well. Just like with research and drafting, trying to revise in one big push is generally ineffective. Identify two to four priorities for revision, begin with one or two of those, proceed methodically, and then move on to new priorities in later revision sessions.

- Edit for continuity and coherence as well as grammar and style. Because this is a longer paper that you will have drafted and revised in stages, it will often need continuity editing that ensures that the various parts are unified and connected. Make sure you have developed your main argument and asserted your voice in each section.

The Recursive Nature of the Research Process

The suggestions above might make the writing of the research paper seem like a straightforward, step-by-step procedure; however, writing an effective research paper, like almost all writing, is a more recursive than linear process. Keep in mind that many of these seemingly discrete tasks are overlapping. When executing a new stage of the process, you may need to return to previous tasks.

Take, for example, doing research and finding sources. Chances are that once you've chosen a topic, your instructor will require you to submit an annotated bibliography in which you document and summarize your sources, often a specific number of them. At this stage, it can feel like the research process is complete, and if you are lucky, it may be. However, producing the annotated bibliography often highlights gaps in your research or points to further questions that need to be addressed before you start drafting. This will require more research. Even as you are drafting or after peer review, you may continue to identify gaps in your knowledge. As a result, you will have to do additional research to shore up your paper.

For additional information and ideas, see *Writing Matters* Chapter 2: "Planning Your Project'"; Chapter 3: "Organizing and Drafting"; Chapter 12: "Planning a Research Project"; and Chapter 15: "Using Information Responsibly."

Choosing and Narrowing a Topic

The process of choosing a topic is another highly challenging part of the research process. While occasionally a writer quickly comes up with a viable, engaging focus, the process of choosing a topic and narrowing its focus can be complex, time-consuming, and – let's admit it – frustrating. Yet producing a successful paper depends greatly on choosing a topic that is clearly defined and engaging. Moreover, having a well-defined topic can make the subsequent stages of the process more focused and efficient.

Here are some guidelines for choosing and narrowing your topic:

- To get started, use whatever idea-generating techniques you find valuable. These can include brainstorming, free-writing, talking to others, or perusing newspapers and magazines.

- Find a topic that truly interests you. Working on something that you are genuinely curious about will make the process far more engaging and rewarding.

- Beware of stale, hand-me-down topics like abortion or capital punishment. While these can be approached in interesting ways, they are overdone and broad, and students often choose them simply because they seem familiar and easy rather than genuinely interesting.

- Revise your topic as you proceed. As you research and acquire knowledge of your subject, your interest and focus will likely shift and narrow. Follow your interests.

- Consider focusing on a sub-topic within your larger topic. This is related to the suggestion above. Often in the process of researching, planning, and even drafting, we discover our topic is too broad. Rather than finding an entirely new topic, the more effective strategy is to focus on a sub-topic, i.e., a topic within your original topic. While students are often reluctant to narrow in this way because they feel they may not have enough to say, the truth is that focusing on a sub-topics often allows the writer to develop a more interesting and complex argument.

- Use sources to identify specific issues or questions. Your topic should be a debatable one, so your sources will, in one form or another, be framing the debatable issues within that topic. You as a writer are entering the conversation these sources are engaged in, so look for the questions and issues the sources are addressing, and feel free to focus on a specific issue that they have identified.

As the above suggestions indicate, finalizing a topic usually involves research, often substantial amounts of it. While it is useful to brainstorm and reflect on your interests in order generate possible topics, you will likely need to do some preliminary research before you can settle comfortably into a topic. Later in the process, as your research becomes more thorough and your knowledge of the subject increases, you may have to refine your topic to reflect your greater understanding.

The process of refining your topic can continue right up to the submission of your final draft. As you draft, go through peer review, and revise your paper, you may realize that you want to focus more on one specific aspect of the topic and will need to re-work your paper accordingly.

A Topic vs. An Issue

While we have thus far spoken primarily of choosing a topic, the term "topic" can be misleading because it is so general. Since you are developing an argument, it might be more helpful to think of addressing an issue or, perhaps even better, answering a question. Looking at the process as choosing a topic can lead us to rather broad and ultimately unmanageable topics. But if we think about addressing an issue or answering a question, we can give our work focus and ensure that we are producing an argumentative essay.

But what's the difference between a topic and an issue? A topic is typically rather general and doesn't necessarily point to a debate, while an issue points to a debate or a debatable question. Here's an example that illustrates the distinction between a topic and an issue and also delineates the process of moving from a topic to a specific issue and question:

Suppose after reading essays by Malcolm X and Carolyn Bird you decide you are interested in the topic of college education. However, writing about "college education" is obviously too broad, so you have to narrow your focus. What has intrigued you perhaps is the suggestion that college education is not necessary or valuable for most people. Now you are moving toward an issue.

This is still somewhat broad, however. Now you might consider why you have asked yourself this question. You realize that you have been challenged by Malcolm X's claim that college life, with its parties and panty raids, is actually a distraction from genuine learning. In addition, Malcolm X demonstrates that he has educated himself better than any college could have, while Bird claims that, because we have such wide access to materials now, pretty much anyone can educate himself or herself in the way colleges promise to. You are torn because you recognize some truth in Malcolm X's and Bird's arguments but also value your own college experience. You know that so much of college life is distracting yet so much is rewarding as well. Now you are refining the issue even further. You might arrive at the following question: "Given the problems and value present in college life, how can colleges create an environment that better fosters the kind of education Malcolm achieved on his own?" This question would point you toward research on the goals of college education, the main problems in student achievement, and the ways these problems have been addressed.

Pragmatic Issues vs. Conceptual Issues
Determining whether you want to approach your topic from a pragmatic or a conceptual angle can help you narrow your focus.

Almost every paper will address both pragmatic and conceptual issues, but most successful ones tend to focus primarily on one or the other. The difference between the two is this: a pragmatic focus will ask readers to do something or adopt a specific action to solve a problem while a conceptual focus will ask readers to gain understanding or adopt a belief regarding an issue or problem.

Conceptual and pragmatic problems of course overlap; you can't solve a problem without some conceptual understanding of the issue, and conceptual thinking can point you to pragmatic solutions. However, it is best to identify whether your main purpose is to create understanding (conceptual) or if it is to urge a solution or action (pragmatic) (Williams and Colomb 70).

Let's return to the topic of college education mentioned earlier in this section. Suppose that in addition to having read Malcolm X and

Carolyn Bird on education, you have read articles about the failure of universities to adequately prepare students for the world of work. You've found general agreement about this. If you were to adopt a *conceptual* approach to the topic, you might research the reasons for this failure: Why are college graduates consistently under-prepared for professional careers? This might involve debates over issues of curriculum, standards, student attitudes, or employer needs. You would focus your research on finding material that addresses these conceptual issues. In your conclusion, you might briefly address the implications of your conceptual analysis for pragmatic solutions, but this would not be the main focus on the paper.

However, you could also tackle this topic from a *pragmatic* angle by examining solutions to the problem: How can colleges better prepare students for careers and the world of work? While this approach would have to address some conceptual issues about the causes of the problem, your main focus – and the overwhelming proportion of your paper – would analyze possible solutions in order to propose the best course of action. What are colleges doing to better prepare students? What seems to be working or not working? Based on your research, what would you recommend as an effective approach or set of approaches to solving this problem?

For further information and suggestions, see *Writing Matters* Chapter 2 section c: "Generating Ideas"; Chapter 2 section d: "Narrowing or Broadening Your Topic"; and Chapter 12 section d: "Drafting Research Questions and Hypotheses."

Library Services at Loyola

Writing a research paper can be daunting task, even for experienced researchers. Fortunately, dedicated help and effective research resources are always available at Loyola libraries. A librarian will be part of your UCWR class this semester, and librarians might participate in other classes you take. Librarians and other library staff are committed to helping students do their best work. For them, no question is too small or silly, so do not hesitate to ask for assistance.

Library Reference Desk

Librarians assist students on the second floor of the Information Commons on the Lakeshore Campus and in Lewis Library at the Water Tower Campus. You can drop by or schedule an appointment in advance. There is also online help; you can access assistance through a chat connection or by sending questions to librarians as text messages.

Details about all of these services are available through the library's website.

Library Circulation Desk
Library staff at the circulation desk in Cudahy and Lewis Libraries will help you check out books, pick up materials on hold or requested through Interlibrary Loan, and check out course reserve materials.

Library Information Resources
A well-written, research-based argument is supported by quality information resources. Locating these resources, especially those from scholarly sources, requires learning about library catalogs and research databases.

Before you are ready to delve into scholarly sources on an unfamiliar topic, you will usually need to consult reference sources, or sources of background information. Many reference sources are available online, but some classic ones still exist only in print. Reference sources may be found using a library catalog or other search aids, but often the best method is simply asking a librarian for a referral. A librarian will suggest at least one reference source to your UCWR class during class with you this semester.

Once you have basic knowledge about a topic, you will be ready to begin searching a library catalog or research database. Our library supports two catalogs, Pegasus and WorldCat Local. Both may be accessed through the library's website. These catalogs help locate books, both print and electronic, in the library's collections. A librarian will introduce the catalogs to your class, but you are encouraged to experiment and contact librarians with your questions.

The library also provides students with access to hundreds of databases, most of them tied to research in specific subject areas. In UCWR classes, librarians will focus on one general database that can be used for nearly any topic. Databases are linked from the library's website, both by title and by subject area through our Research Guides (see below).

Your instructor and the research librarian who works with your class will be eager to help you navigate through the college-level research project. Make good use of these individuals and their expertise. But successful research requires perhaps more independent work than any other type of writing assignment. Because of this, Loyola libraries have created a number of useful web pages that can help facilitate the research project. On the library web page (libraries.luc.edu), you can access "Research Guides" that are organized by disciplines such as Anthropology, Environmental Studies, and Physics. Among these, moreover, is a guide designed especially for UCWR. This guide may be your most useful electronic link.

The Research Guide for UCWR (libguides.luc.edu/UCWR?hs=a) contains a number of extremely useful tabs that address various areas of research. Some of these, such as "Types of Academic Sources," provide helpful overviews. Others, such as "Evaluating Sources" and "The Research Question," reinforce information and skill sets you will need to compose a successful research paper. Perhaps most importantly, other tabs provide links to the most used and most useful databases, as well as the catalogs. Consider opening this page and working from there whenever you are conducting your research. Make it your home base for each research session, and you should be able to navigate swiftly among the various tabs and links the library has designed to serve your research needs.

Works Cited

Bisignani, Dana, and Allen Brizee. "Annotated Bibliographies." *Purdue Online Writing Lab.* 2012. Purdue University. Web. 25 June 2012.

Caputo, Gabrielle. "The Lies We Waste Our Lives On." *Communities in Conversation: Environmental Issues and Green Activism.* Eds. Sherrie Weller, et al. Loyola University Chicago, 2011. 50-51. Print.

Fitzgerald, F. Scott. "The Crack-up." *Esquire* Feb. 1936:41. Print.

Felius, Marleen, et al. "On the Breeds of Cattle—Historic and Current Classifications." *Diversity* 3 (2011): 660-692. *Academic Search Premier.* Web. 26 Sept. 2012.

Graff, Gerald, Cathy Birkenstein, and Russel Durst. *They Say/I Say: The Moves That Matter in Academic Writing with Readings.* 2nd ed. New York: W. W. Norton, 2012.

Hidi, Suzanne, and Valerie Anderson. "Producing Written Summaries: Task Demands, Cognitive Operations, and Implications for Instruction." *Review of Educational Research* 56.4 (Winter 1986): 473-493. *JSTOR.* Web. 25 June 2012.

Howard, Judith. "The Need for Connection." *Communities in Conversation: Environmental Issues and Green Activism.* Eds. Sherrie Weller, et al. Loyola University Chicago, 2011. 47-49. Print.

Howard, Rebecca Moore. *Writing Matters.* New York: McGraw-Hill, 2011. Print.

Maclellan, Effie. "Reading to Learn." *Studies in Higher Education* 22.3 (Oct. 1997): 277-289. *Academic Search Premier*. Web. 28 June 2012.

Mateos, Mar, and Isabel Sol. "Synthesising Information from Various Texts: A Study of Procedures and Products at Different Educational Levels." *European Journal of Psychology of Education* 24.1 (2009) 435-451. Print.

McGinley, William. "The Role of Reading and Writing While Composing from Sources." *International Reading Association* 27.3 (1992) 227-248.

Morgan, Teyana. "Summary Assignment." 27 February 2012. MS.

Ramage, John D., John C. Bean, and June Johnson. *Writing Arguments: A Rhetoric with Readings*. Brief 9th Ed. Boston: Pearson, 2011.

Regannie, Lisa. "A Whole New World." 27 Oct. 2012. MS.

Strahan, Linda, Kathleen Moore, and Michael Heumann. *Write It: A Process Approach to College Essays*. Dubuque: Kendall Hunt, 2011. Print.

Williams, Joseph M., and Gregory G. Colomb. *The Craft of Argument*. 2nd ed. New York: Longman, 2003. Print.

Yu, Guoxing. "The Shifting Sands in the Effects of Source Text Summarizability on Summary Writing." *Assessing Writing* 14 (2009): 116-137. *ScienceDirect*. Web. 25 June 2012.

II

FOUNDATIONS OF ARGUMENT

EXCERPTS FROM *RHETORICA*

Aristotle

Book I

1

1 Rhetoric is the counterpart of Dialectic. Both alike are concerned with such things as come, more or less, within the general ken of all men and belong to no definite science. Accordingly all men make

use, more or less, of both; for to a certain extent all men attempt to discuss statements and to maintain them, to defend themselves and to attack others. Ordinary people do this either at random or through practice and from acquired habit. Both ways being possible, the subject can plainly be handled systematically, for it is possible to inquire the reason why some speakers succeed through practice and others spontaneously; and every one will at once agree that such an inquiry is the function of an art.

Now, the framers of the current treatises on rhetoric have constructed but a small portion of that art. The modes of persuasion are the only true constituents of the art: everything else is merely accessory. These writers, however, say nothing about enthymemes, which are the substance of rhetorical persuasion, but deal mainly with non-essentials. The arousing of prejudice, pity, anger, and similar emotions has nothing to do with the essential facts, but is merely a personal appeal to the man who is judging the case. Consequently if the rules for trials which are now laid down some states-especially in well-governed states-were applied everywhere, such people would have nothing to say. All men, no doubt, think that the laws should prescribe such rules, but some, as in the court of Areopagus, give practical effect to their thoughts and forbid talk about non-essentials. This is sound law and custom. It is not right to pervert the judge by moving him to anger or envy or pity-one might as well warp a carpenter's rule before using it. Again, a litigant has clearly nothing to do but to show that the alleged fact is so or is not so, that it has or has not happened. As to whether a thing is important or unimportant, just or unjust, the judge must surely refuse to take his instructions from the litigants: he must decide for himself all such points as the law-giver has not already defined for him.[...]

Rhetoric is useful (1) because things that are true and things that are just have a natural tendency to prevail over their opposites, so that if the decisions of judges are not what they ought to be, the defeat must be due to the speakers themselves, and they must be blamed accordingly. Moreover, (2) before some audiences not even the possession of the exactest knowledge will make it easy for what we say to produce conviction. For argument based on knowledge implies instruction, and there are people whom one cannot instruct. Here, then, we must use, as our modes of persuasion and argument, notions possessed by everybody, as we observed in the Topics when dealing with the way to handle a popular audience. Further, (3) we must be able to employ persuasion, just as strict reasoning can be employed, on opposite sides of a question, not in order that we may in practice employ it in both ways (for we must not make people believe what is wrong), but in order that we may see clearly what the facts are, and that, if another man argues unfairly, we on our part may be able to confute him. No other of the arts draws opposite conclusions: dialectic and rhetoric alone do this. Both these arts draw opposite conclusions impartially. Nevertheless, the underlying facts do not lend themselves equally well to the contrary views. No; things that are true and things that are better are, by their nature, practically always easier to prove and easier to believe in. Again, (4) it is absurd to hold that a man ought to be ashamed of being unable to defend himself with his limbs, but not of being unable to defend himself with speech and reason, when the use of rational speech is more distinctive of a human being than the use of his limbs. And if it be objected that one who uses such power of speech unjustly might do great harm, that is a charge which may be made in common against all good things except virtue, and above all against the things that are most useful, as strength, health, wealth, generalship. A man can confer the greatest of benefits by a right use of these, and inflict the greatest of injuries by using them wrongly. [...]

2

Rhetoric may be defined as the faculty of observing in any given case the available means of persuasion. This is not a function of any other art. Every other art can instruct or persuade about its own particular subject-matter; for instance, medicine about what is healthy and unhealthy, geometry about the properties of magnitudes, arithmetic about numbers, and the same is true of the other arts and sciences. But rhetoric we look upon as the power of observing the means of persuasion on almost any subject presented to us; and that is why we say that, in its technical character, it is not concerned with any special or definite class of subjects.

5   Of the modes of persuasion some belong strictly to the art of rhetoric and some do not. By the latter I mean such things as are not supplied by the speaker but are there at the outset-witnesses, evidence given under torture, written contracts, and so on. By the former I mean such as we can ourselves construct by means of the principles of rhetoric. The one kind has merely to be used, the other has to be invented.

Of the modes of persuasion furnished by the spoken word there are three kinds. The first kind depends on the personal character of the speaker; the second on putting the audience into a certain frame of mind; the third on the proof, or apparent proof, provided by the words of the speech itself. Persuasion is achieved by the speaker's personal character when the speech is so spoken as to make us think him credible. We believe good men more fully and more readily than others: this is true generally whatever the question is, and absolutely true where exact certainty is impossible and opinions are divided. This kind of persuasion, like the others, should be achieved by what the speaker says, not by what people think of his character before he begins to speak. It is not true, as some writers assume in their treatises on rhetoric, that the personal goodness revealed by the speaker contributes nothing to his power of persuasion; on the contrary, his character may almost be called the most effective means of persuasion he possesses. Secondly, persuasion may come through the hearers, when the speech stirs their emotions. Our judgements when we are pleased and friendly are not the same as when we are pained and hostile. It is towards producing these effects, as we maintain, that present-day writers on rhetoric direct the whole of their efforts. This subject shall be treated in detail when we come to speak of the emotions. Thirdly, persuasion is effected through the speech itself when we have proved a truth or an apparent truth by means of the persuasive arguments suitable to the case in question.

There are, then, these three means of effecting persuasion. The man who is to be in command of them must, it is clear, be able (1) to reason logically, (2) to understand human character and goodness in their various forms, and (3) to understand the emotions-that is, to name them and describe them, to know their causes and the way in which they are excited. It thus appears that rhetoric is an offshoot of dialectic and also of ethical studies. Ethical studies may fairly be called political; and for this reason rhetoric masquerades as political science, and the professors of it as political experts-sometimes from want of education, sometimes from ostentation, sometimes owing to other human failings. As a matter of fact, it is a branch of dialectic and similar to it, as we said at the outset. Neither rhetoric nor dialectic is the scientific study of any one separate subject: both are faculties for providing arguments. This is perhaps a sufficient account of their scope and of how they are related to each other. [...]

A statement is persuasive and credible either because it is directly self-evident or because it appears to be proved from other statements that are so. In either case it is persuasive because there is somebody whom it persuades. But none of the arts theorize about individual cases. Medicine, for instance, does not theorize about what will help to cure Socrates or Callias, but only about what will help to cure any or all of a given class of patients: this alone is business: individual cases are so infinitely various that no systematic knowledge of them is possible. In the same way the theory of rhetoric is concerned not with what seems probable to a given individual like Socrates or Hippias, but with what seems probable to men of a given type; and this is true of dialectic also. Dialectic does not construct its syllogisms out of any haphazard materials, such as the fancies of crazy people, but out of materials that call for discussion; and rhetoric, too, draws upon the regular subjects of debate. The duty of rhetoric is to deal with such matters as we deliberate upon without arts or systems to guide us, in the hearing of persons who cannot take in at a glance a complicated argument, or follow a long chain of reasoning. The subjects of our deliberation are such as seem to present us with alternative possibilities: about things that could not have been, and cannot now or in the future be, other than they are, nobody who takes them to be of this nature wastes his time in deliberation. [...]

3

Rhetoric falls into three divisions, determined by the three classes of listeners to speeches. For of the three elements in speech-making — speaker, subject, and person addressed—it is the last one, the hearer, that determines the speech's end and object. The hearer must be either a judge, with a decision to make about things past or future, or an observer. A member of the assembly decides about future events, a juryman about past events: while those who merely decide on the orator's skill are observers. From this it follows that there are three divisions of oratory—(1) political, (2) forensic, and (3) the ceremonial oratory of display.

10   Political speaking urges us either to do or not to do something: one of these two courses is always taken by private counsellors, as well as by men who address public assemblies. Forensic speaking either attacks or defends somebody: one or other of these two things must always be done by the parties in a case. The ceremonial oratory of display either praises or censures somebody. These three kinds of rhetoric refer to three different kinds of time. The political orator is concerned with the future: it is about things to be done hereafter that he advises, for or against. The party in a case at law is concerned with the past; one man accuses the other, and the other defends himself, with reference

to things already done. The ceremonial orator is, properly speaking, concerned with the present, since all men praise or blame in view of the state of things existing at the time, though they often find it useful also to recall the past and to make guesses at the future.

Rhetoric has three distinct ends in view, one for each of its three kinds. The political orator aims at establishing the expediency or the harmfulness of a proposed course of action; if he urges its acceptance, he does so on the ground that it will do good; if he urges its rejection, he does so on the ground that it will do harm; and all other points, such as whether the proposal is just or unjust, honourable or dishonourable, he brings in as subsidiary and relative to this main consideration. Parties in a law-case aim at establishing the justice or injustice of some action, and they too bring in all other points as subsidiary and relative to this one. Those who praise or attack a man aim at proving him worthy of honour or the reverse, and they too treat all other considerations with reference to this one. [...]

Book II

1

We have now considered the materials to be used in supporting or opposing a political measure, in pronouncing eulogies or censures, and for prosecution and defence in the law courts. We have considered the received opinions on which we may best base our arguments so as to convince our hearers-those opinions with which our enthymemes deal, and out of which they are built, in each of the three kinds of oratory, according to what may be called the special needs of each.

But since rhetoric exists to affect the giving of decisions-the hearers decide between one political speaker and another, and a legal verdict is a decision-the orator must not only try to make the argument of his speech demonstrative and worthy of belief; he must also make his own character look right and put his hearers, who are to decide, into the right frame of mind. Particularly in political oratory, but also in lawsuits, it adds much to an orator's influence that his own character should look right and that he should be thought to entertain the right feelings towards his hearers; and also that his hearers themselves should be in just the right frame of mind. That the orator's own character should look right is particularly important in political speaking: that the audience should be in the right frame of mind, in lawsuits. When people are feeling friendly and placable, they think one sort of thing; when they are feeling angry or hostile, they think either something totally different or the same thing with a different intensity: when they feel friendly to the man who comes before them for judgement, they regard him as having done little wrong, if any; when they feel hostile, they take the opposite view. Again, if they are eager for, and have good hopes of, a thing that will be pleasant if it happens, they think that it certainly will happen and be good for them: whereas if they are indifferent or annoyed, they do not think so.

There are three things which inspire confidence in the orator's own character-the three, namely, that induce us to believe a thing apart from any proof of it: good sense, good moral character, and goodwill. False statements and bad advice are due to one or more of the following three causes. Men either form a false opinion through want of good sense; or they form a true opinion, but because of their moral badness do not say what they really think; or finally, they are both sensible and upright, but not well disposed to their hearers, and may fail in consequence to recommend what they know to be the best course. These are the only possible cases. It follows that any one who is thought to have all three of these good qualities will inspire trust in his audience. The way to make ourselves thought to be sensible and morally good must be gathered from the analysis of goodness already given: the way to establish your own goodness is the same as the way to establish that of others. Good will and friendliness of disposition will form part of our discussion of the emotions, to which we must now turn.

15   The Emotions are all those feelings that so change men as to affect their judgements, and that are also attended by pain or pleasure. Such are anger, pity, fear and the like, with their opposites. We must arrange what we have to say about each of them under three heads. Take, for instance, the emotion of anger: here we must discover (1) what the state of mind of angry people is, (2) who the people are with whom they usually get angry, and (3) on what grounds they get angry with them. It is not enough to know one or even two of these points; unless we know all three, we shall be unable to arouse anger in any one. The same is true of the other emotions. So just as earlier in this work we drew up a list of useful propositions for the orator, let us now proceed in the same way to analyse the subject before us. [...]

Book III

1

In making a speech one must study three points: first, the means of producing persuasion; second, the style, or language, to be used; third, the proper arrangement of the various parts of the speech. We have already specified the sources of persuasion. We have shown that these are three in number; what they are; and why there are only these three: for we have shown that persuasion must in every case be effected either (1) by working on the emotions of the judges themselves, (2) by giving them the right impression of the speakers' character, or (3) by proving the truth of the statements made.

Enthymemes also have been described, and the sources from which they should be derived; there being both special and general lines of argument for enthymemes.

Our next subject will be the style of expression. For it is not enough to know what we ought to say; we must also say it as we ought; much help is thus afforded towards producing the right impression of a speech. The first question to receive attention was naturally the one that comes first naturally-how persuasion can be produced from the facts themselves. The second is how to set these facts out in language. A third would be the proper method of delivery; this is a thing that affects the success of a speech greatly; but hitherto the subject has been neglected. Indeed, it was long before it found a way into the arts of tragic drama and epic recitation: at first poets acted their tragedies themselves. It is plain that delivery has just as much to do with oratory as with poetry. (In connexion with poetry, it has been studied by Glaucon of Teos among others.) It is, essentially, a matter of the right management of the voice to express the various emotions-of speaking loudly, softly, or between the two; of high, low, or intermediate pitch; of the various rhythms that suit various subjects. These are the three things-volume of sound, modulation of pitch, and rhythm-that a speaker bears in mind. It is those who do bear them in mind who usually win prizes in the dramatic contests; and just as in drama the actors now count for more than the poets, so it is in the contests of public life, owing to the defects of our political institutions. No systematic treatise upon the rules of delivery has yet been composed; indeed, even the study of language made no progress till late in the day. Besides, delivery is-very properly-not regarded as an elevated subject of inquiry. Still, the whole business of rhetoric being concerned with appearances, we must pay attention to the subject of delivery, unworthy though it is, because we cannot do without it. The right thing in speaking really is that we should be satisfied not to annoy our hearers, without trying to delight them: we ought in fairness to fight our case with no help beyond the bare facts: nothing, therefore, should matter except the proof of those facts. Still, as has been already said, other things affect the result considerably, owing to the defects of our hearers. The arts of language cannot help having a small but real importance, whatever it is we have to expound to others: the way in which a thing is said does affect its intelligibility. Not, however, so much importance as people think. All such arts are fanciful and meant to charm the hearer. Nobody uses fine language when teaching geometry.

When the principles of delivery have been worked out, they will produce the same effect as on the stage. But only very slight attempts to deal with them have been made and by a few people, as by Thrasymachus in his 'Appeals to Pity'. Dramatic ability is a natural gift, and can hardly be systematically taught. The principles of good diction can be so taught, and therefore we have men of ability in this direction too, who win prizes in their turn, as well as those speakers who excel in delivery-speeches of the written or literary kind owe more of their effect to their direction than to their thought.

20   It was naturally the poets who first set the movement going; for words represent things, and they had also the human voice at their disposal, which of all our organs can best represent other things. Thus the arts of recitation and acting were formed, and others as well. Now it was because poets seemed to win fame through their fine language when their thoughts were simple enough, that the language of oratorical prose at first took a poetical colour, e.g. that of Gorgias. Even now most uneducated people think that poetical language makes the finest discourses. That is not true: the language of prose is distinct from that of poetry. This is shown by the state of things to-day, when even the language of tragedy has altered its character. Just as iambics were adopted, instead of tetrameters, because they are the most prose-like of all metres, so tragedy has given up all those words, not used in ordinary talk, which decorated the early drama and are still used by the writers of hexameter poems. It is therefore ridiculous to imitate a poetical manner which the poets themselves have dropped; and it is now plain that we have not to treat in detail the whole question of style, but may confine ourselves to that part of it which concerns our

present subject, rhetoric. The other—the poetical—part of it has been discussed in the treatise on the Art of Poetry. [...]

13

A speech has two parts. You must state your case, and you must prove it. You cannot either state your case and omit to prove it, or prove it without having first stated it; since any proof must be a proof of something, and the only use of a preliminary statement is the proof that follows it. Of these two parts the first part is called the Statement of the case, the second part the Argument, just as we distinguish between Enunciation and Demonstration. The current division is absurd. For 'narration' surely is part of a forensic speech only: how in a political speech or a speech of display can there be 'narration' in the technical sense? or a reply to a forensic opponent? or an epilogue in closely-reasoned speeches? Again, introduction, comparison of conflicting arguments, and recapitulation are only found in political speeches when there is a struggle between two policies. They may occur then; so may even accusation and defence, often enough; but they form no essential part of a political speech. Even forensic speeches do not always need epilogues; not, for instance, a short speech, nor one in which the facts are easy to remember, the effect of an epilogue being always a reduction in the apparent length. It follows, then, that the only necessary parts of a speech are the Statement and the Argument. These are the essential features of a speech; and it cannot in any case have more than Introduction, Statement, Argument, and Epilogue. 'Refutation of the Opponent' is part of the arguments: so is 'Comparison' of the opponent's case with your own, for that process is a magnifying of your own case and therefore a part of the arguments, since one who does this proves something. The Introduction does nothing like this; nor does the Epilogue-it merely reminds us of what has been said already. If we make such distinctions we shall end, like Theodorus and his followers, by distinguishing 'narration' proper from 'post-narration' and 'pre-narration', and 'refutation' from 'final refutation'. But we ought only to bring in a new name if it indicates a real species with distinct specific qualities; otherwise the practice is pointless and silly, like the way Licymnius invented names in his Art of Rhetoric-'Secundation', 'Divagation', 'Ramification'. [...]

THE METHOD OF SCIENTIFIC INVESTIGATION, 1863

Thomas Henry Huxley

◈

THOMAS HENRY HUXLEY (1825-1895)

Thomas Henry Huxley was born the seventh of eight children in the town of Ealing, Sussex. Huxley's father, a mathematics teacher, lost his position when Huxley was a child, which put a significant financial strain on the family and cut short Huxley's outside education. From that point, he taught himself, doing so with enough success to earn a scholarship as a medical apprentice while a teenager. At 21, Huxley received the opportunity to serve as assistant surgeon on the *HMS Rattlesnake*. During the voyage, he embarked on study of marine invertebrates, work which garnered the attention of some of Britain's scientific elite. Huxley's major fame arose in response to Charles Darwin's assertion of evolutionary theory. In 1860, Huxley faced off against Archbishop Samuel Wilberforce in the "Oxford Debate," in which Huxley's staunch defense of evolution helped to popularize the idea and earn him the nickname "Darwin's Bulldog." As an educator, Huxley also helped to establish biology as a degreed academic discipline. His major writings include *Evidence on Man's Place in Nature* (1863), the first work to consider the question of human evolution, and his 1893 lecture *Evolution and Ethics*.

1   The method of scientific investigation is nothing but the expression of the necessary mode of working of the human mind. It is simply the mode at which all phenomena are reasoned about, rendered precise and exact. There is no more difference, but there is just the same kind of difference, between the mental operations of a man of science and those of an ordinary person, as there is between the operations and methods of a baker or of a butcher weighing out his goods in common scales, and the operations of a chemist in performing a difficult and complex analysis by means of his balance and finely graduated weights.

It is not that the action of the scales in the one case, and the balance in the other, differ in the principles of their construction or manner of working; but the beam of one is set on an infinitely finer axis than the other, and of course turns by the addition of a much smaller weight.

You will understand this better, perhaps, if I give you some familiar example. You have all heard it repeated, I dare say, that men of science work by means of induction and deduction, and that by the help of these operations, they, in a sort of sense, wring from Nature certain other things, which are called natural laws, and causes, and that out of these, by some cunning skill of their own, they build up hypotheses and theories. And it is imagined by many, that the operations of the common mind can be by no means compared with these processes, and that they have to be acquired by a sort of special apprenticeship to the craft. To hear all these large words, you would think that the mind of a man of science must be constituted differently from that of his fellow men; but if you will not be frightened by terms, you will discover that you are quite wrong, and that all these terrible apparatus are being used by yourselves every day and every hour of your lives.

There is a well-known incident in one of Moliere's plays, where the author makes the hero express unbounded delight on being told that he had been talking prose during the whole of his life [*Le bourgeois gentilhomme*]. In the same way, I trust, that you will take comfort, and be delighted with yourselves, on the discovery that you have been acting on the principles of inductive and deductive philosophy during the same period. Probably there is not one here who has not in the course of the day had occasion to set in motion a complex train of reasoning, of the very same kind, as that which a scientific man goes through in tracing the causes of natural phenomena. A very trivial circumstance will serve to exemplify this. Suppose you go into a fruiterer's shop, wanting an apple,--you take up one, and, on biting it, you find it is sour; you look at it, and see that it is hard and green. You take up another one, and that too is hard, green, and sour. The shopman offers you a third; but, before biting it, you examine it, and find that it is hard and green, and you immediately say that you will not have it, as it must be sour, like those that you have already tried.

Nothing can be more simple than that, you think; but if you will take the trouble to analyse and trace out into its logical elements what has been done by the mind, you will be greatly surprised. In the first place you have performed the operation of induction. You have found that, in two experiences, hardness and greenness in apples went together with sourness. It was so in the first case, and it was confirmed by the second. True, it is a very small basis, but still it is enough to make an induction from; you generalise the facts, and you expect to find sourness in apples where you get hardness and greenness. You found upon that a general law that all hard and green apples are sour; and that, as far as it goes, is a perfect induction. Well, having got your natural law in this way, when you are offered another apple which you find is hard and green, you say, 'All hard and green apples are sour; this apple is hard and green, therefore this apple is sour.' That train of reasoning is what logicians call a syllogism, and has all its various parts and terms,--its major premiss, its minor premiss and its conclusion. And, by the help of further reasoning, which, if drawn out, would have to be exhibited in two or three other syllogisms, you arrive at your final determination, 'I will not have that apple.' So that, you see, you have, in the first place, established a law by induction, and upon that you have founded a deduction, and reasoned out the special particular case. Well now, suppose, having got your conclusion of the law, that at some time afterwards, you are discussing the qualities of apples with a friend: you will say to him, 'It is a very curious thing,--but I find that all hard and green apples are sour!' Your friend says to you, 'But how do you know that?' You at once reply, 'Oh, because I have tried them over and over again, and have always found them to be so.' Well, if we were talking science instead of common sense, we should call that an experimental verification. And, if still opposed, you go further, and say, 'I have heard from the people in Somersetshire and Devonshire, where a large number of apples are grown, that they have observed the same thing. It is also found to be the case in Normandy, and in North America. In short, I find it to be the universal experience of mankind wherever attention has been directed to the subject.' Whereupon, your friend, unless he is a very unreasonable man, agrees with you, and is convinced that you are quite right in the conclusion you have drawn. He believes, although perhaps he does not know he believes it, that the more extensive verifications are,--that the more frequently experiments have been made, and the results of the same kind arrived at,--that the more varied the conditions under which the same results are attained, the more certain is the ultimate conclusion. He sees that the experiment has been tried under all sorts of conditions, as to time, place, and people, with the same result; and he says with you, therefore, that the law you have laid down must be a good one, and he must believe it.

❖

THE CHOICE FETISH: BLESSINGS AND CURSES OF A MARKET IDOL

Robert B. Reich

❖

ROBERT B. REICH (1946-)

Economist Robert B. Reich was born in Scranton, Pennsylvania, in 1946. After receiving a B.A. from Dartmouth College in 1968, Reich won a Rhodes Scholarship to study at Oxford University, where he earned his M.A. He next obtained a J.D. from Yale Law School. Reich has served in two presidential administrations, first with the Federal Trade Commission under Jimmy Carter, and later as Secretary of Labor under Bill Clinton. Reich is currently Chancellor's Professor of Public Policy at the University of California, Berkeley's Goldman School of Public Policy; he has also taught at Harvard and Brandeis University. Reich is a prolific writer, contributing to publications including *The Atlantic* and *The New Republic*, while his books include *Locked in the Cabinet* (1997), a recounting of his experience in the Clinton administration, and 2010's *Aftershock: The Next Economy and America's Future*.

Choices are supposed to be liberating. "Freedom of choice" is the 1 economist's favorite tonic, the libertarian's ideal, the classic liberal's alternative to revolution. But are we in danger of overdoing it? Can there be such a thing as too much choice?

My 401(k) plan offers me ten different funds, each one of them featuring several dozen permutations for allocating my savings among an array of equities, bonds, and derivatives. Yet regardless of my choice, the odds of beating a market index are very low. My HMO is competing with many others, each one providing a dizzying set of healthcare options. But basically, I'd be content with a good doctor.

A lot of choices we face today are little more than incremental gradations of quality, based on how much you're willing or able to pay. Which is to say, the market works. Residential communities are beginning to resemble appliances or automobiles, with innumerable options and add-ons available depending on price: A pool is extra; throw in an extra facility—it's more money. You want landscape maintenance? A security guard? There's a bigger tab.

A young couple, new to town, asks me to which preschool they should send their four-year-old. I tell them that the quality of the attention their child will get—how caring, consistent, and stimulating—depends largely on how much they're willing to shell out. Meanwhile, many early boomers like me are making agonizing choices about caring for aging parents—assisted living; cooperative with visiting nurse; independent with home health-care aide; nursing home. Again, quality depends on money. It's agonizing when you can't afford the very best, when that's what they deserve.

5   Even the most intimate decisions are transmuting into commercial choices. Ivy League women are selling their eggs. I saw one advertisement for Ivy League sperm. Soon, there'll be Ivy League uteruses where fetuses can thrive in a superenriched learning environment. At later stages of development, humans can now—with increasing ease— change their noses into almost any shape they wish, lift their faces, reshape their corneas, put hair into balding scalps, get new hips, and fortify their erections. In a few years, maybe you'll be able to replace genes you don't like, and then make a perfect clone of yourself. Even choices of marriage partner are getting down to business: One lawyer I know who specializes in prenuptial agreements tells me business is booming. The number of "personal coaches" has doubled each year since the early 1990s, according to Thomas Leonard, founder of Coach University, which has already trained thousands of them. There has also been an upsurge in online counselors, guides, and spiritual advisors.

Blame it partly on digital technology, which is multiplying choices. Henry Ford's assembly line lowered the cost and democratized consumption of the automobile, but it did so by narrowing choice. "Any customer can have a car painted any color that he wants as long as it is black," he famously offered; now, you can design your own car over the Internet. The first mass-produced shoes in America were called "straights" because, like those that people had worn for centuries, they didn't distinguish between left and right feet; last Christmas, Nordstrom offered a choice of more than 20 million pairs of shoes tailored precisely to customer specifications. A neighbor of mine with a satellite dish atop her garage receives hundreds of television channels; it must take her days just to surf through them. At this writing, there are more than a billion web pages. The most sophisticated search engine plumbs no more than 50 percent of them. Anyone who attempts to surf this ocean risks drowning.

When just about everything can be turned into digits and then rearranged into an almost infinite variety, the consumer is king, or so it's supposed. But the consumer actually becomes a day laborer, breathlessly toiling to make sense of it all. More time and energy is spent deciding on the best deal than enjoying the purchase itself. Tried choosing a new computer lately? You've got to know more than Bill Gates knew ten years ago to figure whether exactly what you need is a 400-megahertz Pentium III with MPEG-2 digital video full-screen playback, a 128-bit graphics accelerator, 32 megabytes of memory, and an external disk drive.

The glut of choice is also being propelled by a new prosperity that equates wealth with the ability to get exactly what you want, and by a deepening cynicism about uniform public services. "School choice" is all the rage—charter, magnet, private, schools specializing in music or science—to which upscale parents add private tutors, semesters abroad, and summer enrichment programs. Even if it is not privatized soon, Social Security has already fallen prey to widespread expectations that its contribution to the retirement income of today's workers will shrink. Coupled with the gradual disappearance of pension plans, private savings—the "third leg" of retirement income—has to bear ever more weight. That's why every big bank and securities dealer is eagerly jumping into the breach.

Public pools and parks are giving way to private health clubs that range from a simple treadmill to manicured golf courses and glass-enclosed tennis and squash courts, accompanied by small armies of personal trainers and attendants. Public roads and police departments are supplanted by gated residential communities with their own maintenance crews and security guards. The budgets of public libraries are being squeezed as the prosperous middle class buys its own books online.

Choices like these are sorting Americans by wealth, health, 10 education, and age. "Public" institutions never completely leveled the field—after all, public schools were long racially segregated in the South by law, and economically segregated in the North by neighborhood—but the ideals of the public school, the public library, public police and fire departments, Social Security, and even the draft at least provided common reference points, and sometimes occasions to meet across the divides.

Even American politics is succumbing to the god of choice. We're losing public deliberation about what's good for all of us in favor of individual choices about what's best for *me*. The "public good" or "public interest" has become a quaint phrase from the era of town meetings, political parties, and democratic clubs. It's now all about opinion polls, e-voting, and ballot propositions.

Instead of liberating us, the new world of choice is making us more dependent on people who specialize in persuading us to choose this or that. A growing portion of the retirement savings we channel to Fidelity or Merrill Lynch or any other financial service goes to advertising and marketing pros who try to convince us there's a significant difference between these giants. A considerable chunk of the health-care dollars we and our employers send to health insurers and HMOs finds its way to the ad agencies that tout them. Politics is now almost completely in the hands of political consultants, lobbyists, publicists, and spin doctors, all of whom are paid large sums to convince us to choose their candidate or their cause over a competing one, even when the differences between them are so small as to be invisible to the naked eye.

I relish my freedom of choice as much as anyone. But my freedom isn't equivalent to the breadth or quantity of my choices. You and I need freedom to make the significant choices—such as what we stand for, to what and to whom we're going to commit our lives, and what we want by way of a community and a society. Too many small choices only divert our attention from these bigger ones, robbing us of the time and energy we need to exercise true freedom. Yet the new technologies, combined with increasing middle-class prosperity and disdain for public institutions, are making fetishes out of tiny choices. Unless we choose what kinds of choices we want to be faced with— both as individuals and as a society—we will soon drown in a rising tide of inconsequential options.

Reprinted from *Civilization* (August/September 2000), by permission of the author

◆

III
PROCESS

DON'T YOU THINK IT'S TIME TO START THINKING?

Northrop Frye

◈

NORTHROP FRYE (1912-1991)

Northrop Frye, one of Canada's most important literary critics and
theorists, was born in Quebec and raised in New Brunswick. After
earning his bachelor's degree from the University of Toronto, he went
on to study theology and was ordained a minister of the United Church
of Canada. Later, Frye earned his M.A. from Oxford, and returned to
the University of Toronto, where he would teach for the remaining years
of his academic career. Frye's first and most significant book, *Fearful
Symmetry* (1947), was an analysis of William Blake's poetry and broke
new ground in scholarship of the poet. Frye's work pioneered the
concept of a systematic theory of criticism, creating a scientific process
out of the discipline of literary criticism. Frye also supported Canadian
literature— in a period in which the field was viewed in a dim light—as
part of a larger interest in understanding the Canadian imagination and
identity.

---

1   A student often leaves high school today without any sense of language
as a structure.

He may also have the idea that reading and writing are elementary
skills that he mastered in childhood, never having grasped the fact
that there are differences in levels of reading and writing as there are
in mathematics between short division and integral calculus.

Yet, in spite of his limited verbal skills, he firmly believes that he
can think, that he has ideas, and that if he is just given the opportunity
to express them he will be all right. Of course, when you look at what
he's written you find it doesn't make any sense. When you tell him this
he is devastated.

Part of his confusion here stems from the fact that we use the word
"think" in so many bad, punning ways. Remember James Thurber's

Walter Mitty who was always dreaming great dreams of glory. When his wife asked him what he was doing he would say, "Has it ever occurred to you that I might be thinking?"

But, of course, he wasn't thinking at all. Because we use it for everything our minds do, worrying, remembering, daydreaming, we imagine that thinking is something that can be achieved without any training. But again it's a matter of practice. How well we can think depends on how much of it we have already done. Most students need to be taught, very carefully and patiently, that there is no such thing as an inarticulate idea waiting to have the right words wrapped around it.

They have to learn that ideas do not exist until they have been incorporated into words. Until that point you don't know whether you are pregnant or just have gas on the stomach.

The operation of thinking is the practice of articulating ideas until they are in the right words. And we can't think at random either. We can only add one more idea to the body of something we have already thought about. Most of us spend very little time doing this, and that is why there are so few people whom we regard as having any power to articulate at all. When such a person appears in public life, like Mr. Trudeau, we tend to regard him as possessing a gigantic intellect.

A society like ours doesn't have very much interest in literacy. It is compulsory to read and write because society must have docile and obedient citizens. We are taught to read so that we can obey the traffic signs and to cipher so that we can make out our income tax, but development of verbal competency is very much left to the individual.

And when we look at our day-to-day existence we can see that there are strong currents at work against the development of powers of articulateness. Young adolescents today often betray a curious sense of shame about speaking articulately, of framing a sentence with a period at the end of it.

Part of the reason for this is the powerful anti-intellectual drive which is constantly present in our society. Articulate speech marks you out as an individual, and in some settings this can be rather dangerous because people are often suspicious and frightened of articulateness. So if you say as little as possible and use only stereotyped, ready-made phrases you can hide yourself in the mass.

Then there are various epidemics sweeping over society which use unintelligibility as a weapon to preserve the present power structure. By making things as unintelligible as possible, to as many people as possible, you can hold the present power structure together. Understanding and articulateness lead to its destruction. This is the kind of thing that George Orwell was talking about, not just in *Nineteen Eighty-Four*, but in all his work on language. The kernel of everything reactionary and tyrannical in society is the impoverishment of the means of verbal communication.

The vast majority of things that we hear today are prejudices and clichés, simply verbal formulas that have no thought behind them but are put up as pretense of thinking. It is not until we realize these things conceal meaning, rather than reveal it, that we can begin to develop our own powers of articulateness.

The teaching of humanities is, therefore, a militant job. Teachers are faced not simply with a mass of misconceptions and unexamined assumptions. They must engage in a fight to help the student confront and reject the verbal formulas and stock responses, to convert passive acceptance into active, constructive power. It is a fight against illiteracy and for the maturation of the mental process, for the development of skills which once acquired will never become obsolete.

SHITTY FIRST DRAFTS

Anne Lamott

ANNE LAMOTT (1954-)

Anne Lamott has lived in the San Francisco area for most of her life. Her father, Kenneth Lamott, was a writer whose death from a brain tumor helped inspire her first novel, *Hard Laughter* (1980). Lamott has subsequently written several novels and works of non-fiction, typically from an autobiographical perspective. Christianity and religion are frequent themes, serving, most obviously, as the focus in *Traveling Mercies* (1999). Her single motherhood has also taken center stage in such works as *Operating Instructions* (1993) and her most recent work *Some Assembly Required* (2012). In 1994's *Bird by Bird: Some Instructions on Writing and Life*, she discusses the writing process and provides advice for those embarking upon it.

Now, practically even better news than that of short assignments is the idea of shitty first drafts. All good writers write them. This is how they end up with good second drafts and terrific third drafts. People tend to look at successful writers, writers who are getting their books published and maybe even doing well financially, and think that they sit down at their desks every morning feeling like a million dollars, feeling great about who they are and how much talent they have and what a great story they have to tell; that they take in a few deep breaths, push back their sleeves, roll their necks a few times to get all the cricks out, and dive in, typing fully formed passages as fast as a court reporter. But this is just the fantasy of the uninitiated. I know some very great writers, writers you love who write beautifully and have made a great deal of money, and not one of them sits down routinely feeling wildly enthusiastic and confident. Not one of them writes elegant first drafts. All right, one of them does, but we do not like her very much. We do not think that she has a rich inner life or that God likes her or can even stand her. (Although when I mentioned this to my priest friend Tom, he said you can safely assume you've created God in your own image when it turns out that God hates all the same people you do.)

Very few writers really know what they are doing until they've done it. Nor do they go about their business feeling dewy and thrilled. They do not type a few stiff warm-up sentences and then find themselves bounding along like huskies across the snow. One writer I know tells me that he sits down every morning and says to himself nicely, "It's not like you don't have a choice, because you do—you can either type or kill yourself." We all often feel like we are pulling teeth, even those writers whose prose ends up being the most natural and fluid. The right words and sentences just do not come pouring out like ticker tape most of the time.

Now, Muriel Spark is said to have felt that she was taking dictation from God every morning—sitting there, one supposes, plugged into a Dictaphone, typing away, humming. But this is a very hostile and aggressive position. One might hope for bad things to rain down on a person like this.

For me and most of the other writers I know, writing is not rapturous. In fact, the only way I can get anything written at all is to write really, really shitty first drafts.

5   The first draft is the child's draft, where you let it all pour out and then let it romp all over the place, knowing that no one is going to see it and that you can shape it later. You just let this childlike part of you channel whatever voices and visions come through and onto the page. If one of the characters wants to say, "Well, so what, Mr. Poopy Pants?," you let her. No one is going to see it. If the kid wants to get into really sentimental, weepy, emotional territory, you let him. Just get it all down on paper, because there may be something great in those six crazy pages that you would never have gotten to by more rational, grown-up means. There may be something in the very last line of the very last paragraph on page six that you just love, that is so beautiful or wild that you now know what you're supposed to be writing about, more or less, or in what direction you might go—but there was no way to get to this without first getting through the first five and a half pages.

I used to write food reviews for *California* magazine before it folded. (My writing food reviews had nothing to do with the magazine folding, although every single review did cause a couple of canceled subscriptions. Some readers took umbrage at my comparing mounds of vegetable puree with various ex-presidents' brains.) These reviews always took two days to write. First I'd go to a restaurant several times with a few opinionated, articulate friends in tow. I'd sit there writing down everything anyone said that was at all interesting or funny. Then on the following Monday I'd sit down at my desk with my notes, and try to write the review. Even after I'd been doing this for years, panic would set in. I'd try to write a lead, but instead I'd write a couple of dreadful sentences, XX them out, try again, XX everything out, and then feel despair and worry settle on my chest like an x-ray apron. It's over, I'd think, calmly. I'm not going to be able to get the magic to work this time. I'm ruined. I'm through. I'm toast. Maybe, I'd think, I can get my old job back as a clerk-typist. But probably not. I'd get up and study my teeth in the mirror for a while. Then I'd stop, remember to breathe, make a few phone calls, hit the kitchen and chow down. Eventually I'd go back and sit down at my desk, and sigh for the next ten minutes. Finally I would pick up my one-inch picture frame, stare into it as if for the answer, and every time the answer would come: all I had to do was to write a really shitty first draft of, say, the opening paragraph. And no one was going to see it.

So I'd start writing without reining myself in. It was almost just typing, just making my fingers move. And the writing would be terrible. I'd write a lead paragraph that was a whole page, even though the entire review could only be three pages long, and then I'd start writing up descriptions of the food, one dish at a time, bird by bird, and the critics would be sitting on my shoulders, commenting like cartoon characters. They'd be pretending to snore, or rolling their eyes at my overwrought descriptions, no matter how hard I tried to tone those descriptions down, no matter how conscious I was of what a friend said to me gently in my early days of restaurant reviewing. "Annie," she said, "it is just a piece of *chicken*. It is just a bit of *cake*."

But because by then I had been writing for so long, I would eventually let myself trust the process—sort of, more or less. I'd write a first draft that was maybe twice as long as it should be, with a self-indulgent and boring beginning, stupefying descriptions of the meal, lots of quotes from my black-humored friends that made them sound more like the Manson girls than food lovers, and no ending to speak of. The whole thing would be so long and incoherent and hideous that for the rest of the day I'd obsess about getting creamed by a car before I could write a decent second draft. I'd worry that people would read what I'd written and believe that the accident had really been a suicide, that I had panicked because my talent was waning and my mind was shot.

The next day, though, I'd sit down, go through it all with a colored pen, take out everything I possibly could, find a new lead somewhere on the second page, figure out a kicky place to end it, and then write a second draft. It always turned out fine, sometimes even funny and weird and helpful. I'd go over it one more time and mail it in.

10   Then, a month later, when it was time for another review, the whole process would start again, complete with the fears that people would find my first draft before I could rewrite it.

Almost all good writing begins with terrible first efforts. You need to start somewhere. Start by getting something—anything—down on paper. A friend of mine says that the first draft is the down draft—you just get it down. The second draft is the up draft—you fix it up. You try to say what you have to say more accurately. And the third draft is the dental draft, where you check every tooth, to see if it's loose or cramped or decayed, or even, God help us, healthy.

What I've learned to do when I sit down to work on a shitty first draft is to quiet the voices in my head. First there's the vinegar-lipped Reader Lady, who says primly, "Well, that's not very interesting, is it?" And there's the emaciated German male who writes these Orwellian memos detailing your thought crimes. And there are your parents, agonizing over your lack of loyalty and discretion; and there's William Burroughs, dozing off or shooting up because he finds you as bold and articulate as a houseplant; and so on. And there are also the dogs; let's not forget the dogs, the dogs in their pen who will surely hurtle and snarl their way out if you ever stop writing, because writing is, for some of us, the latch that keeps the door of the pen closed, keeps those crazy ravenous dogs contained.

Quieting those voices is at least half the battle I fight daily. But this is better than it used to be. It used to be 87 percent. Left to its own devices, my mind spends much of its time having conversations with people who aren't there. I walk along defending myself to people, or exchanging repartee with them, or rationalizing my behavior, or seducing them with gossip, or pretending I'm on their TV talk show or whatever. I speed or run an aging yellow light or don't come to a full stop, and one nanosecond later am explaining to imaginary cops exactly why I had to do what I did, or insisting that I did not in fact do it.

I happened to mention this to a hypnotist I saw many years ago, and he looked at me very nicely. At first I thought he was feeling around on the floor for the silent alarm button, but then he gave me the following exercise, which I still use to this day.

Close your eyes and get quiet for a minute, until the chatter starts   15
up. Then isolate one of the voices and imagine the person speaking
as a mouse. Pick it up by the tail and drop it into a mason jar. Then
isolate another voice, pick it up by the tail, drop it in the jar. And so on.
Drop in any high-maintenance parental units, drop in any contractors,
lawyers, colleagues, children, anyone who is whining in your head.
Then put the lid on, and watch all these mouse people clawing at the
glass, jabbering away, trying to make you feel like shit because you
won't do what they want—won't give them more money, won't be
more successful, won't see them more often. Then imagine that there
is a volume-control button on the bottle. Turn it all the way up for a
moment, and listen to the stream of angry, neglected, guilt-mongering
voices. Then turn it all the way down and watch the frantic mice lunge
at the glass, trying to get to you. Leave it down, and get back to your
shitty first draft.

A writer friend of mine suggests opening the jar and shooting
them all in the head. But I think he's a little angry, and I'm sure nothing
like this would ever occur to you.

Reprinted from *Bird by Bird: Some Instructions on Writing and Life* (1995),
by permission of Pantheon Books, a division of Random House, Inc.

A WAY OF WRITING

William Stafford

WILLIAM STAFFORD (1914-1993)

William Stafford was born in Kansas and earned both a B.A. and M.A. from the University of Kansas. After several years of work in public service, Stafford obtained his Ph.D. from the University of Iowa. Though he was appointed the twentieth Poet Laureate of the United States in 1970, his career in poetry began relatively late in life, with first collection, *Traveling Through the Dark*, published when he was 48. Stafford taught English at Lewis & Clark College in Oregon, retiring in 1980 and subsequently focusing on his poetic career. Stafford's additional works include the essay collections *Writing the Australian Crawl* (1978), *You Must Revise Your Life* (1986), and the children's book *The Animal That Drank Up Sound* (1992).

1   A writer is not so much someone who has something to say as he is someone who has found a process that will bring about new things he would not have thought of if he had not started to say them. That is, he does not draw on a reservoir; instead, he engages in an activity that brings to him a whole succession of unforeseen stories, poems, essays, plays, laws, philosophies, religions, or—but wait!

Back in school, from the first when I began to try to write things, I felt this richness. One thing would lead to another; the world would give and give. Now, after twenty years or so of trying, I live by that certain richness, an idea hard to pin, difficult to say, and perhaps offensive to some. For there are strange implications in it.

One implication is the importance of just plain receptivity. When I write, I like to have an interval before me when I am not likely to be interrupted. For me, this means usually the early morning, before others are awake. I get pen and paper, take a glance out the window (often it is dark out there), and wait. It is like fishing. But I do not wait very long, for there is always a nibble—and this is where receptivity comes in. To get started I will accept anything that occurs to me.

Something always occurs, of course, to any of us. We can't keep from thinking. Maybe I have to settle for an immediate impression: it's cold, or hot, or dark, or bright, or in between! Or—well, the possibilities are endless. If I put down something, that thing will help the next thing come, and I'm off. If I let the process go on, things will occur to me that were not at all in my mind when I started. These things, odd and trivial as they may be, are somehow connected. And if I let them string out, surprising things will happen.

If I let them string out…Along with initial receptivity, then, there is another readiness: I must be willing to fail. If I am to keep on writing, I cannot bother to insist on high standards. I must get into action and not let anything stop me, or even slow me much. By "standards" I do not mean "correctness"—spelling, punctuation, and so on. These details become mechanical for anyone who writes for a while. I am thinking about what many people would consider "important" standards, such matters as social significance, positive values, consistency, etc. I resolutely disregard these. Something better, greater, is happening! I am following a process that leads so wildly and originally into new territory that no judgment can at the moment be made about values, significance, and so on. I am making something new, something that has not been judged before. Later others—and maybe I myself—will make judgments. Now, I am headlong to discover. Any distraction may harm the creating.

So, receptive, careless of failure, I spin out things on the page. And a wonderful freedom comes. If something occurs to me, it is all right to accept it. It has one justification: it occurs to me. No one else can guide me. I must follow my own weak, wandering, diffident impulses.

A strange bonus happens. At times, without my insisting on it, my writings become coherent; the successive elements that occur to me are clearly related. They lead by themselves to new connections. Sometimes the language, even the syllables that happen along, may start a trend. Sometimes the materials alert me to something waiting in my mind, ready for sustained attention. At such times, I allow myself to be eloquent, or intentional, or for great swoops (treacherous! not to be trusted!) reasonable. But I do not insist on any of that; for I know that back of my activity there will be the coherence of my self, and that indulgence of my impulses will bring recurrent patterns and meanings again.

This attitude toward the process of writing creatively suggests a problem for me, in terms of what others say. They talk about "skills" in writing. Without denying that I do have experience, wide reading, automatic orthodoxies and maneuvers of various kinds, I still must insist that I am often baffled about what "skill" has to do with the precious little area of confusion when I do not know what I am going to say and then I found out what I am going to say. That precious interval I am unable to bridge by skill. What can I witness about it? It remains mysterious, just as all of us must feel puzzled about how we are so inventive as to be able to talk along through complexities with our friends, not needing to plan what we are going to say, but never stalled for long in our confident forward progress. Skill? If so, it is the skill we all have, something we must have learned before the age of three or four.

A writer is one who has become accustomed to trusting that grace, or luck, or—skill.

Yet another attitude I find necessary: most of what I write, like most of what I say in casual conversation, will not amount to much. Even I will realize, and even at the time, that it is not negotiable. It will be like practice. In conversation, I allow myself random remarks—in fact, as I recall, that is the way I learned to talk—so in writing I launch many expendable efforts. A result of this free way of writing is that I am not writing for others, mostly; they will not see the product at all unless the activity eventuates in something that later appears to be worthy. My guide is the self, and its adventuring in the language brings about communication.

10   This process-rather-than-substance view of writing invites a final, dual reflection:

1. Writers may not be special—sensitive or talented in any usual sense. They are simply engaged in sustained use of a language skill we all have. Their "creations" come about through confident reliance on stray impulses that will, with trust, find occasional patterns that are satisfying.

2. But writing itself is one of the great, free human activities. There is scope for individuality, and elation, and discovery, in writing. For the person who follows with trust and forgiveness what occurs to him, the world remains always ready and deep, an inexhaustible environment, with the combined vividness of an actuality and flexibility of a dream. Working back and forth between experience and thought, writers have more than space and time can offer. They have the whole unexplored realm of human vision.[...]

Excerpted from "A Way of Writing." *Field: Contemporary Poetry and Poetics*, no. 2. Published by Oberlin College Press.

HOW I CAUSED THAT STORY

Doris Kearns Goodwin

❖

DORIS KEARNS GOODWIN (1943-)

Pulitzer Prize winner Doris Kearns Goodwin was born in Brooklyn, New York in 1943. She received a B.A. from Colby College in 1964 and a Ph.D. in government from Harvard University in 1968. After graduating, she began an internship in Lyndon B. Johnson's White House, which soon became an assistantship to the president himself. Later, she would assist Johnson in writing his memoirs. Following her work in the White House, Goodwin spent 10 years on the faculty at Harvard. During this period, she also wrote her first book, *Lyndon Johnson and the American Dream* (1977) which put her on the map as a popular writer. She followed it with a larger-scale work, *The Fitzgeralds and the Kennedys: an American Saga* (1987); though the book would face charges of plagiarism for a failure to properly cite all passages. Goodwin went on to win the Pulitzer Prize in 1995 for the book's follow-up, *No Ordinary Time: Franklin and Eleanor Roosevelt: the American Homefront during World War II*. Her next major work, 2005's *Team of Rivals: the Political Genius of Abraham Lincoln*, was also award-winning—taking that year's Lincoln Prize for best book about the Civil War and the American History Book Prize from the New York Historical Society. Goodwin's is currently working on a project that focuses on Theodore Roosevelt. In addition to her work as a writer and scholar, Goodwin has served as a commentator on PBS NewsHour and Meet the Press.

---

1   I am a historian. With the exception of being a wife and mother, it is who I am. And there is nothing I take more seriously.

In recent days, questions have been raised about how historians go about crediting their sources, and I have been caught up in the swirl. Ironically, the more intensive and far-reaching a historian's research, the greater the difficulty of citation. As the mountain of material grows, so does the possibility of error.

Fourteen years ago, not long after the publication of my book *The Fitzgeralds and the Kennedys*, I received a communication from author Lynne McTaggart pointing out that material from her book on Kathleen Kennedy had not been properly attributed. I realized that she was right. Though my footnotes repeatedly cited Ms. McTaggart's work, I failed to provide quotation marks for phrases that I had taken verbatim, having assumed that these phrases, drawn from my notes, were my words, not hers. I made the corrections she requested, and the matter was completely laid to rest—until last week, when the *Weekly Standard* published an article reviving the issue. The larger question for those of us who write history is to understand how citation mistakes can happen.

The research and writing for this 900-page book, with its 3,500 footnotes, took place over ten years. At that time, I wrote my books and took my notes in longhand, believing I could not think well on a keyboard. Most of my sources were drawn from a multitude of primary materials: manuscript collections, private letters, diaries, oral histories, newspapers, periodicals, personal interviews. After three years of research, I discovered more than 150 cartons of materials that had been previously stored in the attic of Joe Kennedy's Hyannis Port house. These materials were a treasure trove for a historian— old report cards, thousands of family letters, movie stubs and diaries, which allowed me to cross the boundaries of time and space. It took me two additional years to read, categorize and take notes on these documents.

During this same period, I took handwritten notes on perhaps 300 books. Passages I wanted to quote directly were noted along with general notes on the ideas and story lines of each book. Notes on all these sources were then arranged chronologically and kept in dozens of folders in 25 banker's boxes. Immersed in a flood of papers, I began to write the book. After each section and each chapter was completed, I returned the notes to the boxes along with notations for future footnoting. When the manuscript was finished, I went back to all these sources to check the accuracy of attributions. As a final protection, I revisited the 300 books themselves. Somehow in this process, a few of the books were not fully rechecked. I relied instead on my notes, which combined direct quotes and paraphrased sentences. If I had had the books in front of me, rather than my notes, I would have caught mistakes in the first place and placed any borrowed phrases in direct quotes.

What made this incident particularly hard for me was the fact that I take great pride in the depth of my research and the extensiveness of my citations. The writing of history is a rich process of building on the work of the past with the hope that others will build on what you have done. Through footnotes you point the way to future historians.

The only protection as a historian is to institute a process of research and writing that minimizes the possibility of error. And that I have tried to do, aided by modern technology, which enables me, having long since moved beyond longhand, to use a computer for both organizing and taking notes. I now rely on a scanner, which reproduces the passages I want to cite, and then I keep my own comments on those books in a separate file so that I will never confuse the two again. But the real miracle occurred when my college-age son taught me how to use the mysterious footnote key on the computer, which makes it possible to insert the citations directly into the text while the sources are still in front of me, instead of shuffling through hundreds of folders four or five years down the line, trying desperately to remember from where I derived a particular statistic or quote. Still, there is no guarantee against error. Should one occur, all I can do, as I did 14 years ago, is to correct it as soon as I possibly can, for my own sake and the sake of history. In the end, I am still the same fallible person I was before I made the transition to the computer, and the process of building a lengthy work of history remains a complicated but honorable task.

Reprinted from *Time*, January 22, 2002, by permission of Time, Inc.

◆

Revision Strategies of Student Writers and Experienced Adult Writers

Nancy Sommers

❖

Nancy Sommers

Nancy Sommers received an Ed.D. from Boston University. From 1987 to 2007, she served as head of the Expository Writing Program at Harvard University, and continues to serve on the faculty of Harvard's Graduate School of Education. Sommers has written extensively on the theories and practice of student writing and the process of teaching writing, with her most notable works including *"Revision Strategies of Student and Experienced Writers"* (1980) and *"Responding to Student Writing"* (1982). She has also written several textbooks, and branched out into film with *Shaped by Writing, Across the Drafts*, and *Beyond the Red Ink*.

Although various aspects of the writing process have been studied extensively of late, research on revision has been notably absent. The reason for this, I suspect, is that current models of the writing process have directed attention away from revision. With few exceptions, these models are linear; they separate the writing process into discrete stages. Two representative models are Gordon Rohman's suggestion that the composing process moves from prewriting to writing to rewriting and James Britton's model of the writing process as a series of stages described in metaphors of linear growth, conception—incubation—production.[1] What is striking about these theories of writing is that they model themselves on speech: Rohman defines the writer in a way that cannot distinguish him from a speaker ("A writer is a man who...puts [his] experience into words in his own mind"—p. 15); 1

and Britton bases his theory of writing on what he calls (following Jakobson) the "expressiveness" of speech.[2] Moreover, Britton's study itself follows the "linear model" of the relation of thought and language in speech proposed by Vygotsky, a relationship embodied in the linear movement "from the motive which engenders a thought to the shaping of the thought, *first* in inner speech, *then* in meanings of words, and *finally* in words" (quoted in Britton, p. 40). What this movement fails to take into account in its linear structure—"first…then…finally"—is the recursive shaping of thought by language; what it fails to take into account is *revision*. In these linear conceptions of the writing process revision is understood as a separate stage at the end of the process—a stage that comes after the completion of a first or second draft and one that is temporally distinct from the prewriting and writing stages of the process.[3]

The linear model bases itself on speech in two specific ways. First of all, it is based on traditional rhetorical models, models that were created to serve the spoken art of oratory. In whatever ways the parts of classical rhetoric are described, they offer "stages" of composition that are repeated in contemporary models of the writing process. Edward Corbett, for instance, describes the "five parts of a discourse"—inventio, dispositio, elocutio, memoria, pronuntiatio—and, disregarding the last two parts since "after rhetoric came to be concerned mainly with written discourse, there was no further need to deal with them,"[4] he produces a model very close to Britton's conception [inventio], incubation [dispositio], production [elocutio]. Other rhetorics also follow this procedure, and they do so not simply because of historical accident. Rather, the process represented in the linear model is based on the irreversibility of speech. Speech, Roland Barthes says, "is irreversible":

> "A word cannot be retracted, except precisely by saying that one retracts it. To cross out here is to add: if I want to erase what I have just said, I cannot do it without showing the eraser itself (I must say: 'or rather…' 'I expressed myself badly…'); paradoxically, it is ephemeral speech which is indelible, not monumental writing. All that one can do in the case of a spoken utterance is to tack on another utterance."[5]

What is impossible in speech is *revision*: like the example Barthes gives, revision in speech is an afterthought. In the same way, each stage of the linear model must be exclusive (distinct from the other stages) or else it becomes trivial and counterproductive to refer to these junctures as "stages."

By staging revision after enunciation, the linear models reduce 5 revision in writing, as in speech, to no more than an afterthought. In this way such models make the study of revision impossible. Revision, in Rohman's model, is simply the repetition of writing; or to pursue Britton's organic metaphor, revision is simply the further growth of what is already there, the "preconceived" product. The absence of research on revision, then, is a function of a theory of writing which makes revision both superfluous and redundant, a theory which does not distinguish between writing and speech.

What the linear models do produce is a parody of writing. Isolating revision and then disregarding it plays havoc with the experiences composition teachers have of the actual writing and rewriting of experienced writers. Why should the linear model be preferred? Why should revision be forgotten, superfluous? Why do teachers offer the linear model and students accept it? One reason, Barthes suggests, is that "there is a fundamental tie between teaching a speech," while "writing begins at the point where speech becomes *impossible*."[6] The spoken word cannot be revised. The possibility of revision distinguishes the written text from speech. In fact, according to Barthes, this is the essential difference between writing and speaking. When we must revise, when the very idea is subject to recursive shaping by language, then speech becomes inadequate. This is a matter to which I will return, but first we should examine, theoretically, a detailed exploration of what student writers as distinguished from experienced adult writers *do* when they write and rewrite their work. Dissatisfied with both the linear model of writing and the lack of attention to the process of revision, I conducted a series of studies over the past three years which examined the revision processes of student writers and experienced writers to see what role revision played in their writing processes. In the course of my work the revision process was redefined as *a sequence of changes in a composition—changes which are initiated by cues and occur continually throughout the writing of a work.*

Methodology

I used a case study approach. The student writers were twenty freshmen at Boston University and the University of Oklahoma with SAT verbal scores ranging from 450-600 in their first semester of composition. The twenty experienced adult writers from Boston and Oklahoma City included journalists, editors, and academics. To refer to the two groups, I use the terms *student writers* and *experienced writers* because the principal difference between these two groups is the amount of experience they have had in writing.

Each writer wrote three essays, expressive, explanatory, and persuasive, and rewrote each essay twice, producing nine written products in draft and final form. Each writer was interviewed three times after the final revision of each essay. And each writer suggested revisions for a composition written by an anonymous author. Thus extensive written and spoken documents were obtained from each writer.

The essays were analyzed by counting and categorizing the changes made. Four revision operations were identified: deletion, substitution, addition, and reordering. And four levels of changes were identified: word, phrase, sentence, theme (the extended statement of one idea). A coding system was developed for identifying the frequency of revision by level and operation. In addition, transcripts of the interviews in which the writers interpreted their revisions were used to develop what was called a *scale of concerns* for each writer. This scale enabled me to codify what were the writer's primary concerns, secondary concerns, tertiary concerns, and whether the writers used the same scale of concerns when revising the second or third drafts as they used in revising the first draft.

Revision Strategies of Student Writers

10   Most of the students I studied did not use the terms *revision* or *rewriting*. In fact, they did not seem comfortable using the word *revision* and explained that revision was not a word they used, but the word their teachers used. Instead, most of the students had developed various functional terms to describe the type of changes they made. The following are samples of these definitions:

> *Scratch Out and Do Over Again*: "I say scratch out and do over, and that means what it says. Scratching out and cutting out. I read what I have written and I cross out a word and put another word in; a more decent word or a better word. Then if there is somewhere to use a sentence that I have crossed out, I will put it there."

> *Reviewing*: "Reviewing means just using better words and eliminating words that are not needed. I go over and change words around."

Reviewing: "I just review every word and make sure that everything is worded right. I see if I am rambling; I see if I can put a better word in or leave one out. Usually when I read what I have written, I say to myself, 'that word is so bland or so trite,' and then I go and get my thesaurus."

Redoing: "Redoing means cleaning up the paper and crossing out. It is looking at something and saying, no that has to go, or no, that is not right."

Marking Out: "I don't use the word rewriting because I only   15
write one draft and the changes that I make are made on top of the draft. The changes that I make are usually just marking out words and putting different ones in."

Slashing and Throwing Out: "I throw things out and say they are not good. I like to write like Fitzgerald did by inspiration, and if I feel inspired then I don't need to slash and throw much out."

The predominant concern in these definitions is vocabulary. The students understand the revision process as a rewording activity. They do so because they perceive words as the unit of written discourse. That is, they concentrate on particular words apart from their role in the text. Thus one student quoted above thinks in terms of dictionaries, and, following the eighteenth century theory of words parodied in *Gulliver's Travels*, he imagines a load of things carried about to be exchanged. Lexical changes are the major revision activities of the students because economy is their goal. They are governed, like the linear model itself, by the Law of Occam's razor that prohibits logically needless repetition: redundancy and superfluity. Nothing governs speech more than such superfluities; speech constantly repeats itself precisely because spoken words, as Barthes writes, are expendable in the cause of communication. The aim of revision according to the students' own description is therefore to clean up speech; the redundancy of speech is unnecessary in writing, their logic suggests, because writing, unlike speech, can be reread. Thus one student said, "Redoing means cleaning up the paper and crossing out." The remarkable contradiction of cleaning by marking might, indeed, stand for student revision as I have encountered it.

The students place a symbolic importance on their selection and rejection of words as the determiners of success or failure for their compositions. When revising, they primarily ask themselves: can

I find a better word or phrase? A more impressive, not so clichéd, or less hum-drum word? Am I repeating the same word or phrase too often? They approach the revision process with what could be labeled as a "thesaurus philosophy of writing"; the students consider the thesaurus a harvest of lexical substitutions and believe that most problems in their essays can be solved by rewording. What is revealed in the students' use of the thesaurus is a governing attitude toward their writing: that the meaning to be communicated is already there, already finished, already produced, ready to be communicated, and all that is necessary is a better word "rightly worded." One student defined revision as "redoing"; "redoing" meant "just using better words and eliminating words that are not needed." For the students, writing is translating: the thought to the page, the language of speech to the more formal language of prose, the word to its synonym. Whatever is translated, an original text already exists for students, one which need not be discovered or acted upon, but simply communicated.[7]

The students list repetition as one of the elements they most worry about. This cue signals to them that they need to eliminate the repetition either by substituting or deleting words or phrases. Repetition occurs, in large part, because student writing imitates—transcribes—speech: attention to repetitious words is a manner of cleaning speech. Without a sense of the developmental possibilities of revision (and writing in general) students seek, on the authority of many textbooks, simply to clean up their language and prepare to type. What is curious, however, is that students are aware of lexical repetition, but not conceptual repetition. They only notice the repetition if they can "hear" it; they do not diagnose lexical repetition as symptomatic of problems on a deeper level. By rewording their sentences to avoid the lexical repetition, the students solve the immediate problem, but blind themselves to problems on a textual level; although they are using different words, they are sometimes merely restating the same idea with different words. Such blindness, as I discovered with student writers, is the inability to "see" revision as a process: the inability to "re-view" their work again, as it were, with different eyes, and to start over.

20   The revision strategies described above are consistent with the students' understanding of the revision process as requiring lexical changes but not semantic changes. For the students, the extent to which they revise is a function of their level of inspiration. In fact, they use the word *inspiration* to describe the ease or difficulty with which their essay is written, and the extent to which the essay needs

to be revised. If students feel inspired, if the writing comes easily, and if they don't get stuck on individual words or phrases, then they say that they cannot see any reason to revise. Because students do not see revision as an activity in which they modify and develop perspectives and ideas, they feel that if they know what they want to say, then there is little reason for making revisions.

The only modification of ideas in the students' essays occurred when they tried out two or three introductory paragraphs. This results, in part, because the students have been taught in another version of the linear model of composing to use a thesis statement as a controlling device in their introductory paragraphs. Since they write their introductions and their thesis statements even before they have really discovered what they want to say, their early close attention to the thesis statement, and more generally the linear model, function to restrict and circumscribe not only the development of their ideas, but also their ability to change the direction of these ideas.

Too often as composition teachers we conclude that students do not willingly revise. The evidence from my research suggests that it is not that students are unwilling to revise, but rather that they do what they have been taught to do in a consistently narrow and predictable way. On every occasion when I asked students why they hadn't made any more changes, they essentially replied, "I knew something larger was wrong, but I didn't think it would help to move words around." The students have strategies for handling words and phrases and their strategies helped them on a word or sentence level. What they lack, however, is a set of strategies to help them identify the "something larger" that they sensed was wrong and work from there. The students do not have strategies for handling the whole essay. They lack procedures or heuristics to help them reorder lines of reasoning or ask questions about their purposes and readers. The students view their compositions in a linear way as a series of parts. Even such potentially useful concepts as "unity" or "form" are reduced to the rule that a composition, if it is to have form, must have an introduction, a body, and a conclusion, or the sum total of the necessary parts.

The students decide to stop revising when they decide that they have not violated any of the rules for revising. These rules, such as "Never begin a sentence with a conjunction" or "Never end a sentence with a preposition," are lexically cued and rigidly applied. In general, students will subordinate the demands of the specific problems of their text to the demands of the rules. Changes are made in compliance with abstract rules about the product, rules that quite often do not apply to the specific problems in the text. These revision strategies are teacher-based, directed towards a teacher-reader who expects compliance with rules—with pre-existing "conceptions"—and who will only examine parts of the composition (writing comments about those parts in the margins of their essays) and will cite any violations of rules in those parts. At best the students see their writing altogether passively through the eyes of former teachers or their surrogates, the textbooks, and are bound to the rules which they have been taught.

Revision Strategies of Experienced Writers

One aim of my research has been to contrast how student writers define revision with how a group of experienced writers define their revision processes. Here is a sampling of the definitions from the experienced writers:

25

Rewriting: "It is a matter of looking at the kernel of what I have written, the content, and then thinking about it, responding to it, making decisions, and actually restructuring it."

Rewriting: "I rewrite as I write. It is hard to tell what is a first draft because it is not determined by time. In one draft, I might cross out three pages, write two, cross out a fourth, rewrite it, and call it a draft. I am constantly writing and rewriting. I can only conceptualize so much in my first draft—only so much information can be held in my head at one time; my rewriting efforts are a reflection of how much information I can encompass at one time. There are levels and agenda which I have to attend to in each draft."

Rewriting: "Rewriting means on one level, finding the argument, and on another level, language changes to make the argument more effective. Most of the time I feel as if I can go on rewriting forever. There is always one part of a piece that I could keep working on. It is always difficult to know at what point to abandon a piece of writing. I like this idea that a piece of writing is never finished, just abandoned."

Rewriting: "My first draft is usually very scattered. In rewriting, I find the line of argument. After the argument is resolved, I am much more interested in word choice and phrasing."

Revising: "My cardinal rule in revising is never to fall in love with what I have written in a first or second draft. An idea, sentence, or even a phrase that looks catchy, I don't trust. Part of this idea is to wait a while. I am much more in love with something after I have written it than I am a day or two later. It is much easier to change anything with time."

Revising: "It means taking apart what I have written and putting   30 it back together again. I ask major theoretical questions of my ideas, respond to those questions, and think of proportion and structure, and try to find a controlling metaphor. I find out which ideas can be developed and which should be dropped. I am constantly chiseling and changing as I revise."

The experienced writers describe their primary objective when revising as finding the form or shape of their argument. Although the metaphors vary, the experienced writers often use structural expressions such as "finding a framework," "a pattern," or "a design" for their argument. When questioned about this emphasis, the experienced writers responded that since their first drafts are usually scattered attempts to define their territory, their objective in the second draft is to begin observing general patterns of development and deciding what should be included and what excluded. One writer explained, "I have learned from experience that I need to keep writing a first draft until I figure out what I want to say. Then in a second draft, I begin to see the structure of an argument and how all the various sub-arguments which are buried beneath the surface of all those sentences are related." What is described here is a process in which the writer is both agent and vehicle. "Writing," says Barthes, unlike speech, "develops like a seed, not a line,"[8] and like a seed it confuses beginning and end, conception and production. Thus, the experienced writers say their drafts are "not determined by time," that rewriting is a "constant process," that they feel as if (they) "can go on forever." Revising confuses the beginning and end, the agent and vehicle; it confuses, *in order to find*, the line of argument.

After a concern for form, the experienced writers have a second objective: a concern for their readership. In this way, "production" precedes "conception." The experienced writers imagine a reader (reading their product) whose existence and whose expectations influence their revision process. They have abstracted the standards of a reader and this reader seems to be partially a reflection of themselves and functions as a critical and productive collaborator—a collaborator who has yet to love their work. The anticipation of a reader's judgment causes a feeling of dissonance when the writer recognizes incongruities between intention and execution, and requires these writers to make revisions on all levels. Such a reader gives them just what the students lacked: new eyes to "re-view" their work. The experienced writers believe that they have learned the causes and conditions, the product, which will influence their reader, and their revision strategies are geared towards creating these causes and conditions. They demonstrate a complex understanding of which examples, sentences, or phrases should be included or excluded. For example, one experienced writer decided to delete public examples and add private examples when writing about the energy crisis because "private examples would be less controversial and thus more persuasive." Another writer revised his transitional sentences because "some kinds of transitions are more easily recognized as transitions than others." These examples represent the type of strategic attempts these experienced writers use to manipulate the conventions of discourse in order to communicate to their reader.

But these revision strategies are a process of more than communication; they are part of the process of *discovering meaning* altogether. Here we can see the importance of dissonance; at the heart of revision is the process by which writers recognize and resolve the dissonance they sense in their writing. Ferdinand de Saussure has argued that meaning is differential or "diacritical," based on differences between terms rather than "essential" or inherent qualities of terms. "Phonemes," he said, "are characterized not, as one might think, by their own positive quality but simply by the fact that they are distinct."[9] In fact, Saussure bases his entire *Course in General Linguistics* on these differences, and such differences are dissonant; like musical dissonances which gain their significance from their relationship to the "key" of the composition which itself is determined by the whole language, specific language (parole) gains its meaning from the system of language (langue) of which it is a manifestation and part. The musical composition—a "composition" of parts—creates its "key" as in an over-all structure which determines the value (meaning) of its parts. The analogy with music is readily seen in the compositions of experienced writers: both sorts of composition are based precisely on those structures experienced writers seek in their writing. It is this complicated relationship between the parts and the whole in the work of experienced writers which destroys the linear model; writing cannot develop "like a line" because each addition or deletion is a reconsidering of the whole. Explicating Saussure, Jonathan Culler asserts that "meaning depends on difference of meaning."[10] But student writers constantly struggle to bring their essays into congruence with a predefined meaning. The experienced writers do the opposite: they seek to discover (to create) meaning in the engagement with their writing, in revision. They seek to emphasize and exploit the lack of clarity, the differences of meaning, the dissonance, that writing as opposed to speech allows in the possibility of revision. Writing has spatial and temporal features not apparent in speech—words are recorded in space and fixed in time—which is why writing is susceptible to reordering and later addition. Such features make possible the dissonance that both provokes revision and promises, from itself, new meaning.

For the experienced writers the heaviest concentration of changes is on the sentence level, and the changes are predominantly by addition and deletion. But, unlike the students, experienced writers make changes on all levels and use all revision operations. Moreover, the operations the students fail to use—reordering and addition— seem to require a theory of the revision process as a totality—a theory which, in fact, encompasses the *whole* of the composition. Unlike the students, the experienced writers possess a nonlinear theory in which a sense of the whole writing both precedes and grows out of an examination of the parts. As we saw, one writer said he needed "a first draft to figure out what to say," and "a second draft to see the structure of an argument buried beneath the surface." Such a "theory" is both theoretical and strategical; once again, strategy and theory are conflated in ways that are literally impossible for the linear model. Writing appears to be more like a seed than a line.

Two elements of the experienced writers' theory of the revision process are the adoption of a holistic perspective and the perception that revision is a recursive process. The writers ask: what does my essay as a *whole* need for form, balance, rhythm, or communication. Details are added, dropped, substituted, or reordered according to their sense of what the essay needs for emphasis and proportion. This sense, however, is constantly in flux as ideas are developed and modified; it is constantly "re-viewed" in relation to the parts. As their ideas change, revision becomes an attempt to make their own writing consonant with that changing vision.

The experienced writers see their revision process as a recursive process—a process with significant recurring activities—with different levels of attention and different agenda for each cycle. During the first revision cycle their attention is primarily directed towards narrowing the topic and delimiting their ideas. At this point, they are not as concerned as they are later about vocabulary and style. The experienced writers explained that they get closer to their meaning by not limiting themselves too early to lexical concerns. As one writer commented to explain her revision process, a comment inspired by the summer 1977 New York power failure: "I feel like Con Edison cutting off certain states to keep the generators going. In first and second drafts, I try to cut off as much as I can of my editing generator, and in a third draft, I try to cut off some of my idea generators, so I can make sure that I will actually finish the essay." Although the experienced writers describe their revision process as a series of different levels or cycles, it is inaccurate to assume that they have only one objective for each cycle and that each cycle can be defined by a different objective. The same objectives and sub-processes are present in each cycle, but in different proportions. Even though these experienced writers place the predominant weight upon finding the form of their argument during the first cycle, other concerns exist as well. Conversely, during the later cycles, when the experienced writers' primary attention is focused upon stylistic concerns, they are still attuned, although in a reduced way, to the form of the argument. Since writers are limited in what they can attend to during each cycle (understandings are temporal), revision strategies help balance competing demands on attention. Thus, writers can concentrate on more than one objective at a time by developing strategies to sort out and organize their different concerns in successive cycles of revision.

It is a sense of writing as discovery—a repeated process of beginning over again, starting out new—that the students failed to have. I have used the notion of dissonance because such dissonance, the incongruities between intention and execution, governs both writing and meaning. Students do not see the incongruities. They need to rely on their own internalized sense of good writing and to see their writing with their "own" eyes. Seeing in revision—seeing beyond hearing—is at the root of the word *revision* and the process itself; current dicta on revising blind our students to what is actually involved in revision. In fact, they blind them to what constitutes good writing altogether. Good writing disturbs: it creates dissonance. Students need to seek the dissonance of discovery, utilizing in their writing, as the experienced writers do, the very difference between writing and speech—the possibility of revision.

End Notes

1. D. Gordon Rohman and Albert O. Wlecke, "Pre-writing: The Construction and Application of Models for Concept Formation in Writing," Cooperative Research Project No. 2174, U.S. Office of Education, Department of Health, Education, and Welfare; James Britton, Anthony Burgess, Nancy Martin, Alex McLeod, Harold Rosen, *The Development of Writing Abilities (11-18)* (London: Macmillan Education, 1975).

2. Britton is following Roman Jakobson, "Linguistics and Poetics," in T.A. Sebeok, *Style in Language* (Cambridge, Mass: MIT Press, 1960).

3. For an extended discussion of this issue see Nancy Sommers, "The Need for Theory in Composition Research," *College Composition and Communication*, 30 (February, 1979), 46-49.

4. *Classical Rhetoric for the Modern Student* (New York: Oxford University Press, 1965), p. 27.

5. Roland Barthes, "Writers, Intellectuals, Teachers," in *Image-Music-Text*, trans. Stephen Heath (New York: Hill and Wang, 1977), pp. 190-191.

6. "Writers, Intellectuals, Teachers," p. 190.

7. Nancy Sommers and Ronald Schleifer, "Means and Ends: Some Assumptions of Student Writers," *Composition and Teaching*, II (in press).

8. *Writing Degree Zero* in *Writing Degree Zero and Elements of Semiology*, trans. Annette Lavers and Colin Smith (New York: Hill and Wang, 1968), p. 20.

9. *Course in General Linguistics*, trans. Wade Baskin (New York, 1966), p. 119.

10. Jonathan Culler, *Saussure* (Penguin Modern Masters Series; London: Penguin Books, 1976), p. 70.

Reprinted from *College Composition and Communication, Vol 31, No. 4,* (December 1980), by permission of the National Council of Teachers of English.

Acknowledgment: The author wishes to express her gratitude to Professor William Smith, University of Pittsburgh, for his vital assistance with the research reported in this article and to Patrick Hays, her husband, for extensive discussions and critical editorial help.

IV

EDUCATION

GRADUATION

Maya Angelou

◆

MAYA ANGELOU (1928-)

Maya Angelou, born Marguerite Ann Johnson in St. Louis, Missouri, experienced a childhood and adolescence marked by upheaval and trauma. Her parents divorced when she was 3, and at 8 she was raped by her mother's boyfriend. She gave birth to a son shortly after graduating from high school, and spent the next few years employed in positions ranging from cook to pimp and prostitute. Eventually, Angelou became a performer, working as a dancer, singer, and actress, and soon began to pursue a writing career. In this period, she also became involved in the civil rights movement, working first with Martin Luther King, Jr.'s Southern Christian Leadership Conference and later with Malcolm X shortly before his assassination in 1965. In 1969, Angelou's first and most famous work, the autobiography *I Know Why the Caged Bird Sings*, was published, and subsequently nominated for a National Book Award. She followed this with several more chronologically-ordered autobiographies, including *Gather Together in My Name* (1974), *The Heart of a Woman* (1981), and *A Song Flung Up to Heaven* (2002). Her first poetry collection, *Just Give Me a Cool Drink of Water 'fore I Diiie* (1971), was nominated for a Pulitzer Prize. She has also written numerous articles and short stories, written and directed screenplays and films, and produced spoken-word albums, for which she has received multiple Grammys. Since 1981, Angelou has held the Reynolds Professorship of American Studies at Wake Forest University, teaching classes with a variety of focuses. In 2000, she received the National Medal of Arts, and in 2011 was honored with the Presidential Medal of Freedom.

1   The children in Stamps trembled visibly with anticipation. Some adults were excited too, but to be certain the whole young population had come down with graduation epidemic. Large classes were graduating from both the grammar school and the high school. Even those who were years removed from their own day of glorious release were anxious to help with preparations as a kind of dry run. The junior

students who were moving into the vacating classes' chairs were tradition-bound to show their talents for leadership and management. They strutted through the school and around the campus exerting pressure on the lower grades. Their authority was so new that occasionally if they pressed a little too hard it had to be overlooked. After all, next term was coming, and it never hurt a sixth grader to have a play sister in the eighth grade, or a tenth-year student to be able to call a twelfth grader Bubba. So all was endured in a spirit of shared understanding. But the graduating classes themselves were the nobility. Like travelers with exotic destinations on their minds, the graduates were remarkably forgetful. They came to school without their books, or tablets or even pencils. Volunteers fell over themselves to secure replacements for the missing equipment. When accepted, the willing workers might or might not be thanked, and it was of no importance to the pregraduation rites. Even teachers were respectful of the now quiet and aging seniors, and tended to speak to them, if not as equals, as beings only slightly lower than themselves. After tests were returned and grades given, the student body, which acted like an extended family, knew who did well, who excelled, and what piteous ones had failed.

Unlike the white high school, Lafayette County Training School distinguished itself by having neither lawn, nor hedges, nor tennis court, nor climbing ivy. Its two buildings (main classrooms, the grade school and home economics) were set on a dirt hill with no fence to limit either its boundaries or those of bordering farms. There was a large expanse to the left of the school which was used alternately as a baseball diamond or a basketball court. Rusty hoops on the swaying poles represented the permanent recreational equipment, although bats and balls could be borrowed from the P.E. teacher if the borrower was qualified and if the diamond wasn't occupied.

Over this rocky area relieved by a few shady tall persimmon trees the graduating class walked. The girls often held hands and no longer bothered to speak to the lower students. There was a sadness about them, as if this old world was not their home and they were bound for higher ground. The boys, on the other hand, had become more friendly, more outgoing. A decided change from the closed attitude they projected while studying for finals. Now they seemed not ready to give up the old school, the familiar paths and classrooms. Only a small percentage would be continuing on to college—one of the South's A & M (agricultural and mechanical) schools, which trained Negro youths to be carpenters, farmers, handymen, masons, maids, cooks and baby nurses. Their future rode heavily on their shoulders, and blinded them to the collective joy that had pervaded the lives of the boys and girls in the grammar school graduating class.

Parents who could afford it had ordered new shoes and ready-made clothes for themselves from Sears and Roebuck or Montgomery Ward. They also engaged the best seamstresses to make the floating graduating dresses and to cut down secondhand pants which would be pressed to a military slickness for the important event.

5   Oh, it was important, all right. Whitefolks would attend the ceremony, and two or three would speak of God and home, and the Southern way of life, and Mrs. Parsons, the principal's wife, would play the graduation march while the lower-grade graduates paraded down the aisles and took their seats below the platform. The high school seniors would wait in empty classrooms to make their dramatic entrance.

In the Store I was the person of the moment. The birthday girl. The center. Bailey had graduated the year before, although to do so he had had to forfeit all pleasures to make up for his time lost in Baton Rouge.

My class was wearing butter-yellow piqué dresses, and Momma launched out on mine. She smocked the yoke into tiny crisscrossing puckers, then shirred the rest of the bodice. Her dark fingers ducked in and out of the lemony cloth as she embroidered raised daisies around the hem. Before she considered herself finished she had added a crocheted cuff on the puff sleeves, and a pointy crocheted collar.

I was going to be lovely. A walking model of all the various styles of fine hand sewing and it didn't worry me that I was only twelve years old and merely graduating from the eighth grade. Besides, many teachers in Arkansas Negro schools had only that diploma and were licensed to impart wisdom.

The days had become longer and more noticeable. The faded beige of former times had been replaced with strong and sure colors. I began to see my classmates' clothes, their skin tones, and the dust that waved off pussy willows. Clouds that lazed across the sky were objects of great concern to me. Their shiftier shapes might have held a message that in my new happiness and with a little bit of time I'd soon decipher. During that period I looked at the arch of heaven so religiously my neck kept a steady ache. I had taken to smiling more often, and my jaws hurt from the unaccustomed activity. Between the two physical sore spots, I suppose I could have been uncomfortable, but that was not the case. As a member of the winning team (the graduating class of 1940) I had outdistanced unpleasant sensations by miles. I was headed for the freedom of the open fields.

Youth and social approval allied themselves with me and we trammeled memories of slights and insults. The wind of our swift passage remodeled my features. Lost tears were pounded to mud and then to dust. Years of withdrawal were brushed aside and left behind, as hanging ropes of parasitic moss.

My work alone had awarded me a top place and I was going to be one of the first called in the graduating ceremonies. On the classroom blackboard, as well as on the bulletin board in the auditorium, there were blue stars and white stars and red stars. No absences, no tardinesses, and my academic work was among the best of the year. I could say the preamble to the Constitution even faster than Bailey. We timed ourselves often: "WethepeopleoftheUnited-Statesinordert oformamoreperfectunion…" I had memorized the Presidents of the United States from Washington to Roosevelt in chronological as well as alphabetical order.

My hair pleased me too. Gradually the black mass had lengthened and thickened, so that it kept at last to its braided pattern, and I didn't have to yank my scalp off when I tried to comb it.

Louise and I had rehearsed the exercises until we tired out ourselves. Henry Reed was class valedictorian. He was a small, very black boy with hooded eyes, a long, broad nose and an oddly shaped head. I had admired him for years because each term he and I vied for the best grades in our class. Most often he bested me, but instead of being disappointed I was pleased that we shared top places between us. Like many Southern Black children, he lived with his grandmother, who was as strict as Momma and as kind as she knew how to be. He was courteous, respectful and soft-spoken to elders, but on the playground he chose to play the roughest games. I admired him. Anyone, I reckoned, sufficiently afraid or sufficiently dull could be polite. But to be able to operate at a top level with both adults and children was admirable.

His valedictory speech was entitled "To Be or Not to Be." The rigid tenth-grade teacher helped him to write it. He'd been working on the dramatic stresses for months.

The weeks until graduation were filled with heady activities. A group of small children were to be presented in a play about buttercups and daisies and bunny rabbits. They could be heard throughout the building practicing their hops and their little songs that sounded like silver bells. The older girls (non-graduates, of course) were assigned the task of making refreshments for the night's festivities. A tangy scent of ginger, cinnamon, nutmeg and chocolate wafted around the home economics building as the budding cooks made samples for themselves and their teachers.

In every corner of the workshop, axes and saws split fresh timber as the woodshop boys made sets and stage scenery. Only the graduates were left out of the general bustle. We were free to sit in the library at the back of the building or look in quite detachedly, naturally, on the measures being taken for our event.

Even the minister preached on graduation the Sunday before. His subject was, "Let your light so shine that men will see your good works and praise your Father, Who is in Heaven." Although the sermon was purported to be addressed to us, he used the occasion to speak to backsliders, gamblers, and general ne'er-do-wells. But since he had called our names at the beginning of the service we were mollified.

Among Negroes the tradition was to give presents to children going only from one grade to another. How much more important this was when the person was graduating at the top of the class. Uncle Willie and Momma had sent away for a Mickey Mouse watch like Bailey's. Louise gave me four embroidered handkerchiefs. (I gave her three crocheted doilies.) Mrs. Sneed, the minister's wife, made me an underskirt to wear for graduation, and nearly every customer gave me a nickel or maybe even a dime with the instruction "Keep on moving to higher ground," or some such encouragement.

Amazingly the great day finally dawned and I was out of bed before I knew it. I threw open the back door to see it more clearly, but Momma said, "Sister, come away from that door and put your robe on."

20   I hoped the memory of that morning would never leave me. Sunlight itself was still young, and the day had none of the insistence maturity would bring it in a few hours. In my robe and barefoot in the backyard, under cover of going to see about my new beans, I gave myself up to the gentle warmth and thanked God that no matter what evil I had done in my life He had allowed me to live to see this day. Somewhere in my fatalism I had expected to die, accidentally, and never have the chance to walk up the stairs in the auditorium and gracefully receive my hard-earned diploma. Out of God's merciful bosom I had won reprieve.

Bailey came out in his robe and gave me a box wrapped in Christmas paper. He said he had saved his money for months to pay for it. It felt like a box of chocolates, but I knew Bailey wouldn't save money to buy candy when we had all we could want under our noses.

He was as proud of the gift as I. It was a soft-leather-bound copy of a collection of poems by Edgar Allan Poe, or, as Bailey and I called him, "Eap." I turned to "Annabel Lee" and we walked up and down the garden rows, the cool dirt between our toes, reciting the beautifully sad lines.

Momma made a Sunday breakfast although it was only Friday. After we finished the blessing, I opened my eyes to find the watch on my plate. It was a dream of a day. Everything went smoothly and to my credit I didn't have to be reminded or scolded for anything. Near evening I was too jittery to attend to chores, so Bailey volunteered to do all before his bath.

Days before, we had made a sign for the Store and as we turned out the lights Momma hung the cardboard over the doorknob. It read clearly: CLOSED. GRADUATION.

My dress fitted perfectly and everyone said that I looked like a sunbeam in it. On the hill, going toward the school, Bailey walked behind with Uncle Willie, who muttered, "Go on, Ju." He wanted him to walk ahead with us because it embarrassed him to have to walk so slowly. Bailey said he'd let the ladies walk together, and the men would bring up the rear. We all laughed, nicely. 15

Little children dashed by out of the dark like fireflies. Their crepe-paper dresses and butterfly wings were not made for running and we heard more than one rip, dryly, and the regretful "uh uh" that followed.

The school blazed without gaiety. The windows seemed cold and unfriendly from the lower hill. A sense of ill-fated timing crept over me, and if Momma hadn't reached for my hand I would have drifted back to Bailey and Uncle Willie, and possibly beyond. She made a few slow jokes about my feet getting cold, and tugged me along to the now-strange building.

Around the front steps, assurance came back. There were my fellow "greats," the graduating class. Hair brushed back, legs oiled, new dresses and pressed pleats, fresh pocket handkerchiefs and little hand-bags, all homesewn. Oh, we were up to snuff, all right. I joined my comrades and didn't even see my family go in to find seats in the crowded auditorium.

The school band struck up a march and all classes filed in as had been rehearsed. We stood in front of our seats, as assigned, and on a signal from the choir director, we sat. No sooner had this been accomplished than the band started to play the national anthem.

We rose again and sang the song, after which we recited the pledge of allegiance. We remained standing for a brief minute before the choir director and the principal signaled to us, rather desperately I thought, to take our seats. The command was so unusual that our carefully rehearsed and smooth-running machine was thrown off. For a full minute we fumbled for our chairs and bumped into each other awkwardly. Habits change or solidify under pressure, so in our state of nervous tension we had been ready to follow our usual assembly pattern: the American National Anthem, then the pledge of allegiance, then the song every Black person I knew called the Negro National Anthem. All done in the same key, with the same passion and most often standing on the same foot.

20   Finding my seat at last, I was overcome with a presentiment of worse things to come. Something unrehearsed, unplanned, was going to happen, and we were going to be made to look bad. I distinctly remember being explicit in the choice of pronoun. It was "we," the graduating class, the unit, that concerned me then.

The principal welcomed "parents and friends" and asked the Baptist minister to lead us in prayer. His invocation was brief and punchy, and for a second I thought we were getting back on the high road to right action. When the principal came back to the dais, however, his voice had changed. Sounds always affected me profoundly and the principal's voice was one of my favorites. During assembly it melted and lowed weakly into the audience. It had not been in my plan to listen to him, but my curiosity was piqued and I straightened up to give him my attention.

He was talking about Booker T. Washington, our "late great leader," who said we can be as close as the fingers on the hand, etc.... Then he said a few vague things about friendship and the friendship of kindly people to those less fortunate than themselves. With that his voice nearly faded, thin, away. Like a river diminishing to a stream and then to a trickle. But he cleared his throat and said, "Our speaker tonight, who is also our friend, came from Texarkana to deliver the commencement address, but due to the irregularity of the train schedule, he's going to, as they say, 'speak and run.'" He said that we understood and wanted the man to know that we were most grateful for the time he was able to give us and then something about how we were willing always to adjust to another's program, and without more ado—"I give you Mr. Edward Donleavy."

Not one but two white men came through the door offstage. The shorter one walked to the speaker's platform, and the tall one moved over to the center seat and sat down. But that was our principal's seat, and already occupied. The dislodged gentleman bounced around for a long breath or two before the Baptist minister gave him his chair, then with more dignity than the situation deserved, the minister walked off the stage.

Donleavy looked at the audience once (on reflection, I'm sure that he wanted only to reassure himself that we were really there), adjusted his glasses and began to read from a sheaf of papers.

He was glad "to be here and to see the work going on just as it was   25 in the other schools."

At the first "Amen" from the audience I willed the offender to immediate death by choking on the word. But Amen's and Yes, sir's began to fall around the room like rain through a ragged umbrella.

He told us of the wonderful changes we children in Stamps had in store. The Central School (naturally, the white school was Central) had already granted improvements that would be in use in the fall. A well-known artist was coming from Little Rock to teach art to them. They were going to have the newest microscopes and chemistry equipment for their laboratory. Mr. Donleavy didn't leave us long in the dark over who made these improvements available to Central High. Nor were we to be ignored in the general betterment scheme he had in mind.

He said that he had pointed out to people at a very high level that one of the first-line football tacklers at Arkansas Agricultural and Mechanical College had graduated from good old Lafayette County Training School. Here fewer Amen's were heard. Those few that did break through lay dully in the air with the heaviness of habit.

He went on to praise us. He went on to say how he had bragged that "one of the best basketball players at Fisk sank his first ball right here at Lafayette County Training School."

The white kids were going to have a chance to become Galileos   30 and Madame Curies and Edisons and Gauguins, and our boys (the girls weren't even in on it) would try to be Jesse Owenses and Joe Louises.

Owens and the Brown Bomber were great heroes in our world, but what school official in the white-goddom of Little Rock had the right to decide that those two men must be our only heroes? Who decided that for Henry Reed to become a scientist he had to work like George Washington Carver, as a bootblack, to buy a lousy microscope? Bailey was obviously always going to be too small to be an athlete, so which concrete angel glued to what country seat had decided that if my brother wanted to become a lawyer he had first to pay penance for his skin by picking cotton and hoeing corn and studying correspondence books at night for twenty years?

The man's dead words fell like bricks around the auditorium and too many settled in my belly. Constrained by hard-learned manners I couldn't look behind me, but to my left and right the proud graduating class of 1940 had dropped their heads. Every girl in my row had found something new to do with her handkerchief. Some folded the tiny squares into love knots, some into triangles, but most were wadding them, then pressing them flat on their yellow laps.

On the dais, the ancient tragedy was being replayed. Professor Parsons sat, a sculptor's reject, rigid. His large, heavy body seemed devoid of will or willingness, and his eyes said he was no longer with us. The other teachers examined the flag (which was draped stage right) or their notes, or the windows which opened on our now-famous playing diamond.

Graduation, the hush-hush of magic time of frills and gifts and congratulations and diplomas, was finished for me before my name was called. The accomplishment was nothing. The meticulous maps, drawn in three colors of ink, learning and spelling decasyllabic words, memorizing the whole of *The Rape of Lucrece*—it was nothing. Donleavy had exposed us.

35   We were maids and farmers, handymen and washerwomen, and anything higher that we aspired to was farcical and presumptuous. Then I wished that Gabriel Prosser and Nat Turner had killed all white folks in their beds and that Abraham Lincoln had been assassinated before the signing of the Emancipation Proclamation, and that Harriet Tubman had been killed by that blow on her head and Christopher Columbus had drowned in the *Santa Maria*.

It was awful to be Negro and have no control over my life. It was brutal to be young and already trained to sit quietly and listen to charges brought against my color and no chance of defense. We should all be dead. I thought I should like to see us all dead, one on top of the other. A pyramid of flesh with the whitefolks at the bottom, as the broad base, then the Indians with their silly tomahawks and teepees and wigwams and treaties, the Negroes with their mops and recipes and cotton sacks and spirituals sticking out of their mouths. The Dutch children should all stumble in their wooden shoes and break their necks. The French should choke to death on the Louisiana Purchase (1803) while silkworms ate all the Chinese with their stupid pigtails. As a species, we were an abomination. All of us.

Donleavy was running for election, and assured our parents that if he won we could count on having the only colored paved playing field in that part of Arkansas. Also—he never looked up to acknowledge the grunts of acceptance—also, we were bound to get some new equipment for the home economics building and the workshop.

He finished, and since there was no need to give any more than the most perfunctory thank-you's, he nodded to the men on the stage, and the tall white man who was never introduced joined him at the door. They left with the attitude that now they were off to something really important. (The graduation ceremonies at Lafayette County Training School had been a mere preliminary.)

The ugliness they left was palpable. An uninvited guest who wouldn't leave. The choir was summoned and sang a modern arrangement of "Onward, Christian Soldiers," with new words pertaining to graduates seeking their place in the world. But it didn't work. Elouise, the daughter of the Baptist minister, recited "Invictus," and I could have cried at the impertinence of "I am the master of my fate, I am the captain of my soul."

My name had lost its ring of familiarity and I had to be nudged   40 to go and receive my diploma. All my preparations had fled. I neither marched up to the stage like a conquering Amazon, nor did I look in the audience for Bailey's nod of approval. Marguerite Johnson, I heard the name again, my honors were read, there were noises in the audience of appreciation, and I took my place on stage as rehearsed.

I thought about colors I hated: ecru, puce, lavender, beige and black.

There was shuffling and rustling around me, then Henry Reed was giving his valedictory address, "To Be or Not to Be." Hadn't he heard the whitefolks? We couldn't *be*, so the question was a waste of time. Henry's voice came out clear and strong. I feared to look at him. Hadn't he got the message? There was no "nobler in the mind" for Negroes because the world didn't think we had minds, and they let us know it. "Outrageous fortune"? Now, that was a joke. When the ceremony was over I had to tell Henry Reed some things. That is, if I still cared. Not "rub," Henry, "erase." "Ah, there's the erase." Us.

Henry had been a good student in elocution. His voice rose on tides of promise and fell on waves of warnings. The English teacher had helped him to create a sermon winging through Hamlet's soliloquy. To be a man, a doer, a builder, a leader, or to be a tool, an unfunny joke, a crusher of funky toadstools. I marveled that Henry could go through with the speech as if we had a choice.

I had been listening and silently rebutting each sentence with my eyes closed; then there was a hush, which in an audience warns that something unplanned is happening. I looked up and saw Henry Reed, the conservative, the proper, the A student, turn his back to the audience and turn to us (the proud graduating class of 1940) and sing, nearly speaking,

45   "Lift ev'ry voice and sing
    Till earth and heaven ring
    Ring with the harmonies of Liberty…"

It was the poem written by James Weldon Johnson. It was the music composed by J. Rosamond Johnson. It was the Negro National Anthem. Out of habit we were singing it.

Our mothers and fathers stood in the dark hall and joined the hymn of encouragement. A kindergarten teacher led the small children onto the stage and the buttercups and daisies and bunny rabbits marked time and tried to follow:

    "Stony the road we trod
    Bitter the chastening rod
    Felt in the days when hope, unborn, had died.
    Yet with a steady beat
    Have not our weary feet
    Come to the place for which our fathers sighed?"

Every child I knew had learned that song with his ABC's and along with "Jesus Loves Me This I Know." But I personally had never heard it before. Never heard the words, despite the thousands of times I had sung them. Never thought they had anything to do with me.

50   On the other hand, the words of Patrick Henry had made such an impression on me that I had been able to stretch myself tall and trembling and say, "I know not what course others may take, but as for me, give me liberty or give me death."

And now I heard, really for the first time:

    "We have come over a way that with tears
    has been watered,
    We have come, treading our path through
    the blood of the slaughtered."

While echoes of the song shivered in the air, Henry Reed bowed his head, said "Thank you," and returned to his place in the line. The tears that slipped down many faces were not wiped away in shame.

We were on top again. As always, again. We survived. The depths had been icy and dark, but now a bright sun spoke to our souls. I was no longer simply a member of the proud graduating class of 1940; I was a proud member of the wonderful, beautiful Negro race.

Oh, Black known and unknown poets, how often have your   55
auctioned pains sustained us? Who will compute the lonely nights made less lonely by your songs, or the empty pots made less tragic by your tales?

If we were a people much given to revealing secrets, we might raise monuments and sacrifice to the memories of our poets, but slavery cured us of that weakness. It may be enough, however, to have it said that we survive in exact relationship to the dedication of our poets (include preachers, musicians and blues singers).

From *I Know Why the Caged Bird Sings*. Published by Random House, Inc. Copyright © 1969 by Maya Angelou.

THE ALLEGORY OF THE CAVE

Plato

❖

1   ***Socrates:*** And now, I said, let me show in a figure how far our nature is enlightened or unenlightened: —Behold! human beings living in an underground cave, which has a mouth open towards the light and reaching all along the cave; here they have been from their childhood, and have their legs and necks chained so that they cannot move, and can only see before them, being prevented by the chains from turning round their heads. Above and behind them a fire is blazing at a distance, and between the fire and the prisoners there is a raised way; and you will see, if you look, a low wall built along the way, like the screen which marionette players have in front of them, over which they show the puppets.

Glaucon: I see.

Socrates: And do you see, I said, men passing along the wall carrying all sorts of vessels, and statues and figures of animals made of wood and stone and various materials, which appear over the wall? Some of them are talking, others silent.

Glaucon: You have shown me a strange image, and they are strange prisoners.

Socrates: Like ourselves, I replied; and they see only their own 5 shadows, or the shadows of one another, which the fire throws on the opposite wall of the cave?

Glaucon: True, he said; how could they see anything but the shadows if they were never allowed to move their heads?

Socrates: And of the objects which are being carried in like manner they would only see the shadows?

Glaucon: Yes, he said.

Socrates: And if they were able to converse with one another, would they not suppose that they were naming what was actually before them?

Glaucon: Very true.   10

Socrates: And suppose further that the prison had an echo which came from the other side, would they not be sure to fancy when one of the passers-by spoke that the voice which they heard came from the passing shadow?

Glaucon: No question, he replied.

Socrates: To them, I said, the truth would be literally nothing but the shadows of the images.

Glaucon: That is certain.

15   ***Socrates:*** And now look again, and see what will naturally follow if the prisoners are released and disabused of their error. At first, when any of them is liberated and compelled suddenly to stand up and turn his neck round and walk and look towards the light, he will suffer sharp pains; the glare will distress him, and he will be unable to see the realities of which in his former state he had seen the shadows; and then conceive some one saying to him, that what he saw before was an illusion, but that now, when he is approaching nearer to being and his eye is turned toward more real existence, he has a clearer vision—what will be his reply? And you may further imagine that his instructor is pointing to the objects as they pass and requiring him to name them—will he not be perplexed? Will he not fancy that the shadows which he formerly saw are truer than the objects which are now shown to him?

Glaucon: Far truer.

Socrates: And if he is compelled to look straight at the light, will he not have a pain in his eyes which will make him turn away to take refuge in the objects of vision which he can see, and which he will conceive to be in reality clearer than the things which are now being shown to him?

Glaucon: True, he said.

Socrates: And suppose once more, that he is reluctantly dragged up a steep and rugged ascent, and held fast until he is forced into the presence of the sun himself, is he not likely to be pained and irritated? When he approaches the light his eyes will be dazzled, and he will not be able to see anything at all of what are now called realities.

20   ***Glaucon:*** Not all in a moment, he said.

Socrates: He will require to grow accustomed to the sight of the upper world. And first he will see the shadows best, next the reflections of men and other objects in the water, and then the objects themselves; then he will gaze upon the light of the moon and the stars and the spangled heaven; and he will see the sky and the stars by night better than the sun or the light of the sun by day?

Glaucon: Certainly.

Socrates: Last of all he will be able to see the sun, and not mere reflections of him in the water, but he will see him in his own proper place, and not in another; and he will contemplate him as he is.

Glaucon: Certainly.

Socrates: He will then proceed to argue that this is he who gives   25
the season and the years, and is the guardian of all that is in the visible world, and in a certain way the cause of all things which he and his fellows have been accustomed to behold?

Glaucon: Clearly, he said, he would first see the sun and then reason about him.

Socrates: And when he remembered his old habitation, and the wisdom of the cave and his fellow-prisoners, do you not suppose that he would felicitate himself on the change, and pity them?

Glaucon: Certainly, he would.

Socrates: And if they were in the habit of conferring honors among themselves on those who were quickest to observe the passing shadows and to remark which of them went before, and which followed after, and which were together; and who were therefore best able to draw conclusions as to the future, do you think that he would care for such honors and glories, or envy the possessors of them? Would he not say with Homer, "Better to be the poor servant of a poor master," and to endure anything, rather than think as they do and live after their manner?

Glaucon: Yes, he said, I think that he would rather suffer anything   30
than entertain these false notions and live in this miserable manner.

Socrates: Imagine once more, I said, such an one coming suddenly out of the sun to be replaced in his old situation; would he not be certain to have his eyes full of darkness?

Glaucon: To be sure, he said.

Socrates: And if there were a contest, and he had to compete in measuring the shadows with the prisoners who had never moved out of the cave, while his sight was still weak, and before his eyes had become steady (and the time which would be needed to acquire this new habit of sight might be very considerable) would he not be ridiculous? Men would say of him that up he went and down he came without his eyes; and that it was better not even to think of ascending; and if any one tried to loose another and lead him up to the light, let them only catch the offender, and they would put him to death.

Glaucon: No question, he said.

35   *Socrates:* This entire allegory, I said, you may now append, dear Glaucon, to the previous argument; the prison-house is the world of sight, the light of the fire is the sun, and you will not misapprehend me if you interpret the journey upwards to be the ascent of the soul into the intellectual world according to my poor belief, which, at your desire, I have expressed—whether rightly or wrongly God knows. But, whether true or false, my opinion is that in the world of knowledge the idea of good appears last of all, and is seen only with an effort; and, when seen, is also inferred to be the universal author of all things beautiful and right, parent of light and of the lord of light in this visible world, and the immediate source of reason and truth in the intellectual; and that this is the power upon which he who would act rationally, either in public or private life must have his eye fixed.

Glaucon: I agree, he said, as far as I am able to understand you.

◈

EVERYTHING HAS A NAME

Helen Keller

HELEN KELLER (1880-1968)

Helen Keller, born in Tuscumbia, Alabama in 1880, spent her first nineteen months with the abilities to see and hear. It was only after suffering a severe childhood illness that she emerged blind and deaf, able to communicate only with those closest to her through the use of a personal signing system. When Keller was six, her family was inspired by the story of Laura Bridgman, the first blind and deaf person in the U.S. to receive significant formal education, and sought out similar assistance for their daughter. The assistance came in Anne Sullivan, a young instructor who would soon become Keller's governess and, in adulthood, companion. Keller proved an adept student, and in adulthood became the first deaf and blind person in the United States to obtain a bachelor's degree. She became an avid author and lecturer, most active in political causes, writing and campaigning in support of workers' rights, and co-founding the American Civil Liberties Union in 1920. Keller wrote several autobiographical works, recounting her experiences: *The Story of My Life* (1903), *The World I Live In* (1908), and *My Religion* (1927).

The most important day I remember in all my life is the one on which 1 my teacher, Anne Mansfield Sullivan, came to me. I am filled with wonder when I consider the immeasurable contrast between the two lives which it connects. It was the third of March, 1887, three months before I was seven years old.

On the afternoon of that eventful day, I stood on the porch, dumb, expectant. I guessed vaguely from my mother's signs and from the hurrying to and fro in the house that something unusual was about to happen, so I went to the door and waited on the steps. The afternoon sun penetrated the mass of honeysuckle that covered the porch, and fell on my upturned face. My fingers lingered almost unconsciously on the familiar leaves and blossoms which had just come forth to greet the sweet southern spring. I did not know what the future held of marvel or surprise for me. Anger and bitterness had preyed upon me continually for weeks and a deep languor had succeeded this passionate struggle.

Have you ever been at sea in a dense fog, when it seemed as if a tangible white darkness shut you in, and the great ship, tense and anxious, groped her way toward the shore with plummet and sounding-line, and you waited with beating heart for something to happen? I was like that ship before my education began, only I was without compass or sounding-line, and had no way of knowing how near the harbour was. "Light! give me light!" was the wordless cry of my soul, and the light of love shone on me in that very hour.

I felt approaching footsteps. I stretched out my hand as I supposed to my mother. Some one took it, and I was caught up and held close in the arms of her who had come to reveal all things to me, and, more than all things else, to love me.

5   The morning after my teacher came she led me into her room and gave me a doll. The little blind children at the Perkins Institution had sent it and Laura Bridgman [the first deaf and blind person in the United States to receive an education] had dressed it; but it did not know this until afterward. When I had played with it a little while, Miss Sullivan slowly spelled into my hand the word "d-o-l-l." I was at once interested in this finger play and tried to imitate it. When I finally succeeded in making the letters correctly I was flushed with childish pleasure and pride. Running downstairs to my mother I held up my hand and made the letters for doll. I did not know that I was spelling a word or even that words existed: I was simply making my fingers go in monkey-like imitation. In the days that followed I learned to spell in this uncomprehending way a great many words, among them *pin*, *hat*, *cup*, and a few verbs like *sit*, *stand* and *walk*. But my teacher had been with me several weeks before I understood that everything has a name.

One day, while I was playing with my new doll, Miss Sullivan put my big rag doll into my lap also, spelled "d-o-l-l" and tried to make me understand that "d-o-l-l" applied to both. Earlier in the day we had had a tussle over the words "m-u-g" and "w-a-t-e-r." Miss Sullivan had tried to impress it upon me that "m-u-g" is *mug* and that "w-a-t-e-r" is *water*, but I persisted in confounding the two. In despair she had dropped the subject for the time, only to renew it at the first opportunity. I became impatient at her repeated attempts and, seizing the new doll, I dashed it upon the floor. I was keenly delighted when I felt the fragments of the broken doll at my feet. Neither sorrow nor regret followed my passionate outburst. I had not loved the doll. In the still, dark world in which I lived there was no strong sentiment or tenderness. I felt my teacher sweep the fragments to one side of the hearth, and I had a sense of satisfaction that the cause of my discomfort was removed. She brought me my hat, and I knew I was going out into the warm sunshine. This thought, if a wordless sensation may be called a thought, made me hop and skip with pleasure.

We walked down the path to the well-house, attracted by the fragrance of the honeysuckle with which it was covered. Some one was drawing water and my teacher placed my hand under the spout. As the cool stream gushed over one hand she spelled into the other the word *water*, first slowly, then rapidly. I stood still, my whole attention fixed upon the motions of her fingers. Suddenly I felt a misty consciousness as of something forgotten—a thrill of returning thought; and somehow the mystery of language was revealed to me. I knew then that "w-a-t-e-r" meant the wonderful cool something that was flowing over my hand. That living word awakened my soul, gave it light, hope, joy, set it free! There were barriers still, it is true, but barriers that could in time be swept away.

I left the well-house eager to learn. Everything had a name, and each name gave birth to a new thought. As we returned to the house every object which I touched seemed to quiver with life. That was because I saw everything with the strange, new sight that had come to me. On entering the door I remembered the doll I had broken. I felt my way to the hearth and picked up the pieces. I tried vainly to put them together. Then my eyes filled with tears; for I realized what I had done, and for the first time I felt repentance and sorrow.

I learned a great many new words that day. I do not remember what they all were; but I do know that *mother*, *father*, *sister*, *teacher* were among them—words that were to make the world blossom for me, "like Aaron's rod, with flowers." It would have been difficult to find a happier child than I was as I lay in my crib at the close of that eventful day and lived over the joys it had brought me, and for the first time longed for a new day to come.

From *The Story of My Life* published by Doubleday, a division of Bantam Double Dell Publishing Groups, Inc.

A HOMEMADE EDUCATION

Malcolm X

MALCOLM X (1925-1965)

Human rights activist, writer, and clergyman Malcolm X (aka Malcom Little) was born in Omaha, Nebraska in 1925. When Malcolm was six, his father, Baptist preacher and activist Earl Little, was killed in an accident believed to have been a deliberate Ku Klux Klan action. In 1938, Malcolm's mother, Louise, was institutionalized following a nervous breakdown and Malcolm and his six siblings were sent to separate foster homes. Malcolm dropped out of school in eighth grade after being dissuaded from his dream of becoming a lawyer, and spent several years moving between homes and working assorted jobs. Malcolm was arrested for burglary in 1946, and during the period of his imprisonment from 1947-1952, he was introduced to the Nation of Islam—a black unification and separatist movement led by Elijah Muhammad—and converted to Islam. His conversion was accompanied by his adoption of the name Malcolm X, to signify unnamed ancestors; he would also use the name Malik El-Shabazz. After his release from prison, Malcolm became a clergyman in the Nation of Islam and, as an activist, was perhaps the most prominent face of the movement. In 1964, disillusionment with the Nation of Islam and leader Elijah Muhammad led Malcolm to leave the movement and become a Sunni Muslim, also departing from his previous public stance of radical racial separatism. Soon after, on February 21, 1965, Malcolm was assassinated by three members of the Nation of Islam. Malcolm X's best-known work is *The Autobiography of Malcolm X*, co-written with Alex Haley (1965). Additional posthumously-published writings include *Malcolm X Talks to Young People* (1965) and *Malcolm X on Afro-American History* (1967).

1   It was because of my letters that I happened to stumble upon starting to acquire some kind of a homemade education.

I became increasingly frustrated at not being able to express what I wanted to convey in letters that I wrote, especially to Mr. Elijah Muhammad. In the street, I had been the most articulate hustler out there—I had commanded attention when I said something. But now, trying to write simple English, I not only wasn't articulate, I wasn't even functional. How would I sound writing in slang, the way I would *say* it, something such as, "Look, daddy, let me pull your coat about a cat, Elijah Muhammad—"

Many who today hear me somewhere in person, or on television, or those who read something I've said, will think I went to school far beyond the eighth grade. This impression is due entirely to my prison studies.

It had really begun back in the Charlestown Prison, when Bimbi first made me feel envy of his stock of knowledge. Bimbi had always taken charge of any conversations he was in, and I had tried to emulate him. But every book I picked up had few sentences which didn't contain anywhere from one to nearly all of the words that might as well have been in Chinese. When I just skipped those words, of course, I really ended up with little idea of what the book said. So I had come to the Norfolk Prison Colony still going through only book-reading motions. Pretty soon, I would have quit even these motions, unless I had received the motivation that I did.

I saw that the best thing I could do was get hold of a dictionary—   5
to study, to learn some words. I was lucky enough to reason also that I should try to improve my penmanship. It was sad. I couldn't even write in a straight line. It was both ideas together that moved me to request a dictionary along with some tablets and pencils from the Norfolk Prison Colony school.

I spent two days just rifling uncertainly through the dictionary's pages. I'd never realized so many words existed! I didn't know *which* words I needed to learn. Finally, just to start some kind of action, I began copying.

In my slow, painstaking, ragged handwriting, I copied into my tablet everything printed on that first page, down to the punctuation marks. I believe it took me a day. Then, aloud, I read back to myself, everything I'd written on the tablet. Over and over, aloud, to myself, I read my own handwriting.

I woke up the next morning, thinking about those words—immensely proud to realize that not only had I written so much at one time, but I'd written words that I never knew were in the world. Moreover, with a little effort, I also could remember what many of these words meant. I reviewed the words whose meanings I didn't remember. Funny thing, from the dictionary first page right now, that "aardvark" springs to my mind. The dictionary had a picture of it, a long-tailed, long-eared, burrowing African mammal, which lives off termites caught by sticking out its tongue as an anteater does for ants.

I was so fascinated that I went on—I copied the dictionary's next page. And the same experience came when I studied that. With every succeeding page, I also learned of people and places and events from history. Actually the dictionary is like a miniature encyclopedia. Finally the dictionary's A section had filled a whole tablet—and I went on into the B's. That was the way I started copying what eventually became the entire dictionary. It went a lot faster after so much practice helped me to pick up handwriting speed. Between what I wrote in my tablet, and writing letters, during the rest of my time in prison I would guess I wrote a million words.

10   I suppose it was inevitable that as my word-base broadened, I could for the first time pick up a book and read and now begin to understand what the book was saying. Anyone who has read a great deal can imagine the new world that opened. Let me tell you something, from then until I left that prison, in every free moment I had, if I was not reading in the library, I was reading on my bunk. You couldn't have gotten me out of books with a wedge. Between Mr. Muhammad's teachings, my correspondence, my visitors—usually Ella and Reginald—and my reading of books, months passed without my even thinking about being imprisoned. In fact, up to then, I never had been so truly free in my life.

The Norfolk Prison Colony's library was in the school building. A variety of classes were taught there by instructors who came from such places as Harvard and Boston universities. The weekly debates between inmate teams were also held in the school building. You would be astonished to know how worked up convict debaters and audiences would get over subjects like "Should Babies Be Fed Milk?"

Available on the prison library's shelves were books on just about every general subject. Much of the big private collection that Parkhurst had willed to the prison was still in crates and boxes in the back of the library—thousands of old books. Some of them looked ancient: covers faded; old-time parchment-looking bindings. Parkhurst, I've mentioned, seemed to have been principally interested in history and religion. He had the money and the special interest to have a lot of books that you wouldn't have in general circulation. Any college library would have been lucky to get that collection.

As you can imagine, especially in a prison where there was heavy emphasis on rehabilitation, an inmate was smiled upon if he demonstrated an unusually intense interest in books. There was a sizable number of well-read inmates, especially the popular debaters. Some were said by many to be practically walking encyclopedias. They were almost celebrities. No university would ask any student to devour literature as I did when this new world opened to me; of being able to read and *understand*.

I read more in my room than in the library itself. An inmate who was known to read a lot could check out more than the permitted maximum number of books. I preferred reading in the total isolation of my own room.

When I had progressed to really serious reading, every night at   15 about ten p.m., I would be outraged with the "lights out." It always seemed to catch me right in the middle of something engrossing.

Fortunately, right outside my door was a corridor light that cast a glow into my room. The glow was enough to read by, once my eyes adjusted to it. So when "lights out" came, I would sit on the floor where I could continue reading in that glow.

At one-hour intervals the night guards paced past every room. Each time I heard the approaching footsteps, I jumped into bed and feigned sleep. And as soon as the guard passed, I got back out of bed onto the floor area of that light-glow, where I would read for another fifty-eight minutes—until the guard approached again. That went on until three or four every morning. Three or four hours of sleep a night was enough for me. Often in the years in the streets I had slept less than that.

The teachings of Mr. Muhammad stressed how history had been "whitened"—when white men had written history books, the black man simply had been left out. Mr. Muhammad couldn't have said anything that would have struck me much harder. I had never forgotten how when my class, me and all of those whites, had studied seventh-grade United States history back in Mason, the history of the Negro had been covered in one paragraph, and the teacher had gotten a big laugh with his joke, "Negroes' feet are so big that when they walk, they leave a hole in the ground."

This is one reason why Mr. Muhammad's teachings spread so swiftly all over the United States, among *all* Negroes, whether or not they became followers of Mr. Muhammad. The teachings ring true— to every Negro. You can hardly show me a black adult in America— or a white one, for that matter—who knows from the history books anything like the truth about the black man's role. In my own case, once I heard of the "glorious history of the black man," I took special pains to hunt in the library for books that would inform me on details about black history.

20   I can remember accurately the very first set of books that really impressed me. I have since bought that set of books and I have it at home for my children to read as they grow up. It's called *Wonders of the World*. It's full of pictures of archeological finds, statues that depict, usually, non-European people.

I found books like Will Durant's *Story of Civilization*. I read H. G. Wells' *Outline of History*. *Souls of Black Folk* by W.E.B. Du Bois gave me a glimpse into the black people's history before they came to this country. Carter G. Woodson's *Negro History* opened my eyes about black empires before the black slave was brought to the United States, and the early Negro struggles for freedom.

J. A. Rogers' three volumes of *Sex and Race* told about race-mixing before Christ's time; about Aesop being a black man who told fables; about Egypt's Pharaohs; about the great Coptic Christian Empires; about Ethiopia, the earth's oldest continuous black civilization; as China is the oldest continuous civilization.

Mr. Muhammad's teaching about how the white man had been created led me to *Findings in Genetics* by Gregor Mendel. (The dictionary's G section was where I had learned what "genetics" meant.) I really studied this book by the Austrian monk. Reading it over and over, especially certain sections, helped me to understand that if you started with a black man, a white man could be produced; but starting with a white man, you never could produce a black man—because the white chromosome is recessive. And since no one disputes that there was but one Original Man, the conclusion is clear.

During the last year or so, in the *New York Times*, Arnold Toynbee used the word "bleached" in describing the white man. (His words were: White [i.e. bleached] human beings of North European origin....") Toynbee also referred to the European geographic area as only a peninsula of Asia. He said there is no such thing as Europe. And if you look at the globe, you will see for yourself that America is only an extension of Asia. (But at the same time Toynbee is among those who have helped to bleach history. He has written that Africa was the only continent that produced no history. He won't write that again. Every day now, the truth is coming to light.)

25   I never will forget how shocked I was when I began reading about slavery's total horror. It made such an impact upon me that it later became one of my favorite subjects when I became a minister of Mr. Muhammad's. The world's most monstrous crime, the sin and

the blood on the white man's hands are almost impossible to believe. Books like the one by Frederick Olmstead opened my eyes to the horrors suffered when the slave was landed in the United States. The European woman, Fannie Kimball, who had married a Southern white slaveowner, described how human beings were degraded. Of course I read *Uncle Tom's Cabin*. In fact, I believe that's the only novel I have ever read since I started serious reading.

Parkhurst's collection also contained some bound pamphlets of the Abolitionist Anti-Slavery Society of New England. I read descriptions of atrocities, saw those illustrations of black slave women tied up and flogged with whips; of black mothers watching their babies being dragged off, never to be seen by their mothers again; of dogs after slaves, and of the fugitive slave catchers, evil white men with whips and clubs and chains and guns. I read about the slave preacher Nat Turner, who put the fear of God into the white slavemaster. Nat Turner wasn't going around preaching pie-in-the-sky and "non-violent" freedom for the black man. There in Virginia one night in 1831, Nat and seven other slaves started out at his master's home and through the night they went from one plantation "big house" to the next, killing, until by the next morning 57 white people were dead and Nat had about 70 slaves following him. White people, terrified for their lives, fled from their homes, locked themselves up in public buildings, hid in the woods, and some even left the state. A small army of soldiers took two months to catch and hang Nat Turner. Somewhere I have read where Nat Turner's example is said to have inspired John Brown to invade Virginia and attack Harper's Ferry nearly thirty years later, with thirteen white men and five Negroes.

I read Herodotus, the father of "History," or, rather, I read *about* him. And I read the histories of various nations, which opened my eyes gradually, then wider and wider, to how the whole world's white men had indeed acted like devils, pillaging and raping and bleeding and draining the whole world's non-white people. I remember, for instance, books such as Will Durant's *The Story of Oriental Civilization*, and Mahatma Gandhi's accounts of the struggle to drive the British out of India.

Book after book showed me how the white man had brought upon the world's black, brown, red, and yellow peoples every variety of the sufferings of exploitation. I saw how since the sixteenth century, the so-called "Christian trader" white man began to ply the seas in his lust for Asian and African empires, and plunder, and power. I read, I saw, how the white man never has gone among the non-white peoples bearing the Cross in the true manner and spirit of Christ's teachings—meek, humble, and Christlike.

I perceived, as I read, how the collective white man had been actually nothing but a piratical opportunist who used Faustian machinations to make his own Christianity his initial wedge in criminal conquests. First, always, "religiously," he branded "heathen" and "pagan" labels upon ancient non-white cultures and civilizations. The stage thus set, he then turned upon his non-white victims his weapons of war.

30   I read how, entering India—half a *billion* deeply religious brown people—the

British white man, by 1759, through promises, trickery and manipulations, controlled much of India through Great Britain's East India Company. The parasitical British administration kept tentacling out to half of the subcontinent. In 1857, some of the desperate people of India finally mutinied—and, excepting the African slave trade, nowhere has history recorded any more unnecessary bestial and ruthless human carnage than the British suppression of the nonwhite Indian people.

Over 115 million African blacks—close to the 1930s population of the United

State—were murdered or enslaved during the slave trade. And I read how when the slave market was glutted, the cannibalistic white powers of Europe next carved up, as their colonies, the richest areas of the black continent. And Europe's chancelleries for the next century played a chess game of naked exploitation and power from Cape Horn to Cairo.

Ten guards and the warden couldn't have torn me out of those books. Not even Elijah Muhammad could have been more eloquent than those books were in providing indisputable proof that the collective white man had acted like a devil in virtually every contact he had with the world's collective non-white man. I listen today to the radio, and watch television, and read the headlines about the collective white man's fear and tension concerning China. When the white man professes ignorance about why the Chinese hate him so, my mind can't help flashing back to what I read, there in prison, about how the blood forebears of this same white man raped China at a time when China was trusting and helpless. Those original white "Christian traders" sent into China millions of pounds of opium. By 1839, so many of the Chinese were addicts that China's desperate government destroyed twenty thousand chests of opium. The first Opium War was promptly declared by the white man. Imagine! Declaring *war* upon someone who objects to being narcotized! The Chinese were severely beaten, with Chinese-invented gunpowder.

The Treaty of Nanking made China pay the British white man for   35 the destroyed opium: forced open China's major ports to British trade; forced China to abandon Hong Kong; fixed China's import tariffs so low that cheap British articles soon flooded in, maiming China's industrial development.

After a second Opium War, the Tientsin Treaties legalized the ravaging opium trade, legalized a British-French-American control of China's customs. China tried delaying that Treaty's ratification; Peking was looted and burned.

"Kill the foreign white devils!" was the 1901 Chinese war cry in the Boxer Rebellion. Losing again, this time the Chinese were driven from Peking's choicest areas. The vicious, arrogant white man put up the famous signs, "Chinese and dogs not allowed."

Red China after World War II closed its doors to the Western white world. Massive Chinese agricultural, scientific, and industrial efforts are described in a book that *Life* magazine recently published. Some observers inside Red China have reported that the world never has known such a hate-white campaign as is now going on in this non-white country where, present birthrates continuing, in fifty more years Chinese will be half the earth's population. And it seems that some Chinese chickens will soon come home to roost, with China's recent successful nuclear tests.

Let us face reality. We can see in the United Nations a new world order being shaped, along color lines—an alliance among the nonwhite nations. America's U.N. Ambassador Adlai Stevenson complained not long ago that in the United Nations "a skin game" was being played. He was right. He was facing reality. A "skin game" *is* being played. But Ambassador Stevenson sounded like Jesse James accusing the marshal of carrying a gun. Because who in the world' history ever has played a worse "skin game" than the white man?

Mr. Muhammad, to whom I was writing daily, had no idea of what   40 a new world had opened up to me through my efforts to document his teachings in books.

When I discovered philosophy, I tried to touch all the landmarks of philosophical development. Gradually, I read most of the old philosophers, Occidental and Oriental. The Oriental philosophers were the ones I came to prefer; finally, my impression was that most Occidental philosophy had largely been borrowed from the Oriental thinkers. Socrates, for instance, traveled in Egypt. Some sources even say that Socrates was initiated into some of the Egyptian mysteries. Obviously Socrates got some of his wisdom among the East's wise men.

I have often reflected upon the new vistas that reading opened to me. I knew right there in prison that reading had changed forever the course of my life. As I see it today, the ability to read awoke inside me some long dormant craving to be mentally alive. I certainly wasn't seeking any degree, the way a college confers a status symbol upon its students. My homemade education gave me, with every additional book that I read, a little bit more sensitivity to the deafness, dumbness, and blindness that was afflicting the black race in America. Not long ago, an English writer telephoned me from London, asking questions. One was, "What's your alma mater?" I told him, "Books." You will never catch me with a free fifteen minutes in which I'm not studying something I feel might be able to help the black man.

Yesterday I spoke in London, and both ways on the plane across the Atlantic

I was studying a document about how the United Nations proposes to insure the human rights of the oppressed minorities of the world. The American black man is the world's most shameful case of minority oppression. What makes the black man think of himself as only an internal United States issue is just a catch-phrase, two words, "civil rights." How is the black man going to get "civil rights" before first he wins his *human* rights? If the American black man will start thinking about his human rights, and then start thinking of himself as part of one of the world's great peoples, he will see he has a case for the United Nations.

45   I can't think of a better case! Four hundred years of black blood and sweat invested here in America, and the white man still has the black man begging for what every immigrant fresh off the ship can take for granted the minute he walks down the gangplank.

But I'm digressing. I told the Englishman that my alma mater was books, a good library. Every time I catch a plane, I have with me a book that I want to read—and that's a lot of books these days. If I weren't out here every day battling the white man, I could spend the rest of my life reading, just satisfying my curiosity—because you can hardly mention anything I'm not curious about. I don't think anybody ever got more out of going to prison than I did. In fact, prison enabled me to study far more intensively than I would have if my life had gone differently and I had attended some college. I imagine that one of the biggest troubles with colleges is there are too many distractions, too much panty-raiding, fraternities, and boola-boola and all of that. Where else but in a prison could I have attacked my ignorance by being able to study intensely sometimes as much as fifteen hours a day?

The Case Against College

Caroline Bird

◆

Caroline Bird (1915-2011)

Caroline Bird was born in New York City to Hobart Stanley Bird, a journalist and activist, and Ida Brattrud. Bird spent two years at Vassar before leaving to marry, but later received a B.A. in American History from the University of Toledo in 1938, followed by an M.A. in comparative literature from the University of Wisconsin. Bird published her first work, a poetry collection called *Rhythms*, at age 9. Her first adult book, *The Invisible Scar*, was published in 1966. She followed this with *Born Female: The High Cost of Keeping Women Down*, and in 1975 *The Case Against College*, her most controversial work. Bird's later books, articles, and studies, included *Second Careers: New Ways to Work After Fifty* (1992) and *Lives of Our Own: Secrets of Salty Old Women* (1995).

---

1   The case *for* college has been accepted without question for more than a generation. All high school graduates ought to go, says Conventional Wisdom and statistical evidence, because college will help them earn more money, become "better" people, and learn to be more responsible citizens than those who don't go.

But college has never been able to work its magic for everyone. And now that close to half our high school graduates are attending, those who don't fit the pattern are becoming more numerous, and more obvious. College graduates are selling shoes and driving taxis; college students sabotage each other's experiments and forge letters of recommendation in the intense competition for admission to graduate school. Others find no stimulation in their studies, and drop out—often encouraged by college administrators.

Some observers say the fault is with the young people themselves—they are spoiled, stoned, overindulged, and expecting too much. But that's mass character assassination, and doesn't explain all campus unhappiness. Others blame the state of the world, and they are partly right. We've been told that young people have to go to college because our economy can't absorb an army of untrained eighteen-year-olds. But disillusioned graduates are learning that it can no longer absorb an army of untrained twenty-two-year-olds, either....

The ultimate defense of college has always been that while it may not teach you anything vocationally useful, it will somehow make you a better person, able to do anything better, and those who make it through the process are initiated into the "fellowship of educated men and women." In a study intended to probe what graduates seven years out of college thought their colleges should have done for them, the Carnegie Commission found that most alumni expected the "development of my abilities to think and express myself." But if such respected educational psychologists as Bruner and Piaget are right, specific learning skills have to be acquired very early in life, perhaps even before formal schooling begins.

So, when pressed, liberal-arts defenders speak instead about   5 something more encompassing, and more elusive. "College changed me inside," one graduate told us fervently. The authors of a Carnegie Commission report, who obviously struggled for a definition, concluded that one of the common threads in the perceptions of a liberal education is that it provides "an integrated view of the world which can serve as an inner guide." More simply, alumni say that college should have "helped me to formulate the values and goals of my life."

In theory, a student is taught to develop these values and goals himself, but in practice, it doesn't work quite that way. All but the wayward and saintly take their sense of the good, the true, and the beautiful from the people around them. When we speak of students acquiring "values" in college, we often mean that they will acquire the values—and sometimes that means only the tastes—of their professors. The values of professors may be "higher" than many students will encounter elsewhere, but they may not be relevant to situations in which students find themselves in college and later.

Of all the forms in which ideas are disseminated, the college professor lecturing a class is the slowest and most expensive. You don't have to go to college to read the great books or learn about the great ideas of Western Man. Today you can find them everywhere—in paperbacks, in the public libraries, in museums, in public lectures, in adult-education courses, in abridged, summarized, or adapted form in magazines, films, and television. The problem is no longer one of access to broadening ideas; the problem is the other way around: how to choose among the many courses of action proposed to us, how to edit the stimulations that pour into our eyes and ears every waking hour. A college experience that piles option on option and stimulation on stimulation merely adds to the contemporary nightmare.

What students and graduates say that they did learn on campus comes under the heading of personal, rather than intellectual, development. Again and again I was told that the real value of college is learning to get along with others, to practice social skills, to "sort out my head," and these have nothing to do with curriculum.

For whatever impact the academic experience used to have on college students, the sheer size of many undergraduate classes... dilutes faculty-student dialogue, and, more often than not, they are taught by teachers who were hired when colleges were faced with a shortage of qualified instructors, during their years of expansion and when the big rise in academic pay attracted the mediocre and the less than dedicated.

10   On the social side, colleges are withdrawing from responsibility for feeding, housing, policing, and protecting students at a time when the environment of college may be the most important service it could render. College officials are reluctant to "intervene" in the personal lives of the students. They no longer expect to take over from parents, but often insist that students—who have, most often, never lived away from home before—take full adult responsibility for their plans, achievements, and behavior.

Most college students do not live in the plush, comfortable country-clublike surroundings their parents envisage, or, in some cases, remember. Open dorms, particularly when they are coeducational, are noisy, usually overcrowded, and often messy. Some students desert the institutional "zoos" (their own word for dorms) and move into run-down, over-priced apartments. Bulletin boards in student centers are littered with notices of apartments to share and the drift of conversation suggests that a lot of money is dissipated in scrounging for food and shelter.

Taxpayers now provide more than half of the astronomical sums that are spent on higher education. But less than half of today's high school graduates go on, raising a new question of equity: Is it fair to make all the taxpayers pay for the minority who actually go to college? We decided long ago that it is fair for childless adults to pay school taxes because everyone, parents and nonparents alike, profits by a literate population. Does the same reasoning hold true for state-supported higher education? There is no conclusive evidence on either side.

Young people cannot be expected to go to college for the general good of mankind. They may be more altruistic than their elders, but no great numbers are going to spend four years at hard intellectual labor, let alone tens of thousands of family dollars, for "the advancement of human capability in society at large," one of the many purposes invoked by the Carnegie Commission report. Nor do any considerable number of them want to go to college to beat the Russians to Jupiter, improve the national defense, increase the Gross National Product, lower the crime rate, improve automobile safety, or create a market for the arts—all of which have been suggested at one time or other as benefits taxpayers get for supporting higher education.

One sociologist said that you don't have to have a reason for going to college because it's an institution. His definition of an institution is something everyone subscribes to without question. The burden of proof is not on why you should go to college, but why anyone thinks there might be a reason for not going. The implication—and some educators express it quite frankly—is that an eighteen-year-old high school graduate is still too young and confused to know what he wants to do, let alone what is good for him.

Mother knows best, in other words.   15

It had always been comfortable for students to believe that authorities, like Mother, or outside specialists, like educators, could determine what was best for them. However, specialists and authorities no longer enjoy the credibility former generations accorded them. Patients talk back to doctors and are not struck suddenly dead. Clients question the lawyer's bills and sometimes get them reduced. It is no longer self-evident that all adolescents must study a fixed curriculum that was constructed at a time when all educated men could agree on precisely what it was that made them educated.

The same with college. If high school graduates don't want to continue their education, or don't want to continue it right away, they may perceive more clearly than their elders that college is not for them.

College is an ideal place for those young adults who love learning for its own sake, who would rather read than eat, and who like nothing better than writing research papers. But they are a minority, even at the prestigious colleges, which recruit and attract the intellectually oriented.

The rest of our high school graduates need to look at college more closely and critically, to examine it as a consumer product, and decide if the cost in dollars, in time, in continued dependency, and in future returns, is worth the very large investment each student—and his family—must make.

Dead Men's Path

Chinua Achebe

◈

Chinua Achebe (1930-)

Widely viewed as the father of modern African writing, Chinua Achebe was born Albert Chinụalụmọgụ Achebe in Nigeria in 1930. Achebe attended University College (today the University of Ibadan), Nigeria's first university, where he studied English, history, and theology. After graduating in 1953, Achebe taught English for a period in Oba before relocating to the then-capital city of Lagos and joining the Nigerian Broadcasting Service as a scriptwriter. It was during this period that Achebe began work on his first novel, *Things Fall Apart*, which examines the life of a man in a late nineteenth-century Igbo village and the encroaching impact of colonialism and Christian missionaries on village life. Upon its publication in 1958, the book was met with swift critical acclaim, and was followed shortly by *No Longer at Ease* (1960), a look at modern Nigeria featuring the grandson of the first novel's protagonist. Achebe's literary work, which also includes novels, story collections, and poetry, draws heavily upon Igbo oral tradition, with references derived from folk tales, folk songs, and proverbs. The themes often center on Igbo culture itself, colonialism and conflict between African tradition and (generally European) modernity, and gender roles. Achebe has gained additional notability for his academic work. One lecture, 1975's "An Image of Africa: Racism in Conrad's Heart of Darkness," generated controversy in the West for its claims that Conrad dehumanizes Africans in his work, which had generally been viewed as anti-imperialist. Today, however, Achebe's position has become more widely accepted. Achebe has served on the faculty of several institutions, including the University of Nigeria, the University of Massachusetts Amherst, and Bard College. In 2009, he was named David and Marianna Fisher University Professor and professor of Africana studies at Brown University.

Michael Obi's hopes were fulfilled much earlier than he had expected. 1
He was appointed headmaster of Ndume Central School in January 1949. It had always been an unprogressive school, so the Mission

authorities decided to send a young and energetic man to run it. Obi accepted this responsibility with enthusiasm. He had many wonderful ideas and this was an opportunity to put them into practice. He had had sound secondary school education which designated him a "pivotal teacher" in the official records and set him apart from the other headmasters in the mission field. He was outspoken in his condemnation of the narrow views of these older and often less-educated ones.

"We shall make a good job of it, shan't we?" he asked his young wife when they first heard the joyful news of his promotion.

"We shall do our best," she replied. "We shall have such beautiful gardens and everything will be just *modern* and delightful…" In their two years of married life she had become completely infected by his passion for "modern methods" and his denigration of "these old and superannuated people in the teaching field who would be better employed as traders in the Onitsha market." She began to see herself already as the admired wife of the young headmaster, the queen of the school.

The wives of the other teachers would envy her position. She would set the fashion in everything…. Then, suddenly, it occurred to her that there might not be other wives. Wavering between hope and fear, she asked her husband, looking anxiously at him.

5   "All our colleagues are young and unmarried," he said with enthusiasm which for once she did not share. "Which is a good thing," he continued.

"Why?"

"Why? They will give all their time and energy to the school."

Nancy was downcast. For a few minutes she became skeptical about the new school; but it was only for a few minutes. Her little personal misfortune could not blind her to her husband's happy prospects. She looked at him as he sat folded up in a chair. He was stoop-shouldered and looked frail. But he sometimes surprised people with sudden bursts of physical energy. In his present posture, however, all his bodily strength seemed to have retired behind his deep-set eyes, giving them an extraordinary power of penetration. He was only twenty-six, but looked thirty or more. On the whole, he was not unhandsome.

"A penny for your thoughts, Mike," said Nancy after a while, imitating the woman's magazine she read.

"I was thinking what a grand opportunity we've got at last to show these people how a school should be run."

Ndume School was backward in every sense of the word. Mr. Obi   10
put his whole life into the work, and his wife hers too. He had two
aims. A high standard of teaching was insisted upon, and the school
compound was to be turned into a place of beauty. Nancy's dream-
gardens came to life with the coming of the rains, and blossomed.
Beautiful hibiscus and allamanda hedges in brilliant red and yellow
marked out the carefully tended school compound from the rank
neighborhood bushes.

One evening as Obi was admiring his work he was scandalized to
see an old woman from the village hobble right across the compound,
through a marigold flower-bed and the hedges. On going up there he
found faint signs of an almost disused path from the village across the
school compound to the bush on the other side.

"It amazes me," said Obi to one of his teachers who had been three
years in the school, "that you people allowed the villagers to make use
of this footpath. It is simply incredible." He shook his head.

"The path," said the teacher apologetically, "appears to be very
important to them. Although it is hardly used, it connects the village
shrine with their place of burial."

"And what has that got to do with the school?" asked the
headmaster.

"Well, I don't know," replied the other with a shrug of the   15
shoulders. "But I remember there was a big row some time ago when
we attempted to close it."

"That was some time ago. But it will not be used now," said Obi as
he walked away. "What will the Government Education Officer think
of this when he comes to inspect the school next week? The villagers
might, for all I know, decide to use the schoolroom for a pagan ritual
during the inspection."

Heavy sticks were planted closely across the path at the two places
where it entered and left the school premises. These were further
strengthened with barbed wire.

Three days later the village priest of *Ani* called on the headmaster.
He was an old man and walked with a slight stoop. He carried a
stout walking-stick which he usually tapped on the floor, by way of
emphasis, each time he made a new point in his argument.

"I have heard," he said after the usual exchange of cordialities,
"that our ancestral footpath has recently been closed...."

"Yes," replied Mr. Obi. "We cannot allow people to make a highway   20
of our school compound."

"Look here, my son," said the priest bringing down his walking stick, "this path was here before you were born and before your father was born. The whole life of this village depends on it. Our dead relatives depart by it and our ancestors visit us by it. But most important, it is the path of children coming in to be born...."

Mr. Obi listened with a satisfied smile on his face.

"The whole purpose of our school," he said finally, "is to eradicate just such beliefs as that. Dead mean do not require footpaths. The whole idea is just fantastic. Our duty is to teach your children to laugh at such ideas."

"What you say may be true," replied the priest, "but we follow the practices of our fathers. If you reopen the path we shall have nothing to quarrel about. What I always say is: let the hawk perch and let the eagle perch." He rose to go.

25   "I am sorry," said the young headmaster. "But the school compound cannot be a thoroughfare. It is against our regulations. I would suggest your constructing another path, skirting our premises. We can even get our boys to help in building it. I don't suppose the ancestors will find the little detour too burdensome."

"I have no more words to say," said the old priest, already outside.

Two days later a young woman in the village died in child bed. A diviner was immediately consulted and he prescribed heavy sacrifices to propitiate ancestors insulted by the fence.

Obi woke up next morning among the ruins of his work. The beautiful hedges were torn up not just near the path but right round the school, the flowers trampled to death and one of the school buildings pulled down.... That day, the white Supervisor came to inspect the school and wrote a nasty report on the state of the premises but more seriously about the "tribal-war situation developing between the school and the village, arising in part from the misguided zeal of the new headmaster."

V
LANGUAGE

POLITICS AND THE ENGLISH LANGUAGE

George Orwell

GEORGE ORWELL (1903-1950)

George Orwell was born Eric Blair in India to an English member of the Indian Civil Service. At the age of one, he was taken by his mother to England, where he remained until young adulthood. At 19, he passed the exam to enter the Indian Police Service, and spent the next five years on the service in Burma. He subsequently returned to Europe in 1927 and, while dividing time between England and Paris, established a career as a journalist, frequently entering the world of the impoverished to better understand and empathize with his subject matter. In 1937, he fought in Spain during the Spanish Civil War, an event that would lead him to question all totalitarian governments regardless of party philosophy. Reflective of his journalistic aims and experiences, Orwell's writing was typically political in nature; his most famous and influential works of fiction are the satire *Animal Farm* (1945) and dystopian novel *1984* (1949). His major non-fiction books include 1937's *The Road to Wigan Pier* and 1938's *Homage to Catalonia*, which outlines Orwell's experiences in the Spanish Civil War and his subsequent disillusionment.

---

1   Most people who bother with the matter at all would admit that the English language is in a bad way, but it is generally assumed that we cannot by conscious action do anything about it. Our civilization is decadent and our language—so the argument runs—must inevitably share in the general collapse. It follows that any struggle against the abuse of language is a sentimental archaism, like preferring candles to electric light or hansom cabs to airplanes. Underneath this lies the half-conscious belief that language is a natural growth and not an instrument which we shape for our own purposes.

Now, it is clear that the decline of a language must ultimately have political and economic causes: it is not due simply to the bad influence of this or that individual writer. But an effect can become a cause, reinforcing the original cause and producing the same effect in an intensified form, and so on indefinitely. A man may take to drink because he feels himself to be a failure, and then fail all the more completely because he drinks. It is rather the same thing that is happening to the English language. It becomes ugly and inaccurate because our thoughts are foolish, but the slovenliness of our language makes it easier for us to have foolish thoughts. The point is that the process is reversible. Modern English, especially written English, is full of bad habits which spread by imitation and which can be avoided if one is willing to take the necessary trouble. If one gets rid of these habits one can think more clearly, and to think clearly is a necessary first step toward political regeneration: so that the fight against bad English is not frivolous and is not the exclusive concern of professional writers. I will come back to this presently, and I hope that by that time the meaning of what I have said here will have become clearer. Meanwhile, here are five specimens of the English language as it is now habitually written.

These five passages have not been picked out because they are especially bad—I could have quoted far worse if I had chosen—but because they illustrate various of the mental vices from which we now suffer. They are a little below the average, but are fairly representative examples. I number them so that I can refer back to them when necessary:

(1) *"I am not, indeed, sure whether it is not true to say that the Milton who once seemed not unlike a seventeenth-century Shelley had not become, out of an experience ever more bitter in each year, more alien [sic] to the founder of that Jesuit sect which nothing could induce him to tolerate."*
    Professor Harold Laski (Essay in *Freedom of Expression*)

(2) *"Above all, we cannot play ducks and drakes with a native battery* 5
    of idioms which prescribes such egregious collocations of vocables as the Basic put up with for tolerate or put at a loss for bewilder."
    Professor Lancelot Hogben (*Interglossia*)

(3) *"On the one side we have the free personality: by definition it is not neurotic, for it has neither conflict nor dream. Its desires, such as they are, are transparent, for they are just what institutional approval keeps in the forefront of consciousness; another institutional pattern*

would alter their number and intensity; there is little in them that is natural, irreducible, or culturally dangerous. But on the other side, the social bond itself is nothing but the mutual reflection of these self-secure integrities. Recall the definition of love. Is not this the very picture of a small academic? Where is there a place in this hall of mirrors for either personality or fraternity?"

Essay on psychology in *Politics* (New York)

(4) *"All the 'best people' from the gentlemen's clubs, and all the frantic fascist captains, united in common hatred of Socialism and bestial horror at the rising tide of the mass revolutionary movement, have turned to acts of provocation, to foul incendiarism, to medieval legends of poisoned wells, to legalize their own destruction of proletarian organizations, and rouse the agitated petty-bourgeoise to chauvinistic fervor on behalf of the fight against the revolutionary way out of the crisis."*

Communist pamphlet

(5) *"If a new spirit is to be infused into this old country, there is one thorny and contentious reform which must be tackled, and that is the humanization and galvanization of the B.B.C. Timidity here will bespeak canker and atrophy of the soul. The heart of Britain may be sound and of strong beat, for instance, but the British lion's roar at present is like that of Bottom in Shakespeare's A Midsummer Night's Dream—as gentle as any sucking dove. A virile new Britain cannot continue indefinitely to be traduced in the eyes or rather ears, of the world by the effete languors of Langham Place, brazenly masquerading as 'standard English'. When the Voice of Britain is heard at nine o'clock, better far and infinitely less ludicrous to hear aitches honestly dropped than the present priggish, inflated, inhibited, school-ma'amish arch braying of blameless bashful mewing maidens!"*

Letter in Tribune

Each of these passages has faults of its own, but, quite apart from avoidable ugliness, two qualities are common to all of them. The first is staleness of imagery; the other is lack of precision. The writer either has a meaning and cannot express it, or he inadvertently says something else, or he is almost indifferent as to whether his words mean anything or not. This mixture of vagueness and sheer incompetence is the most marked characteristic of modern English prose, and especially of any kind of political writing. As soon as certain topics are raised, the concrete melts into the abstract and no one seems able to think of turns of speech that are not hackneyed: prose consists less and less of *words* chosen for the sake of their meaning, and more and more of *phrases* tacked together like the sections of a prefabricated henhouse. I list below, with notes and examples, various of the tricks by means of which the work of prose-construction is habitually dodged:

Dying metaphors. A newly invented metaphor assists thought by [10] evoking a visual image, while on the other hand a metaphor which is technically "dead" (e.g. *iron resolution*) has in effect reverted to being an ordinary word and can generally be used without loss of vividness. But in between these two classes there is a huge dump of worn-out metaphors which have lost all evocative power and are merely used because they save people the trouble of inventing phrases for themselves. Examples are: *Ring the changes on, take up the cudgels for, toe the line, ride roughshod over, stand shoulder to shoulder with, play into the hands of, no axe to grind, grist to the mill, fishing in troubled waters, on the order of the day, Achilles' heel, swan song, hotbed.* Many of these are used without knowledge of their meaning (what is a "rift," for instance?), and incompatible metaphors are frequently mixed, a sure sign that the writer is not interested in what he is saying. Some metaphors now current have been twisted out of their original meaning without those who use them even being aware of the fact. For example, *toe the line* is sometimes written as *tow the line*. Another example is *the hammer and the anvil*, now always used with the implication that the anvil gets the worst of it. In real life it is always the anvil that breaks the hammer, never the other way about: a writer who stopped to think what he was saying would avoid perverting the original phrase.

Operators or verbal false limbs. These save the trouble of picking out appropriate verbs and nouns, and at the same time pad each sentence with extra syllables which give it an appearance of symmetry. Characteristic phrases are: *render inoperative, militate against, make contact with, be subjected to, give rise to, give grounds for, have the effect of, play a leading part (role) in, make itself felt, take effect, exhibit a tendency to, serve the purpose of, etc., etc.* The keynote is the elimination of simple verbs. Instead of being a single word, such as *break, stop, spoil, mend, kill,* a verb becomes a *phrase,* made up of a noun or adjective tacked on to some general-purpose verbs such as *prove, serve, form, play, render.* In addition, the passive voice is wherever possible used in preference to the active, and noun constructions are used instead of gerunds (*by examination* of instead of *by examining*). The range of verbs is further cut down by means of the *-ize* and *de-* formations, and the banal statements are given an appearance of profundity by means of the *not un-* formation. Simple conjunctions and prepositions are replaced by such phrases as *with respect to, having regard to, the fact that, by dint of, in view of, in the interests of, on the hypothesis that*; and the ends of sentences are saved by anticlimax by such resounding commonplaces as *greatly to be desired, cannot be left out of account, a development to be expected in the near future, deserving of serious consideration, brought to a satisfactory conclusion*, and so on and so forth.

Pretentious diction. Words like *phenomenon, element, individual (as noun), objective, categorical, effective, virtual, basic, primary, promote, constitute, exhibit, exploit, utilize, eliminate, liquidate*, are used to dress up a simple statement and give an air of scientific impartiality to biased judgments. Adjectives like *epoch-making, epic, historic, unforgettable, triumphant, age-old, inevitable, inexorable, veritable*, are used to dignify the sordid process of international politics, while writing that aims at glorifying war usually takes on an archaic color, its characteristic words being: *realm, throne, chariot, mailed fist, trident, sword, shield, buckler, banner, jackboot, clarion*. Foreign words and expressions such as *cul de sac, ancien régime, deus ex machina, mutatis mutandis, status quo, gleichschaltung, weltanschauung*, are used to give an air of culture and elegance. Except for the useful abbreviations *i.e., e.g.,* and *etc.*, there is no real need for any of the hundreds of foreign phrases now current in the English language. Bad writers, and especially scientific, political, and sociological writers, are nearly always haunted by the notion that Latin or Greek words are grander than Saxon ones, and unnecessary words like *expedite, ameliorate, predict, extraneous, deracinated, clandestine, subaqueous*, and hundreds of others constantly gain ground from their Anglo-Saxon numbers. The jargon peculiar to Marxist writing (*hyena, hangman, cannibal, petty bourgeois, these gentry, lackey, flunkey, mad dog, White Guard*, etc.) consists largely of words translated from Russian, German, or French; but the normal way of coining a new word is to use Latin or Greek root with the appropriate affix and, where necessary, the *-ize* formation. It is often easier to make up words of this kind (*deregionalize, impermissible, extramarital, non-fragmentary* and so forth) than to think up the English words that will cover one's meaning. The result, in general, is an increase in slovenliness and vagueness.

Meaningless words. In certain kinds of writing, particularly in art criticism and literary criticism, it is normal to come across long passages which are almost completely lacking in meaning. Words like *romantic, plastic, values, human, dead, sentimental, natural, vitality*, as used in art criticism, are strictly meaningless in the sense that they not only do not point to any discoverable object, but are hardly ever expected to do so by the reader. When one critic writes, "The outstanding feature of Mr. X's work is its living quality," while another writes, "The immediately striking thing about Mr. X's work is its peculiar deadness," the reader accepts this as a simple difference of opinion. If words like *black* and *white* were involved, instead of the jargon words *dead* and *living*, he would see at once that language was being used in an improper way. Many political words are similarly abused. The word *Fascism* has now no meaning except in so far as it signifies "something not desirable." The words *democracy, socialism, freedom, patriotic, realistic, justice*, have each of them several different meanings which cannot be reconciled with one another. In the case of a word like *democracy*, not only is there no agreed definition, but the attempt to make one is resisted from all sides. It is almost universally felt that when we call a country democratic we are praising it: consequently the defenders of every kind of regime claim that it is a democracy, and fear that they might have to stop using that word if it were tied down to any one meaning. Words of this kind are often used in a consciously dishonest way. That is, the person who uses them has his own private definition, but allows his hearer to think he means something quite different. Statements like *Marshal Pétain was a true patriot, The Soviet press is the freest in the world, The Catholic Church is opposed to persecution*, are almost always made with intent to deceive. Other words used in variable meanings, in most cases more or less dishonestly, are: *class, totalitarian, science, progressive, reactionary, bourgeois, equality*.

Now that I have made this catalogue of swindles and perversions, let me give another example of the kind of writing that they lead to. This time it must of its nature be an imaginary one. I am going to translate a passage of good English into modern English of the worst sort. Here is a well-known verse from *Ecclesiastes*:

> "I returned and saw under the sun, that the race is not to the   15
> swift, nor the battle to the strong, neither yet bread to the wise,
> nor yet riches to men of understanding, nor yet favour to men
> of skill; but time and chance happeneth to them all."

Here it is in modern English:

> *"Objective consideration of contemporary phenomena compels the conclusion that success or failure in competitive activities exhibits no tendency to be commensurate with innate capacity, but that a considerable element of the unpredictable must invariably be taken into account."*

This is a parody, but not a very gross one. Exhibit (3) above, for instance, contains several patches of the same kind of English. It will be seen that I have not made a full translation. The beginning and ending of the sentence follow the original meaning fairly closely, but in the middle the concrete illustrations—race, battle, bread— dissolve into the vague phrase "success or failure in competitive activities." This had to be so, because no modern writer of the kind I am discussing— no one capable of using phrases like "objective considerations of contemporary phenomena"—would ever tabulate his thoughts in that precise and detailed way. The whole tendency of modern prose is away from concreteness. Now analyze these two sentences a little more closely. The first contains forty-nine words but only sixty syllables, and all its words are those of everyday life. The second contains thirty-eight words of ninety syllables: eighteen of those words are from Latin roots, and one from Greek. The first sentence contains six vivid images, and only one phrase ("time and chance") that could be called vague. The second contains not a single fresh, arresting phrase, and in spite of its ninety syllables it gives only a shortened version of the meaning contained in the first. Yet without a doubt it is the second kind of sentence that is gaining ground in modern English. I do not want to exaggerate. This kind of writing is not yet universal, and outcrops of simplicity will occur here and there in the worst-written page. Still, if you or I were told to write a few lines on the uncertainty of human fortunes, we should probably come much nearer to my imaginary sentence than to the one from *Ecclesiastes*.

As I have tried to show, modern writing at its worst does not consist in picking out words for the sake of their meaning and inventing images in order to make the meaning clearer. It consists in gumming together long strips of words which have already been set in order by someone else, and making the results presentable by sheer humbug. The attraction of this way of writing is that it is easy. It is easier— even quicker, once you have the habit—to say *In my opinion it is a not unjustifiable assumption that* than to say *I think*. If you use ready-made phrases, you not only don't have to hunt about for words; you also don't have to bother with the rhythms of your sentences, since these phrases are generally so arranged as to be more or less euphonious. When you are composing in a hurry—when you are dictating to a stenographer, for instance, or making a public speech—it is natural to fall into a pretentious, Latinized style. Tags like *a consideration which we should do well to bear in mind or a conclusion to which all of us would readily assent* will save many a sentence from coming down with a bump. By using stale metaphors, similes, and idioms, you save much mental effort, at the cost of leaving your meaning vague, not only for your reader but for yourself. This is the significance of mixed metaphors. The sole aim of a metaphor is to call up a visual image. When these images clash—as in *The Fascist octopus has sung its swan song, the jackboot is thrown into the melting pot*—it can't be taken as certain that the writer is not seeing a mental image of the objects he is naming; in other words he is not really thinking. Look again at the examples I gave at the beginning of this essay. Professor Laski (1) uses five negatives in fifty-three words.

One of these is superfluous, making nonsense of the whole   20 passage, and in addition there is the slip *alien* for akin, making further nonsense, and several avoidable pieces of clumsiness which increase the general vagueness. Professor Hogben (2) plays ducks and drakes with a battery which is able to write prescriptions, and, while disapproving of the everyday phrase *put up with*, is unwilling to look *egregious* up in the dictionary and see what it means; (3), if one takes an uncharitable attitude towards it, is simply meaningless: probably one could work out its intended meaning by reading the whole of the article in which it occurs. In (4), the writer knows more or less what he wants to say, but an accumulation of stale phrases chokes him like tea leaves blocking a sink. In (5), words and meaning have almost parted company. People who write in this manner usually have a general emotional meaning—they dislike one thing and want to express solidarity with another—but they are not interested in the detail of what they are saying. A scrupulous writer, in every sentence that he writes, will ask himself at least four questions, thus: What am I trying to say? What words will express it? What image or idiom will make it clearer? Is this image fresh enough to have an effect? And he will probably ask himself two more: Could I put it more shortly? Have I said anything that is avoidably ugly? But you are not obliged to go to all this trouble. You can shirk it by simply throwing your mind open and letting the ready-made phrases come crowding in. They will construct your sentences for you—even think your thoughts for you, to a certain extent—and at need they will perform the important service of partially concealing your meaning even from yourself. It is at this point that the special connection between politics and the debasement of language becomes clear.

In our time it is broadly true that political writing is bad writing. Where it is not true, it will generally be found that the writer is some kind of rebel, expressing his private opinions and not a "party line." Orthodoxy, of whatever color, seems to demand a lifeless, imitative style. The political dialects to be found in pamphlets, leading articles, manifestoes, White Papers and the speeches of under-secretaries do, of course, vary from party to party, but they are all alike in that one almost never finds in them a fresh, vivid, home-made turn of speech. When one watches some tired hack on the platform mechanically repeating the familiar phrases—*bestial atrocities, iron heel, bloodstained tyranny, free peoples of the world, stand shoulder to shoulder*—one often has a curious feeling that one is not watching a live human being but some kind of dummy: a feeling which suddenly becomes stronger at moments when the light catches the speaker's spectacles and turns them into blank discs which seem to have no eyes behind them. And this is not altogether fanciful. A speaker who uses that kind of phraseology has gone some distance toward turning himself into a machine. The appropriate noises are coming out of his larynx, but his brain is not involved as it would be if he were choosing his words for himself. If the speech he is making is one that he is accustomed to make over and over again, he may be almost unconscious of what he is saying, as one is when one utters the responses in church.

And this reduced state of consciousness, if not indispensable, is at any rate favorable to political conformity.

In our time, political speech and writing are largely the defense of the indefensible. Things like the continuance of British rule in India, the Russian purges and deportations, the dropping of the atom bombs on Japan, can indeed be defended, but only by arguments which are too brutal for most people to face, and which do not square with the professed aims of the political parties. Thus political language has to consist largely of euphemism, question-begging and sheer cloudy vagueness. Defenseless villages are bombarded from the air, the inhabitants driven out into the countryside, the cattle machine-gunned, the huts set on fire with incendiary bullets: this is called *pacification*. Millions of peasants are robbed of their farms and sent trudging along the roads with no more than they can carry: this is called *transfer of population* or *rectification of frontiers*. People are imprisoned for years without trial, or shot in the back of the neck or sent to die of scurvy in Arctic lumber camps: this is called *elimination of unreliable elements*. Such phraseology is needed if one wants to name things without calling up mental pictures of them. Consider for instance some comfortable English professor defending Russian totalitarianism. He cannot say outright, "I believe in killing off your opponents when you can get good results by doing so." Probably, therefore, he will say something like this:

> "While freely conceding that the Soviet régime exhibits certain features which the humanitarian may be inclined to deplore, we must, I think, agree that a certain curtailment of the right to political opposition is an unavoidable concomitant of transitional periods, and that the rigors which the Russian people have been called upon to undergo have been amply justified in the sphere of concrete achievement."

The inflated style itself is a kind of euphemism. A mass of Latin 25 words falls upon the facts like soft snow, blurring the outline and covering up all the details. The great enemy of clear language is insincerity. When there is a gap between one's real and one's declared aims, one turns as it were instinctively to long words and exhausted idioms, like a cuttlefish spurting out ink. In our age there is no such thing as "keeping out of politics." All issues are political issues, and politics itself is a mass of lies, evasions, folly, hatred, and schizophrenia. When the general atmosphere is bad, language must suffer. I should expect to find—this is a guess which I have not sufficient knowledge to verify—that the German, Russian and Italian languages have all deteriorated in the last ten or fifteen years, as a result of dictatorship.

But if thought corrupts language, language can also corrupt thought. A bad usage can spread by tradition and imitation even among people who should and do know better. The debased language that I have been discussing is in some ways very convenient. Phrases like a *not unjustifiable assumption, leaves much to be desired, would serve no good purpose, a consideration which we should do well to bear in mind*, are a continuous temptation, a packet of aspirins always at one's elbow. Look back through this essay, and for certain you will find that I have again and again committed the very faults I am protesting against. By this morning's post I have received a pamphlet dealing with conditions in Germany. The author tells me that he "felt impelled" to write it. I open it at random, and here is almost the first sentence that I see: "[The Allies] have an opportunity not only of achieving a radical transformation of Germany's social and political structure in such a way as to avoid a nationalistic reaction in Germany itself, but at the same time of laying the foundations of a co-operative and unified Europe." You see, he "feels impelled" to write—feels, presumably, that he has something new to say—and yet his words, like cavalry horses answering the bugle, group themselves automatically into the familiar dreary pattern. This invasion of one's mind by ready-made phrases (*lay the foundations, achieve a radical transformation*) can only be prevented if one is constantly on guard against them, and every such phrase anaesthetizes a portion of one's brain.

I said earlier that the decadence of our language is probably curable. Those who deny this would argue, if they produced an argument at all, that language merely reflects existing social conditions, and that we cannot influence its development by any direct tinkering with words and constructions. So far as the general tone or spirit of a language goes, this may be true, but it is not true in detail. Silly words and expressions have often disappeared, not through any evolutionary process but owing to the conscious action of a minority. Two recent examples were *explore every avenue* and *leave no stone unturned*, which were killed by the jeers of a few journalists. There is a long list of fly-blown metaphors which could similarly be got rid of if enough people would interest themselves in the job; and it should also be possible to laugh the *not un-* formation out of existence, to reduce the amount of Latin and Greek in the average sentence, to drive out foreign phrases and strayed scientific words, and, in general, to make pretentiousness unfashionable. But all these are minor points. The defence of the English language implies more than this, and perhaps it is best to start by saying what it does not imply.

To begin with it has nothing to do with archaism, with the salvaging of obsolete words and turns of speech, or with the setting up of a "standard English" which must never be departed from. On the contrary, it is especially concerned with the scrapping of every word or idiom which has outworn its usefulness. It has nothing to do with correct grammar and syntax, which are of no importance so long as one makes one's meaning clear, or with the avoidance of Americanisms, or with having what is called a "good prose style." On the other hand, it is not concerned with fake simplicity and the attempt to make written English colloquial. Nor does it even imply in every case preferring the Saxon word to the Latin one, though it does imply using the fewest and shortest words that will cover one's meaning. What is above all needed is to let the meaning choose the word, and not the other way about. In prose, the worst thing one can do with words is surrender to them. When you think of a concrete object, you think wordlessly, and then, if you want to describe the thing you have been visualizing you probably hunt about until you find the exact words that seem to fit it. When you think of something abstract you are more inclined to use words from the start, and unless you make a conscious effort to prevent it, the existing dialect will come rushing in and do the job for you, at the expense of blurring or even changing your meaning. Probably it is better to put off using words as long as possible and get one's meaning as clear as one can through pictures and sensations. Afterward one can choose—not simply *accept*—the phrases that will best cover the meaning, and then switch round and decide what impressions one's words are likely to make on another person. This last effort of the mind cuts out all stale or mixed images, all prefabricated phrases, needless repetitions, and humbug and vagueness generally. But one can often be in doubt about the effect of a word or a phrase, and one needs rules that one can rely on when instinct fails. I think the following rules will cover most cases:

i.   Never use a metaphor, simile, or other figure of speech which you are used to seeing in print.

ii.   Never use a long word where a short one will do.

iii.   If it is possible to cut a word out, always cut it out.

iv.   Never use the passive where you can use the active.

v.   Never use a foreign phrase, a scientific word or a jargon word if you can

vi.   think of an everyday English equivalent.

vii.   Break any of these rules sooner than say anything outright barbarous.

These rules sound elementary, and so they are, but they demand a deep change of attitude in anyone who has grown used to writing in the style now fashionable. One could keep all of them and still write bad English, but one could not write the kind of stuff that I quoted in those five specimens at the beginning of this article.

30   I have not here been considering the literary use of language, but merely language as an instrument for expressing and not for concealing or preventing thought. Stuart Chase and others have come near to claiming that all abstract words are meaningless, and have used this as a pretext for advocating a kind of political quietism. Since you don't know what Fascism is, how can you struggle against Fascism? One need not swallow such absurdities as this, but one ought to recognize that the present political chaos is connected with the decay of language, and that one can probably bring about some improvement by starting at the verbal end. If you simplify your English, you are freed from the worst follies of orthodoxy. You cannot speak any of the necessary dialects, and when you make a stupid remark its stupidity will be obvious, even to yourself. Political language—and with variations this is true of all political parties, from Conservatives to Anarchists—is designed to make lies sound truthful and murder respectable, and to give an appearance of solidity to pure wind. One cannot change this all in a moment, but one can at least change one's own habits, and from time to time one can even, if one jeers loudly enough, send some worn-out and useless phrase—some *jackboot, Achilles' heel, hotbed, melting pot, acid test, veritable inferno*, or other lump of verbal refuse—into the dustbin, where it belongs.

◇

WE ARE OUR
OWN METAPHOR

Mary Catherine Bateson

◈

MARY CATHERINE BATESON (1939-)

Mary Catherine Bateson is the daughter of anthropologists Margaret Mead and Gregory Bateson. She received a B.A. from Radcliffe College in 1960 and a Ph.D. from Harvard in 1963. She has written several works of cultural anthropology, as well as a biography of her parents, *With a Daughter's Eye: A Memoir of Margaret Mead and Gregory Bateson* (1984). Bateson has taught at institutions including George Mason University, Harvard University, and Amherst College. She is a fellow of the Internet-based International Leadership Forum, as well as president of the Institute for Intercultural Studies, established by Mead. Bateson's most recent book is *Composing a Further Life: The Age of Active Wisdom* (2010).

The Gaia hypothesis, developed by James Lovelock and Lynn 1
Margulis, asserts that this planet is alive. This integrates a vast amount of information in a single image: What we are talking about is life. It wiggles. It may bite. The Gaian metaphor provides a bridge from high technical specificity to all the experiences that go with direct contact with a living being.

Above all, the Gaia hypothesis evokes the powerful ancient metaphor of Mother Earth. In the early seventies, there was a poster of the Earth as seen from space, the picture that has become so familiar and beloved, and underneath was written, "Your Mother—Love Her or Leave Her!" That was a brilliant but confusing poster, because every young American male knows what he is supposed to do with his mother: grow up and leave her. After all, his entire socialization is geared to achieving independence. The poster fed right into the fantasy that if we messed up this planet we could climb into spaceships and zoom to another one or perhaps to a space platform. That poster was an invitation to believe in the possibility of leaving, in the self as separate and separable.

Since the early years of the space program, the fantasy of solving environmental problems by leaving this planet behind has faded, as has the metaphor of Earth as a spaceship, but we still may not have found the metaphor that leads to effective attention. A metaphor can obscure as well as reveal. In contemporary culture, I doubt that the best way to elicit caring and responsible behavior from adults is to remind them of childhood, the retrospective dumping ground of problems and resentments. I may feel that having the Earth thought of as female enhances me or allows me to empathize a little more deeply, but I hate to expose the planet further to the danger of rape or evoke the ambivalence that people feel about mothers.

The use of a personal name, Gaia, suggests that the planet can evoke the attitudes we reserve for identified human individuals. Do we love Gaia? Does she love or trust in return? What does it add to understanding or confusion that Gaia is the name of a deity from an ancient and polytheistic system no longer widely worshiped, the most primitive layer of Greek religion? The original Gaia was inclined to devour her own offspring, many of whom were monsters.

5   Perhaps we could empathize more if the metaphor were differently conceived. Because the life span of a planet is potentially so long, we might learn to think of the planet as a young child that requires care and attention but has an unknown future. Such a metaphor would underline the need to protect future possibilities, not only for our human descendants but for all life on Earth, and might make accepting the limitations on knowledge and control less painful.

When we use a metaphor that is drawn from human relations, it is well to look carefully for all its hidden implications, for we run the risk of evoking human conflicts. If we are going to think of the Earth as female, it behooves us to take a good look at gender relations, because gender relations of dominance and exploitation will infect, have already infected, the relationship with the planet. Images of children often do evoke protectiveness and caring, yet we have been willing to incur massive debts our children will have to pay, and all too many parents exploit or abuse children and even more feel they have a right to determine a child's future. If we are going to use family images, let us take some responsibility for constructing human families that offer metaphors of mutuality and hope.

To me, the most important thing that the Gaia hypothesis proposes that was absent from earlier metaphors like "spaceship Earth" is that we are immersed in, brought into being by, a living reality, not a mechanical one. We are completely dependent, as we would be in a spaceship, but we do not have full blueprints and we cannot expect to be in complete control.

The Gaia hypothesis demands that we are totally contained in and sustained by a single living system, in which all the parts are interconnected and everything we do resonates with the whole. Nothing is fully localized. The destruction of an ecosystem or a species is an amputation and, like the amputation of a limb, can trigger fatal shock or, at the least, require learning new ways to function. One extraneous item introduced in the wrong place in a living body can trigger pathology. The Gaia hypothesis becomes, at every level of its metaphorical evocation, a reminder that the world we live in is a biological, or if you like a biologized world, a sacred process in which we share, a community to participate in, not an object to be used.

The Gaia hypothesis pulls the data together, but it goes further by offering a metaphor for organizing awareness of the interconnections. It proposes empathy as a way of knowing and imaging connections about which we cannot yet be explicit. It cannot, however, guarantee love or respect any more than centuries of religion and philosophy have been able to end the exploitation by human beings of one another. We continue to be unable to provide adequate care either for the old, our parents, or for the young, our children, to whom we will entrust the future, so it is no wonder we mistake the planet that represents both source and destiny for a shopping mall. What would it be like to walk through the woods or the city in the presence of—aware of—Gaia? Part of that awareness can be built up by letting children look through microscopes, germinate seeds, learn about soil chemistry, but part of it comes into being through the experiences of loving and being loved, resolving quarrels, learning new ways of family life, attending patiently to things we do not understand.

All thought relies on metaphor, on ways of noticing similarity   10 so that what has been learned in one situation can be transferred to another. Scientists try to purge metaphor and intuition from their publications, but the speech of scientists is like all human speech and thought, full of metaphors, often unconscious and unexamined.

The solution is not to purge metaphors from speech; the solution is to take responsibility for the choice of metaphors, to savor them and ponder their suggestions, above all to live with many and take no one metaphor as absolute. There are truths to be discovered in equating one's mother with a toad; there are truths to be discovered in looking at a butchered sheep and recognizing heart and lungs and death itself as common.

Not long ago, in 1988, a group of parents in Tennessee brought a lawsuit protesting that their children were being taught the religion of "secular humanism" in the schools, and objecting to the use of fantasy and mythology in education. A picture from a reading primer that showed a little boy and a little girl sitting at a kitchen table, with the little boy putting a piece of bread into a toaster, was cited as undermining traditional concepts of the family. This may seem extreme, yet these parents were right in their understanding of how people think and learn. Not only does such a picture undermine traditional concepts of the family but it undermines traditional concepts of God, for male dominance over females has long provided a model for the relationship between God and humankind. They would also be right to resist the metaphor of the dryad, along with any other suggestion of sacred presence immanent in the natural world, as undermining the idea of God as transcendent, ruling from outside and above.

Family systems, the organization of institutions, the way we run our country, the way we respond to other cultures and races, and the uses of political and military power—all these things are based on interlocking sets of metaphors. Our many relationships are isomorphic: they have the same form. There is a pattern that connects, and it is a pattern of dominance and exploitation, taught again and again in the most ordinary human arrangements. That pattern is expressed in the fierce and ultimately self-destructive attack on this planet that we cannot rule because we are a part of it.

In effect, because knowledge and perception are so dependent on available models, they cannot be changed without a commitment to changing basic patterns of social life. This is the most significant sense in which we are our own metaphor.

TWO KINDS

Amy Tan

AMY TAN (1952-)

Amy Tan was born in Oakland, California, to two Chinese immigrants. The experiences of her mother in particular helped inspire Tan's first and best-known book, 1989's *The Joy Luck Club*, which explores the cultural differences between a group of Chinese immigrant mothers and their American daughters. When Tan was a teenager, her family suffered the loss of both brother and father to brain tumors in a two-year span, and her mother moved Tan and her brother to Switzerland. After finishing high school abroad, Tan returned to the West Coast, where, after attending several institutions, working, and marrying, she eventually obtained a double B.A. in English and linguistics from San Jose State University in 1972. A M.A. in linguistics followed a year later. Tan subsequently pursued doctoral linguistics studies at the University of California, Berkeley, though never completed her degree. Tan has written several best-selling works, including *The Kitchen God's Wife* (1991) and *The Bonesetter's Daughter* (2001), which was adapted into an opera in 2008. Her short fiction and essays have also appeared in several leading publications, such as The New Yorker and The Atlantic. Her latest book is 2012's *The Valley of Amazement*.

My mother believed you could be anything you wanted to be in 1
America. You could open a restaurant. You could work for the government and get good retirement. You could buy a house with almost no money down. You could become rich. You could become instantly famous.

"Of course you can be prodigy, too," my mother told me when I was nine. "You can be best anything. What does Auntie Lindo know? Her daughter, she is only best tricky."

America was where all my mother's hopes lay. She had come here in 1949 after losing everything in China: her mother and father, her family home, her first husband, and two daughters, twin baby girls.

But she never looked back with regret. There were so many ways for things to get better.

We didn't immediately pick the right kind of prodigy. At first my mother thought I could be a Chinese Shirley Temple. We'd watch Shirley's old movies on TV as though they were training films. My mother would poke my arm and say, "*Ni kan*"—You watch. And I would see Shirley tapping her feet, or singing a sailor song, or pursing her lips into a very round O while saying, "Oh my goodness."

5   "*Ni kan*," said my mother as Shirley's eyes flooded with tears. "You already know how. Don't need talent for crying!"

Soon after my mother got this idea about Shirley Temple, she took me to a beauty training school in the Mission district and put me in the hands of a student who could barely hold the scissors without shaking. Instead of getting big fat curls, I emerged with an uneven mass of crinkly black fuzz. My mother dragged me off to the bathroom and tried to wet down my hair.

"You look like Negro Chinese," she lamented, as if I had done this on purpose.

The instructor of the beauty training school had to lop off these soggy clumps to make my hair even again. "Peter Pan is very popular these days," the instructor assured my mother. I now had hair the length of a boy's, with straight-across bangs that hung at a slant two inches above my eyebrows. I liked the haircut and it made me actually look forward to my future fame.

In fact, in the beginning, I was just as excited as my mother, maybe even more so. I pictured this prodigy part of me as many different images, trying each one on for size. I was a dainty ballerina girl standing by the curtains, waiting to hear the right music that would send me floating on my tiptoes. I was like the Christ child lifted out of the straw manger, crying with holy indignity. I was Cinderella stepping from her pumpkin carriage with sparkly cartoon music filling the air.

10   In all of my imaginings, I was filled with a sense that I would soon become *perfect*. My mother and father would adore me. I would be beyond reproach. I would never feel the need to sulk for anything.

But sometimes the prodigy in me became impatient. "If you don't hurry up and get me out of here, I'm disappearing for good," it warned. "And then you'll always be nothing."

Every night after dinner, my mother and I would sit at the Formica kitchen table. She would present new tests, taking her examples from stories of amazing children she had read in *Ripley's Believe It or Not*, or *Good Housekeeping*, *Reader's Digest*, and a dozen other magazines she kept in a pile in our bathroom. My mother got these magazines from people whose houses she cleaned. And since she cleaned many houses each week, we had a great assortment. She would look through them all, searching for stories about remarkable children.

The first night she brought out a story about a three-year-old boy who knew the capitals of all the states and even most of the European countries. A teacher was quoted as saying the little boy could also pronounce the names of the foreign cities correctly.

"What's the capital of Finland?" my mother asked me, looking at the magazine story.

All I knew was the capital of California, because Sacramento was   15 the name of the street we lived on in Chinatown. "Nairobi!" I guessed, saying the most foreign word I could think of. She checked to see if that was possibly one way to pronounce "Helsinki" before showing me the answer.

The tests got harder—multiplying numbers in my head, finding the queen of hearts in a deck of cards, trying to stand on my head without using my hands, predicting the daily temperatures in Los Angeles, New York, and London.

One night I had to look at a page from the Bible for three minutes and then report everything I could remember. "Now Jehoshaphat had riches and honor in abundance and…that's all I remember, Ma," I said.

And after seeing my mother's disappointed face once again, something inside of me began to die. I hated the tests, the raised hopes and failed expectations. Before going to bed that night, I looked in the mirror above the bathroom sink and when I saw only my face staring back—and that it would always be this ordinary face—I began to cry. Such a sad, ugly girl! I made high-pitched noises like a crazed animal, trying to scratch out the face in the mirror.

And then I saw what seemed to be the prodigy side of me— because I had never seen that face before. I looked at my reflection, blinking so I could see more clearly. The girl staring back at me was angry, powerful. This girl and I were the same. I had new thoughts, willful thoughts, or rather thoughts filled with lots of won'ts. I won't let her change me, I promised myself. I won't be what I'm not.

So now on nights when my mother presented her tests, I performed   20 listlessly, my head propped on one arm. I pretended to be bored. And I was. I got so bored I started counting the bellows of the foghorns out on the bay while my mother drilled me in other areas. The sound was comforting and reminded me of the cow jumping over the moon. And the next day, I played a game with myself, seeing if my mother would give up on me before eight bellows. After a while I usually counted only one, maybe two bellows at most. At last she was beginning to give up hope.

Two or three months had gone by without any mention of my being a prodigy again. And then one day my mother was watching "The Ed Sullivan Show" on TV. The TV was old and the sound kept shorting out. Every time my mother got halfway up from the sofa to adjust the set, the sound would go back on and Ed would be talking. As soon as she sat down, Ed would go silent again. She got up, the TV broke into loud piano music. She sat down. Silence. Up and down, back and forth, quiet and loud. It was like a stiff embraceless dance between her and the TV set. Finally she stood by the set with her hand on the sound dial.

She seemed entranced by the music, a little frenzied piano piece with this mesmerizing quality, sort of quick passages and then teasing lilting ones before it returned to the quick playful parts.

"*Ni kan*," my mother said, calling me over with hurried hand gestures. "Look here."

I could see why my mother was fascinated by the music. It was being pounded out by a little Chinese girl, about nine years old, with a Peter Pan haircut. The girl had the sauciness of a Shirley Temple. She was proudly modest like a proper Chinese child. And she also did this fancy sweep of a curtsy, so that the fluffy skirt of her white dress cascaded slowly to the floor like the petals of a large carnation.

25   In spite of these warning signs, I wasn't worried. Our family had no piano and we couldn't afford to buy one, let alone reams of sheet music and piano lessons. So I could be generous in my comments when my mother bad-mouthed the little girl on TV.

"Play note right, but doesn't sound good! No singing sound," complained my mother.

"What are you picking on her for?" I said carelessly. "She's pretty good. Maybe she's not the best, but she's trying hard." I knew almost immediately I would be sorry I said that.

"Just like you," she said. "Not the best. Because you not trying." She gave a little huff as she let go of the sound dial and sat down on the sofa.

The little Chinese girl sat down also to play an encore of "Anitra's Dance" by Grieg. I remember the song because later on I had to learn how to play it.

Three days after watching "The Ed Sullivan Show," my mother 30 told me what my schedule would be for piano lessons and piano practice. She had talked to Mr. Chong, who lived on the first floor of our apartment building. Mr. Chong was a retired piano teacher and my mother had traded housecleaning services for weekly lessons and a piano for me to practice on every day, two hours a day, from four until six.

When my mother told me this, I felt as though I had been sent to hell. I whined and then kicked my foot a little when I couldn't stand it anymore.

"Why don't you like me the way I am? I'm *not* a genius! I can't play the piano. And even if I could, I wouldn't go on TV if you paid me a million dollars!" I cried.

My mother slapped me. "Who ask you be genius?" she shouted. "Only ask you be your best. For you sake. You think I want you be genius? Hnnh! What for! Who ask you!"

"So ungrateful," I heard her mutter in Chinese. "If she had as much talent as she has temper, she would be famous now."

Mr. Chong, whom I secretly nicknamed Old Chong, was very 35 strange, always tapping his fingers to the silent music of an invisible orchestra. He looked ancient in my eyes. He had lost most of the hair on top of his head and he wore thick glasses and had eyes that always looked tired and sleepy. But he must have been younger than I thought, since he lived with his mother and was not yet married.

I met Old Lady Chong once and that was enough. She had this peculiar smell like a baby that had done something in its pants. And her fingers felt like a dead person's, like an old peach I once found in the back of the refrigerator; the skin just slid off the meat when I picked it up.

I soon found out why Old Chong had retired from teaching piano. He was deaf. "Like Beethoven!" he shouted to me. "We're both listening only in our head!" And he would start to conduct his frantic silent sonatas.

Our lessons went like this. He would open the book and point to different things, explaining their purpose: "Key! Treble! Bass! No sharps or flats! So this is C major! Listen now and play after me!"

And then he would play the C scale a few times, a simple chord, and then, as if inspired by an old, unreachable itch, he gradually added more notes and running trills and a pounding bass until the music was really something quite grand.

40   I would play after him, the simple scale, the simple chord and then I just played some nonsense that sounded like a cat running up and down on top of garbage cans. Old Chong smiled and applauded and then said, "Very good! But now you must learn to keep time!"

So that's how I discovered that Old Chong's eyes were too slow to keep up with the wrong notes I was playing. He went through the motions in half-time. To help me keep rhythm, he stood behind me, pushing down on my right shoulder for every beat. He balanced pennies on top of my wrists so I would keep them still as I slowly played scales and arpeggios. He had me curve my hand around an apple and keep that shape when playing chords. He marched stiffly to show me how to make each finger dance up and down, staccato like an obedient little shoulder.

He taught me all these things, and that was how I also learned I could be lazy and get away with mistakes, lots of mistakes. If I hit the wrong notes because I hadn't practiced enough, I never corrected myself. I just kept playing in rhythm. And Old Chong kept conducting his own private reverie.

So maybe I never really gave myself a fair chance. I did pick up the basics pretty quickly, and I might have become a good pianist at that young age. But I was so determined not to try, not to be anybody different that I learned to play only the most ear-splitting preludes, the most discordant hymns.

Over the next year, I practiced like this, dutifully in my own way. And then one day I heard my mother and her friend Lindo Jong both talking in a loud bragging tone of voice so others could hear. It was after church, and I was leaning against the brick wall wearing a dress with stiff white petticoats. Auntie Lindo's daughter, Waverly, who was about my age, was standing farther down the wall about five feet away. We had grown up together and shared all the closeness of two sisters squabbling over crayons and dolls. In other words, for the most part, we hated each other. I thought she was snotty. Waverly Jong had gained a certain amount of fame as "Chinatown's Littlest Chinese Chess Champion."

45   "She bring home too many trophy," lamented Auntie Lindo that Sunday. "All day she play chess. All day I have no time do nothing but dust off her winnings." She threw a scolding look at Waverly, who pretended not to see her.

"You lucky you don't have this problem," said Auntie Lindo with a sigh to my mother.

And my mother squared her shoulders and bragged: "Our problem worser than yours. If we ask Jing-mei wash dish, she hear nothing but music. It's like you can't stop this natural talent."

And right then, I was determined to put a stop to her foolish pride.

A few weeks later, Old Chong and my mother conspired to have me play in a talent show which would be held in the church hall. By then, my parents had saved up enough to buy me a secondhand piano, a black Wurlitzer spinet with a scarred bench. It was the showpiece of our living room.

For the talent show, I was to play a piece called "Pleading Child"   50 from Schumann's *Scenes from Childhood*. It was a simple, moody piece that sounded more difficult than it was. I was supposed to memorize the whole thing, playing the repeat parts twice to make the piece sound longer. But I dawdled over it, playing a few bars and then cheating, looking up to see what notes followed, I never really listened to what I was playing. I daydreamed about being somewhere else, about being someone else.

The part I liked to practice best was the fancy curtsy: right foot out, touch the rose on the carpet with a pointed foot, sweep to the side, left leg bends, look up and smile.

My parents invited all the couples from the Joy Luck Club to witness my debut. Auntie Lindo and Uncle Tin were there. Waverly and her two older brothers had also come. The first two rows were filled with children both younger and older than I was. The littlest ones got to go first. They recited simple nursery rhythms, squawked out tunes on miniature violins, twirled Hula Hoops, pranced in pink ballet tutus, and when they bowed or curtsied, the audience would sigh in unison, "Awww," and then clap enthusiastically.

When my turn came, I was very confident. I remember my childish excitement. It was as if I knew, without a doubt, that the prodigy side of me really did exist. I had no fear whatsoever, no nervousness. I remember thinking to myself, This is it! I looked out over the audience, at my mother's blank face, my father's yawn, Auntie Lindo's stiff-lipped smile, Waverly's sulky expression. I had on a white dress layered with sheets of lace, and a pink bow in my Peter Pan haircut. As I sat down I envisioned people jumping to their feet and Ed Sullivan rushing up to introduce me to everyone on TV.

And I started to play. It was so beautiful. I was so caught up in how lovely I looked that at first I didn't worry how I would sound: So it was a surprise to me when I hit the first wrong note and I realized something didn't sound quite right. And then I hit another and another followed that. A chill started at the top of my head and began to trickle down. Yet I couldn't stop playing, as though my hands were bewitched. I kept thinking my fingers would adjust themselves back, like a train switching to the right track. I played this strange jumble through two repeats, the sour notes staying with me all the way to the end.

55   When I stood up, I discovered my legs were shaking. Maybe I had just been nervous and the audience, like Old Chong, had seen me go through the right motions and had not heard anything wrong at all. I swept my right foot out, went down on my knee, looked up and smiled. The room was quiet, except for Old Chong, who was beaming and shouting, "Bravo! Bravo! Well done!" But then I saw my mother's face, her stricken face. The audience clapped weakly, and as I walked back to my chair, with my whole face quivering as I tried not to cry, I heard a little boy whisper loudly to his mother, "That was awful," and the mother whispered back, "Well, she certainly tried."

And now I realized how many people were in the audience, the whole world it seemed. I was aware of eyes burning into my back. I felt the shame of my mother and father as they sat stiffly throughout the rest of the show.

We could have escaped during intermission. Pride and some strange sense of honor must have anchored my parents to their chairs. And so we watched it all: the eighteen-year-old boy with a fake mustache who did a magic show and juggled flaming hoops while riding a unicycle. The breasted girl with white makeup who sang from *Madame Butterfly* and got honorable mention. And the eleven-year-old boy who won first prize playing a tricky violin song that sounded like a busy bee.

After the show, the Hsus, the Jongs, and the St. Clairs from the Joy Luck Club came up to my mother and father.

"Lots of talented kids," Auntie Lindo said vaguely, smiling broadly.

60   "That was somethin' else," said my father, and I wondered if he was referring to me in a humorous way, or whether he even remembered what I had done.

Waverly looked at me and shrugged her shoulders. "You aren't a genius like me," she said matter-of-factly. And if I hadn't felt so bad, I would have pulled her braids and punched her stomach.

But my mother's expression was what devastated me: a quiet, blank look that said she had lost everything. I felt the same way, and it seemed as if everybody were now coming up, like gawkers at the scene of an accident, to see what parts were actually missing. When we got on the bus to go home, my father was humming the busy-bee tune and my mother was silent. I kept thinking she wanted to wait until we got home before shouting at me. But when my father unlocked the door to our apartment, my mother walked in and then went to the back, into the bedroom. No accusations. No blame. And in a way, I felt disappointed. I had been waiting for her to start shouting, so I could shout back and cry and blame her for all her misery.

I assumed my talent-show fiasco meant I never had to play the piano again. But two days later, after school, my mother came out of the kitchen and saw me watching TV.

"Four clock," she reminded me as if it were any other day. I was stunned, as though she were asking me to go through the talent-show torture again. I wedged myself more tightly in front of the TV.

"Turn off TV," she called from the kitchen five minutes later.   65

I didn't budge. And then I decided. I didn't have to do what my mother said anymore. I wasn't her slave. This wasn't China. I had listened to her before and look what happened. She was the stupid one.

She came out from the kitchen and stood in the arched entryway of the living room. "Four clock," she said once again, louder.

"I'm not going to play anymore," I said nonchalantly. "Why should I? I'm not a genius."

She walked over and stood in front of the TV. I saw her chest was heaving up and down in an angry way.

"No!" I said, and I now felt stronger, as if my true self had finally   70 emerged. So this was what had been inside me all along.

"No! I won't!" I screamed.

She yanked me by the arm, pulled me off the floor, snapped off the TV. She was frighteningly strong, half pulling, half carrying me toward the piano as I kicked the throw rugs under my feet. She lifted me up and onto the hard bench. I was sobbing by now, looking a t her bitterly. Her chest was heaving even more and her mouth was open, smiling crazily as if she were pleased I was crying.

"You want me to be someone that I'm not!" I sobbed. "I'll never be the kind of daughter you want me to be!"

"Only two kinds of daughters," she shouted in Chinese. "Those who are obedient and those who follow their own mind! Only one kind of daughter can live in this house. Obedient daughter!"

"Then I wish I wasn't your daughter. I wish you weren't my   75 mother," I shouted. As I said these things I got scared. I felt like worms and toads and slimy things were crawling out of my chest, but it also felt good, as if this awful side of me had surfaced, at last.

"Too late change this," said my mother shrilly.

And I could sense her anger rising to its breaking point. I wanted to see it spill over. And that's when I remembered the babies she had lost in China, the ones we never talked about. "Then I wish I'd never been born!" I shouted. "I wish I were dead! Like them."

It was as if I had said the magic words. Alakazam!—and her face went blank, her mouth closed, her arms went slack, and she backed out of the room, stunned, as if she were blowing away like a small brown leaf, thin, brittle, lifeless.

It was not the only disappointment my mother felt in me. In the years that followed, I failed her so many times, each time asserting my own will, my right to fall short of expectations. I didn't get straight A's. I didn't become class president. I didn't get into Stanford. I dropped out of college.

80   For unlike my mother, I did not believe I could be anything I wanted to be. I could only be me.

And for all those years, we never talked about the disaster at the recital or my terrible accusations afterward at the piano bench. All that remained unchecked, like a betrayal that was now unspeakable. So I never found a way to ask her why she had hoped for something so large that failure was inevitable.

And even worse, I never asked her what frightened me the most: Why had she given up hope?

For after our struggle at the piano, she never mentioned my playing again. The lessons stopped. The lid to the piano was closed, shutting out the dust, my misery, and her dreams.

So she surprised me. A few years ago, she offered to give me the piano, for my thirtieth birthday. I had not played in all those years. I saw the offer as a sign of forgiveness, a tremendous burden removed.

85   "Are you sure?" I asked shyly. "I mean, won't you and Dad miss it?"

"No, this your piano," she said firmly. "Always your piano. You only one can play."

"Well, I probably can't play anymore," I said. "It's been years."

"You pick up fast," said my mother, as if she knew this was certain. "You have natural talent. You could been genius if you want to."

"No I couldn't."

"You just not trying," said my mother. And she was neither 90 angry nor sad. She said it as if to announce a fact that could never be disproved. "Take it," she said.

But I didn't at first. It was enough that she had offered it to me. And after that, every time I saw it in my parents' living room, standing in front of the bay windows, it made me feel proud, as if it were a shiny trophy I had won back.

Last week I sent a tuner over to my parents' apartment and had the piano reconditioned, for purely sentimental reasons. My mother had died a few months before and I had been getting things in order for my father, a little bit at a time. I put the jewelry in special silk pouches. The sweaters she had knitted in yellow, pink, bright orange—all the colors I hated—I put those in moth-proof boxes. I found some old Chinese silk dresses, the kind with little slits up the sides. I rubbed the old silk against my skin, then wrapped them in tissue and decided to take them home with me.

After I had the piano tuned, I opened the lid and touched the keys. It sounded even richer than I remembered. Really, it was a very good piano. Inside the bench were the same exercise notes with handwritten scales, the same secondhand music books with their covers held together with yellow tape.

I opened up the Schumann book to the dark little piece I had played at the recital. It was on the left-hand side of the page. "Pleading Child." It looked more difficult than I remembered. I played a few bars, surprised at how easily the notes came back to me.

And for the first time, or so it seemed, I noticed the piece on the 95 right-hand side. It was called "Perfectly Contented." I tried to play this one as well. It had a lighter melody but the same flowing rhythm and turned out to be quite easy. "Pleading Child" was shorter but slower; "Perfectly Contented" was longer but faster. And after I played them both a few times, I realized they were two halves of the same song.

From *The Joy Luck Club* by Amy Tan. Published by The Putnam Publishing Group. Copyright © 1989 by Amy Tan.

PUBLIC AND PRIVATE LANGUAGE

Richard Rodriguez

RICHARD RODRIGUEZ (1944-)

Born into a Mexican immigrant family in San Francisco in 1944, Rodriguez spent his first six years in a Spanish-speaking household before entering Catholic school. The writer, whose first and best-known work is the autobiography *Hunger of Memory: The Education of Richard Rodriguez* (1982), earned his B.A. from Stanford University and M.A. from Columbia University. He was also a Ph.D. candidate in English Renaissance literature at University of California, Berkeley, and received a Fulbright scholarship to attend the Warburg Institute in London. However, Rodriguez ultimately chose to pursue a career in freelance journalism rather than academia, with his writing appearing in publications such as Harper's and Time. While Rodriguez's first book received critical acclaim, his stances against bilingual education and affirmative action also brought controversy. He followed his first book with *Mexico's Children* (1990) and a second autobiographical work, the National Book Award-nominated *Days of Obligation: An Argument with My Mexican Father* (1992). His 2002 book Brown: The Last Discovery of America, which was nominated for a National Book Critics Award, focuses on the "browning of America," the idea of Latino and American culture mixing and coloring each other. Rodriguez has also worked in television, with his writing for *NewsHour* winning a George Foster Peabody Award in 1997. His next book is set to focus on the development of the three major monotheistic religions–Judaism, Christianity, and Islam–in the desert

---

1   I remember to start with that day in Sacramento—a California now nearly thirty years past—when I first entered a classroom, able to understand some fifty stray English words.

The third of four children, I had been preceded to a neighborhood Roman Catholic school by an older brother and sister. But neither of them had revealed very much about their classroom experiences. Each afternoon they returned, as they left in the morning, always together, speaking in Spanish as they climbed the five steps of the porch. And their mysterious books, wrapped in shopping-bag paper, remained on the table next to the door, closed firmly behind them.

An accident of geography sent me to a school where all my classmates were white, many the children of doctors and lawyers and business executives. All my classmates certainly must have been uneasy on that first day of school—as most children are uneasy—to find themselves apart from their families in the first institution of their lives. But I was astonished.

The nun said, in a friendly but oddly impersonal voice, "Boys and girls, this is Richard Rodriguez." (I heard her sound out: *Rich-heard Road-ree-guess.*) It was the first time I had heard anyone name me in English. "Richard," the nun repeated more slowly, writing my name down in her black leather book. Quickly I turned to see my mother's face dissolve in a watery blur behind the pebbled glass door.

Many years later there is something called bilingual education—a   5
scheme proposed in the late 1960s by Hispanic-American social activists, later endorsed by a congressional vote. It is a program that seeks to permit non-English-speaking children, many from lower-class homes, to use their family language as the language of school. (Such is the goal its supporters announce.) I hear them and am forced to say no: It is not possible for a child—any child—ever to use his family's language in school. Not to understand this is to misunderstand the public uses of schooling and to trivialize the nature of intimate life—a family's "language."

Memory teaches me what I know of these matters; the boy reminds the adult. I was a bilingual child, a certain kind—socially disadvantaged—the son of working-class parents, both Mexican immigrants.

In the early years of my boyhood, my parents coped very well in America. My father had steady work. My mother managed at home. They were nobody's victims. Optimism and ambition led them to a house (our home) many blocks from the Mexican south side of town. We lived among *gringos* and only a block from the biggest, whitest houses. It never occurred to my parents that they couldn't live wherever they chose. Nor was the Sacramento of the fifties bent on teaching them a contrary lesson. My mother and father were more annoyed than intimidated by those two or three neighbors who tried initially to make us unwelcome. ("Keep your brats away from my sidewalk!") But despite all they achieved, perhaps because they had so much to achieve, any deep feeling of ease, the confidence of "belonging" in public was withheld from them both. They regarded the people at work, the faces in crowds, as very distant from us. They were the others, *los gringos*. That term was interchangeable in their speech with another, even more telling, *los americanos*.

I grew up in a house where the only regular guests were my relations. For one day, enormous families of relatives would visit and there would be so many people that the noise and the bodies would spill out to the backyard and front porch. Then, for weeks, no one came by. (It was usually a salesman who rang the doorbell.) Our house stood apart. A gaudy yellow in a row of white bungalows. We were the people with the noisy dog. The people who raised pigeons and chickens. We were the foreigners on the block. A few neighbors smiled and waved. We waved back. But no one in the family knew the names of the old couple who lived next door; until I was seven years old, I did not know the names of the kids who lived across the street.

In public, my father and mother spoke a hesitant, accented, not always grammatical English. And they would have to strain—their bodies tense—to catch the sense of what was rapidly said by *los gringos*. At home they spoke Spanish. The language of their Mexican past sounded in counterpoint to the English of public society. The words would come quickly, with ease. Conveyed through those sounds was the pleasing, soothing, consoling reminder of being at home.

10   During those years when I was first conscious of hearing, my mother and father addressed me only in Spanish; in Spanish I learned to reply. By contrast, English (*inglés*), rarely heard in the house, was the language I came to associate with *gringos*. I learned my first words of English overhearing my parents speak to strangers. At five years age, I knew just enough English for my mother to trust me on errands to stores one block away. No more.

I was a listening child, careful to hear the very different sounds of Spanish and English. Wide-eyed with hearing, I'd listen to sounds more than words. First, there were English (*gringo*) sounds. So many words were still unknown that when the butcher or the lady at the drugstore said something to me, exotic polysyllabic sounds would bloom in the midst of their sentences. Often, the speech of people in public seemed to me very loud, booming with confidence. The man behind the counter would literally ask, "What can I do for you?" But by being so firm and so clear, the sound of his voice said that he was a *gringo*; he belonged in public society.

I would also hear then the high nasal notes of middle-class American speech. The air stirred with sound. Sometimes, even now, when I have been traveling abroad for several weeks, I will hear what I heard as a boy. In hotel lobbies or airports, in Turkey or Brazil, some Americans will pass, and suddenly I will hear it again—the high sound of American voices. For a few seconds I will hear it with pleasure, for it is now the sound of *my* society—a reminder of home. But inevitably—already on the flight headed for home—the sound fades with repetition. I will be unable to hear it anymore.

When I was a boy, things were different. The accent of *los gringos* was never pleasing nor was it hard to hear. Crowds at Safeway or at bus stops would be noisy with sound. And I would be forced to edge away from the chirping chatter above me.

I was unable to hear my own sounds, but I knew very well that I spoke English poorly. My words could not stretch far enough to form complete thoughts. And the words I did speak I didn't know well enough to make into distinct sounds. (Listeners would usually lower their heads, better to hear what I was trying to say.) But it was one thing for *me* to speak English with difficulty. It was more troubling for me to hear my parents speak in public: their high-whining vowels and guttural consonants; their sentences that got stuck with "ch" and "ah" sounds; the confused syntax; the hesitant rhythm of sounds so different from the way *gringos* spoke. I'd notice, moreover, that my parents' voices were softer than those of *gringos* we'd meet.

I am tempted now to say that none of this mattered. In adulthood   15 I am embarrassed by my childhood fears. And, in a way, it didn't matter very much that my parents could not speak English with ease. Their linguistic difficulties had no serious consequences. My mother and father made themselves understood at the county hospital clinic and at government offices. And yet, in another way, it mattered very much—it was unsettling to hear my parents struggle with English. Hearing them, I'd grow nervous, my clutching trust in their protection and power weakened.

There were many times like the night at a brightly lit gasoline station (a blaring white memory) when I stood uneasily, hearing my father. He was talking to a teenaged attendant. I do not recall what they were saying, but I cannot forget the sounds my father made as he spoke. At one point his words slid together to form one word— sounds as confused as the threads of blue and green oil in the puddle next to my shoes. His voice rushed through what he had left to say. And, toward the end, reached falsetto notes, appealing to his listener's understanding. I looked away to the lights of passing automobiles. I tried not to hear anymore. But I heard only too well the calm, easy tones in the attendant's reply. Shortly afterward, walking toward home with my father, I shivered when he put his hand on my shoulder. The very first chance that I got, I evaded his grasp and ran on ahead into the dark, skipping with feigned boyish exuberance.

But then there was Spanish. *Español*: my family's language. *Español*: the language that seemed to me a private language. I'd hear strangers on the radio and in the Mexican Catholic church across town speaking in Spanish, but I couldn't really believe that Spanish was a public language, like English. Spanish speakers, rather, seemed related to me, for I sensed that we shared—through our language—the experience of feeling apart from *los gringos*. It was thus a ghetto Spanish that I heard and I spoke. Like those whose lives are bound by a barrio, I was reminded by Spanish of my separateness from *los ostros, los gringos* in power. But more intensely than for most barrio children—because I did not live in a barrio—Spanish seemed to me the language of home. (Most days it was only at home that I'd hear it.) It became the language of joyful return.

A family member would say something to me and I would feel myself specially recognized. My parents would say something to me and I would feel embraced by the sounds of their words. Those sounds said: *I am speaking with ease in Spanish. I am addressing you in words I never use with* los gringos. *I recognize you as someone special, close, like no one outside. You belong with us. In the family.*

(Ricardo.)

20   At the age of five, six, well past the time when most other children no longer easily notice the difference between sounds uttered at home and words spoken in public, I had a different experience. I lived in a world magically compounded of sounds. I remained a child longer than most; I lingered too long, poised at the edge of language—often frightened by the sounds of *los gringos*, delighted by the sounds of Spanish at home. I shared with my family a language that was startlingly different from that used in the great city around us.

For me there were none of the gradations between public and private society so normal to a maturing child. Outside the house was public society; inside the house was private. Just opening or closing the screen door behind me was an important experience. I'd rarely leave home all alone or without reluctance. Walking down the sidewalk, under the canopy of tall trees, I'd warily notice the—suddenly—silent neighborhood kids who stood warily watching me. Nervously, I'd arrive at the grocery store to hear there the sounds of the *gringo*—foreign to me—reminding me that in this world so big, I was a foreigner. But then I'd return. Walking back toward our house, climbing the steps from the sidewalk, when the front door was open in summer, I'd hear voices beyond the screen door talking in Spanish. For a second or two, I'd stay, linger there, listening. Smiling, I'd hear my mother call out, saying in Spanish (words): "Is that you, Richard?" All the while her sounds would assure me: *You are home now; come closer; inside. With us.*

"Sí," I'd reply.

Once more inside the house I would resume (assume) my place in the family. The sounds would dim, grow harder to hear. Once more at home, I would grow less aware of that fact. It required, however, no more than the blurt of the doorbell to alert me to listen to sounds all over again. The house would turn instantly still while my mother went to the door. I'd hear her hard English sounds. I'd wait to hear her voice return to soft-sounding Spanish, which assured me, as surely as did the clicking tongue of the lock on the door, that the stranger was gone.

Plainly, it is not healthy to hear such sounds so often. It is not healthy to distinguish public words from private sounds so easily. I remained cloistered by sounds, timid and shy in public, too dependent on voices at home. And yet it needs to be emphasized: I was an extremely happy child at home. I remember many nights when my father would come back from work, and I'd hear him call out to my mother in Spanish, sounding relieved. In Spanish, he'd sound light and free notes he never could manage in English. Some nights I'd jump up just at hearing his voice. With *mis hermanos* I would come running into the room where he was with my mother. Our laughing (so deep was the pleasure!) became screaming. Like others who know the pain of public alienation, we transformed the knowledge of our public separateness and made it consoling—the reminder of intimacy. *We are speaking now the way we never speak out in public. We are alone—together*, voices sounded, surrounded to tell me. Some nights, no one seemed willing to loosen the hold sounds had on us. At dinner, we invented new words. (Ours sounded Spanish, but made sense only to us.) We pieced together new words by taking, say, an English verb and giving it Spanish endings. My mother's instructions at bedtime would be lacquered with mock-urgent tones. Or a word like *sí* would become, in several notes, able to convey added measures of feeling.

Tongues explored the edges of words, especially the fat vowels. And we happily sounded that military drum roll, the twirling roar of the Spanish *rr*. Family language: my family's sounds. The voices of my parents and sisters and brother. Their voices insisting: *You belong here. We are family members. Related. Special to one another. Listen!* Voices singing and sighing, rising, straining, then surging, teeming with pleasure that burst syllables into fragments of laughter. At times it seemed there was steady quiet only when, from another room, the rustling whispers of my parents faded and I moved closer to sleep.

25   Supporters of bilingual education today imply that students like me miss a great deal by not being taught in their family's language. What they seem not to recognize is that, as a socially disadvantaged child, I considered Spanish to be a private language. What I needed to learn in school was that I had the right—and the obligation—to speak the public language of *los gringos*. The odd truth is that my first-grade classmates could have become bilingual, in the conventional sense of that word, more easily than I. Had they been taught (as upper-middle-class children are often taught early) a second language like Spanish or French, they could have regarded it simply as that: another public language. In my case such bilingualism could not have been so quickly achieved. What I did not believe was that I could speak a single public language.

Without question, it would have pleased me to hear my teachers address me in Spanish when I entered the classroom. I would have felt much less afraid. I would have trusted them and responded with ease. But I would have delayed—for how long postponed?—having to learn the language of public society. I would have evaded—and for how long could I have afforded to delay?—learning the great lesson of school, that I had a public identity.

Fortunately, my teachers were unsentimental about their responsibility. What they understood was that I needed to speak a public language. So their voices would search me out, asking me questions. Each time I'd hear them, I'd look up in surprise to see a nun's face frowning at me. I'd mumble, not really meaning to answer. The nun would persist, "Richard, stand up. Don't look at the floor. Speak up. Speak to the entire class, not just to me!" But I couldn't believe that the English language was mine to use. (In part, I did not want to believe it.) I continued to mumble. I resisted the teacher's demands. (Did I somehow suspect that once I learned public language my pleasing family life would be changed?) Silent, waiting for the bell to sound, I remained dazed, diffident, afraid.

Because I wrongly imagined that English was intrinsically a public language and Spanish an intrinsically private one, I easily noted the difference between classroom language and the language of home. At school, words were directed to a general audience of listeners. ("Boys and girls.") Words were meaningfully ordered. And the point was not self-expression alone but to make oneself understood by many others. The teacher quizzed: "Boys and girls, why do we use that word in this sentence? Could we think of a better word to use there? Would the sentence change its meaning if the words were differently arranged? And wasn't there a better way of saying much the same thing?" (I couldn't say. I wouldn't try to say.)

Three months. Five. Half a year passed. Unsmiling, ever watchful, my teachers noted my silence. They began to connect my behavior with the difficult progress my older sister and brother were making. Until one Saturday morning three nuns arrived at the house to talk to our parents. Stiffly, they sat on the blue living room sofa. From the doorway of another room, spying the visitors, I noted the incongruity—the clash of two worlds, the faces and voices of school intruding upon the familiar setting of home. I overheard one voice gently wondering, "Do your children speak only Spanish at home, Mrs. Rodriguez?" While another voice added, "That Richard especially seems so timid and shy."

That Rich-heard!   30

With great tact the visitors continued, "Is it possible for you and your husband to encourage your children to practice their English when they are home?" Of course, my parents complied. What would they not do for their children's well-being? And how could they have questioned the Church's authority which those women represented? In an instant, they agreed to give up the language (the sounds) that had revealed and accentuated our family's closeness. The moment after the visitors left, the change was observed. "*Ahora*, speak to us *en inglés*," my father and mother united to tell us.

At first, it seemed a kind of game. After dinner each night, the family gathered to practice "our" English. (It was still then *inglés*, a language foreign to us, so we felt drawn as strangers to it.) Laughing, we would try to define words we could not pronounce. We played with strange English sounds, often overanglicizing our pronunciations. And we filled the smiling gaps of our sentences with familiar Spanish sounds. But that was cheating, somebody shouted. Everyone laughed.

In school, meanwhile, like my brother and sister, I was required to attend a daily tutoring session. I needed a full year of special attention. I also needed my teachers to keep my attention from straying in class by calling out, *Rich-heard*—their English voices slowly prying loose my ties to my other name, its three notes, *Ri-car-do*. Most of all I needed to hear my mother and father speak to me in a moment of seriousness in broken—suddenly heartbreaking—English. The scene was inevitable: One Saturday morning I entered the kitchen where my parents were talking in Spanish. I did not realize that they were talking in Spanish however until, at the moment they saw me, I heard their voices change to speak English. Those *gringo* sounds they uttered startled me. Pushed me away. In that moment of trivial misunderstanding and profound insight, I felt my throat twisted by unsounded grief. I turned quickly and left the room. But I had no place to escape to with Spanish. (The spell was broken.) My brother and sisters were speaking English in another part of the house.

Again and again in the days following, increasingly angry, I was obliged to hear my mother and father: "Speak to us *en inglés*. (*Speak.*)" Only then did I determine to learn classroom English. Weeks after, it happened: One day in school I raised my hand to volunteer an answer. I spoke out in a loud voice. And I did not think it remarkable when the entire class understood. That day, I moved very far from the disadvantaged child I had been only days earlier. The belief, the calming assurance that I belonged in public, had at last taken hold.

Shortly after, I stopped hearing the high and loud sounds of *los gringos*. A more and more confident speaker of English, I didn't trouble to listen to *how* strangers sounded, speaking to me. And there simply were too many English-speaking people in my day for me to hear American accents anymore. Conversations quickened. Listening to persons who sounded eccentrically pitched voices, I usually noted their sounds for an initial few seconds before I concentrated on *what* they were saying. Conversations became content-full. Transparent. Hearing someone's *tone* of voice—angry or questioning or sarcastic or happy or sad—I didn't distinguish it from the words it expressed. Sound and word were thus tightly wedded. At the end of a day, I was often bemused, always relieved to realize how "silent," though crowded with words, my day in public had been. (This public silence measured and quickened the change in my life.)

35   At last, seven years old, I came to believe what had been technically true since my birth: I was an American citizen.

But the special feeling of closeness at home was diminished by then. Gone was the desperate, urgent, intense feeling of being at home; rare was the experience of feeling myself individualized by family intimates. We remained a loving family, but one greatly changed. No longer so close; no longer bound tight by the pleasing and troubling knowledge of our public separateness. Neither my older brother nor sister rushed home after school anymore. Nor did I. When I arrived home there would often be neighborhood kids in the house. Or the house would be empty of sounds.

The silence at home, however, was finally more than a literal silence. Fewer words passed between parent and child, but more profound was the silence that resulted from my inattention to sounds. At about the time I no longer bothered to listen with care to the sounds of English in public, I grew careless about listening to the sounds family members made when they spoke. Most of the time I heard someone speaking at home and didn't distinguish his sounds from the words people uttered in public. I didn't even pay much attention to my parents' accented and ungrammatical speech. At least not at home. Only when I was with them in public would I grow alert to their accents. Though, even then, their sounds caused me less and less concern. For I was increasingly confident of my own public identity.

I would have been happier about my public success had I not sometimes recalled what it had been like earlier, when my family had conveyed its intimacy through a set of conveniently private sounds. Sometimes in public, hearing a stranger, I'd hark back to my past. A Mexican farmworker approached me downtown to ask directions to somewhere. "*¿Hijito…?*" he said. And his voice summoned deep longing. Another time, standing beside my mother in the visiting room of a Carmelite convent, before the dense screen which rendered the nuns shadowy figures, I heard several Spanish-speaking nuns—their busy, singsong overlapping voices—assure us that yes, yes, we were remembered, all our family was remembered in their prayers. (Their voices echoed faraway family sounds.) Another day, a dark-faced old woman—her hand light on my shoulder—steadied herself against me as she boarded a bus. She murmured something I couldn't quite comprehend. Her Spanish voice came near, like the face of a never-before-seen relative in the instant before I was kissed. Her voice, like so many of the Spanish voices I'd hear in public, recalled the golden age of my youth. Hearing Spanish then, I continued to be a careful, if sad, listener to sounds. Hearing a Spanish-speaking family walking behind me, I turned to look. I smiled for an instant, before my glance found the Hispanic-looking faces of strangers in the crowd going by.

Today I hear bilingual educators say that children lose a degree of "individuality" by becoming assimilated into public society. (Bilingual schooling was popularized in the seventies, that decade when middle-class ethnics began to resist the process of assimilation—the American melting pot.) But the bilingualists simplistically scorn the value and necessity of assimilation. They do not seem to realize that there are *two ways* a person is individualized. So they do not realize that while one suffers a diminished sense of *private* individuality by becoming assimilated into public society, such assimilation makes possible the achievement of *public* individuality.

40   The bilingualists insist that a student should be reminded of his difference from others in mass society, his heritage. But they equate mere separateness with individuality. The fact is that only in private—with intimates—is separateness from the crowd a prerequisite for individuality. (An intimate draws me apart, tells me that I am unique, unlike all others.) In public, by contrast, full individuality is achieved, paradoxically, by those who are able to consider themselves members of the crowd. Thus it happened for me: Only when I was able to think of myself as an American, no longer an alien in *gringo* society, could I seek the rights and opportunities necessary for full public individuality. The social and political advantages I enjoy as a man result from the day that I came to believe that my name, indeed, is *Rich-heard Road-ree-guess*. It is true that my public society today is often impersonal. (My public society is usually mass society.) Yet despite the anonymity of the crowd and despite the fact that the individuality I achieve in public is often tenuous—because it depends on my being one in a crowd—I celebrate the day I acquired my new name. Those middle-class ethnics who scorn assimilation seem to me filled with decadent self-pity, obsessed by the burden of public life. Dangerously, they romanticize public separateness and they trivialize the dilemma of the socially disadvantaged.

VI

CHALLENGES

THE MEANING OF JULY FOURTH FOR THE NEGRO

Frederick Douglas

FREDERICK DOUGLASS (c.1818-1895)

Abolitionist leader, writer, and orator Frederick Douglass was born Frederick Augustus Washington Bailey c. 1818 to an enslaved mother from whom he was separated as an infant. He learned the alphabet from his master's wife and the basics of reading and writing from white neighborhood children, subsequently further educating himself through access to newspapers and other materials. After falling in love with Anna Murray, a free black woman, in 1838, he escaped from slavery by disguising himself as a free black sailor and boarding a train north. He and Murray married soon after, with the couple then adopting the surname Douglass. Douglass published his first memoir, *Narrative of the Life of Frederick Douglass, an American Slave* in 1845. He also became a publisher of abolitionist newspapers, and in 1848 was the only African American to attend the Seneca Falls Convention for women's rights, at which he spoke in support of women's suffrage. During the Civil War, Douglass consulted with President Lincoln on issues relating to black Union soldiers and liberated slaves in the South. Douglass's profile attained such renown over the decades that in 1872 he was nominated as vice president on Victoria Woodhull's Equal Rights Party ticket. Throughout the post-war years, Douglass served several government positions, including president of the Freedman's Savings Bank (1874); U.S. Marshal (1877-1881); Recorder of Deeds for the District of Columbia (1881); and chargé d'affaires to the Dominican Republic (1889-1891). Douglass also continued his efforts as a writer and orator until his death in Washington D.C. in 1895. Among his other major works are *My Bondage and My Freedom* (1855) and *Life and Times of Frederick Douglass* (1881). On July 5, 1852, Douglass delivered an address to the Ladies of the Rochester Anti-Slavery Sewing Society which would become one of his most important speeches, "What to a slave is the 4th of July?" or, "The Meaning of July Fourth for The Negro."

Rochester, New York, July 5, 1852

Mr. President, Friends and Fellow Citizens:

He who could address this audience without a quailing sensation,   1
has stronger nerves than I have. I do not remember ever to have appeared as a speaker before any assembly more shrinkingly, nor with greater distrust of my ability, than I do this day. A feeling has crept over me quite unfavorable to the exercise of my limited powers of speech. The task before me is one which requires much previous thought and study for its proper performance. I know that apologies of this sort are generally considered flat and unmeaning. I trust, however, that mine will not be so considered. Should I seem at ease, my appearance would much misrepresent me. The little experience I have had in addressing public meetings, in country school houses, avails me nothing on the present occasion.

The papers and placards say that I am to deliver a Fourth of July Oration. This certainly sounds large, and out of the common way, for me. It is true that I have often had the privilege to speak in this beautiful Hall, and to address many who now honor me with their presence. But neither their familiar faces, nor the perfect gage I think I have of Corinthian Hall seems to free me from embarrassment.

The fact is, ladies and gentlemen, the distance between this platform and the slave plantation, from which I escaped, is considerable—and the difficulties to be overcome in getting from the latter to the former are by no means slight. That I am here to-day is, to me, a matter of astonishment as well as of gratitude. You will not, therefore, be surprised, if in what I have to say I evince no elaborate preparation, nor grace my speech with any high sounding exordium. With little experience and with less learning, I have been able to throw my thoughts hastily and imperfectly together; and trusting to your patient and generous indulgence I will proceed to lay them before you.

This, for the purpose of this celebration, is the Fourth of July. It is the birthday of your National Independence, and of your political freedom. This, to you, as what the Passover was to the emancipated people of God. It carries your minds back to the day, and to the act of your great deliverance; and to the signs, and to the wonders, associated with that act, and that day. This celebration also marks the beginning of another year of your national life; and reminds you that the Republic of America is now 76 years old. I am glad, fellow-citizens, that your nation is so young. Seventy-six years, though a good old age for a man, is but a mere speck in the life of a nation. Three score years and ten is the allotted time for individual men; but nations number their years by thousands. According to this fact, you are, even now, only in the beginning of your national career, still lingering in the period of childhood. I repeat, I am glad this is so. There is hope in the thought, and hope is much needed, under the dark clouds which lower above the horizon. The eye of the reformer is met with angry flashes, portending disastrous times; but his heart may well beat lighter at the thought that America is young, and that she is still in the impressible stage of her existence. May he not hope that high lessons of wisdom, of justice and of truth, will yet give direction to her destiny? Were the nation older, the patriot›s heart might be sadder, and the reformer›s brow heavier. Its future might be shrouded in gloom, and the hope of its prophets go out in sorrow. There is consolation in the thought that America is young.—Great streams are not easily turned from channels, worn deep in the course of ages. They may sometimes rise in quiet and stately majesty, and inundate the land, refreshing and fertilizing the earth with their mysterious properties. They may also rise in wrath and fury, and bear away, on their angry waves, the accumulated wealth of years of toil and hardship. They, however, gradually flow back to the same old channel, and flow on as serenely as ever. But, while the river may not be turned aside, it may dry up, and leave nothing behind but the withered branch, and the unsightly rock, to howl in the abyss-sweeping wind, the sad tale of departed glory. As with rivers so with nations.

5   Fellow-citizens, I shall not presume to dwell at length on the associations that cluster about this day. The simple story of it is, that, 76 years ago, the people of this country were British subjects. The style and title of your «sovereign people» (in which you now *glory*) was not then born. You were under the British Crown. Your fathers esteemed the English Government as the home government; and England as the fatherland. This home government, you know, although a considerable distance from your home, did, in the exercise of its parental prerogatives, impose upon its colonial children, such restraints, burdens and limitations, as, in its mature judgment, it deemed wise, right and proper.

But your fathers, who had not adopted the fashionable idea of this day, of the infallibility of government, and the absolute character of its acts, presumed to differ from the home government in respect to the wisdom and the justice of some of those burdens and restraints. They went so far in their excitement as to pronounce the measures of government unjust, unreasonable, and oppressive, and altogether such as ought not to be quietly submitted to. I scarcely need say, fellow-citizens, that my opinion of those measures fully accords with that of your fathers. Such a declaration of agreement on my part would not be worth much to anybody. It would certainly prove nothing as to what part I might have taken had I lived during the great controversy of 1776. To say now that America was right, and England wrong, is exceedingly easy. Everybody can say it; the dastard, not less than the noble brave, can flippantly discant on the tyranny of England towards the American Colonies. It is fashionable to do so; but there was a time when, to pronounce against England, and in favor of the cause of the colonies, tried men's souls. They who did so were accounted in their day plotters of mischief, agitators and rebels, dangerous men. To side with the right against the wrong, with the weak against the strong, and with the oppressed against the oppressor! here lies the merit, and the one which, of all others, seems unfashionable in our day. The cause of liberty may be stabbed by the men who glory in the deeds of your fathers. But, to proceed.

Feeling themselves harshly and unjustly treated, by the home government, your fathers, like men of honesty, and men of spirit, earnestly sought redress. They petitioned and remonstrated; they did so in a decorous, respectful, and loyal manner. Their conduct was wholly unexceptionable. This, however, did not answer the purpose. They saw themselves treated with sovereign indifference, coldness and scorn. Yet they persevered. They were not the men to look back.

As the sheet anchor takes a firmer hold, when the ship is tossed by the storm, so did the cause of your fathers grow stronger as it breasted the chilling blasts of kingly displeasure. The greatest and best of British statesmen admitted its justice, and the loftiest eloquence of the British Senate came to its support. But, with that blindness which seems to be the unvarying characteristic of tyrants, since Pharaoh and his hosts were drowned in the Red Sea, the British Government persisted in the exactions complained of.

The madness of this course, we believe, is admitted now, even by England; but we fear the lesson is wholly lost on our present rulers.

Oppression makes a wise man mad. Your fathers were wise men,   10
and if they did not go mad, they became restive under this treatment. They felt themselves the victims of grievous wrongs, wholly incurable in their colonial capacity. With brave men there is always a remedy for oppression. Just here, the idea of a total separation of the colonies from the crown was born! It was a startling idea, much more so than we, at this distance of time, regard it. The timid and the prudent (as

has been intimated) of that day were, of course, shocked and alarmed by it.

Such people lived then, had lived before, and will, probably, ever have a place on this planet; and their course, in respect to any great change (no matter how great the good to be attained, or the wrong to be redressed by it), may be calculated with as much precision as can be the course of the stars. They hate all changes, but silver, gold and copper change! Of this sort of change they are always strongly in favor.

These people were called Tories in the days of your fathers; and the appellation, probably, conveyed the same idea that is meant by a more modern, though a somewhat less euphonious term, which we often find in our papers, applied to some of our old politicians.

Their opposition to the then dangerous thought was earnest and powerful; but, amid all their terror and affrighted vociferations against it, the alarming and revolutionary idea moved on, and the country with it.

On the 2nd of July, 1776, the old Continental Congress, to the dismay of the lovers of ease, and the worshipers of property, clothed that dreadful idea with all the authority of national sanction. They did so in the form of a resolution; and as we seldom hit upon resolutions, drawn up in our day, whose transparency is at all equal to this, it may refresh your minds and help my story if I read it.

15   *"Resolved, That these united colonies are, and of right, ought to be free and Independent States; that they are absolved from all allegiance to the British Crown; and that all political connection between them and the State of Great Britain is, and ought to be, dissolved."*

Citizens, your fathers made good that resolution. They succeeded; and to-day you reap the fruits of their success. The freedom gained is yours; and you, therefore, may properly celebrate this anniversary. The 4th of July is the first great fact in your nation's history—the very ringbolt in the chain of your yet undeveloped destiny.

Pride and patriotism, not less than gratitude, prompt you to celebrate and to hold it in perpetual remembrance. I have said that the Declaration of Independence is the ringbolt to the chain of your nation's destiny; so, indeed, I regard it. The principles contained in that instrument are saving principles. Stand by those principles, be true to them on all occasions, in all places, against all foes, and at whatever cost.

From the round top of your ship of state, dark and threatening clouds may be seen. Heavy billows, like mountains in the distance, disclose to the leeward huge forms of flinty rocks! That bolt drawn, that chain broken, and all is lost. Cling to this day—cling to it, and to its principles, with the grasp of a storm-tossed mariner to a spar at midnight.

The coming into being of a nation, in any circumstances, is an interesting event. But, besides general considerations, there were peculiar circumstances which make the advent of this republic an event of special attractiveness. The whole scene, as I look back to it, was simple, dignified and sublime. The population of the country, at the time, stood at the insignificant number of three millions. The country was poor in the munitions of war. The population was weak and scattered, and the country a wilderness unsubdued. There were then no means of concert and combination, such as exist now. Neither steam nor lightning had then been reduced to order and discipline. From the Potomac to the Delaware was a journey of many days. Under these, and innumerable other disadvantages, your fathers declared for liberty and independence and triumphed.

Fellow-citizens, I am not wanting in respect for the fathers of this   20 republic. The signers of the Declaration of Independence were brave men. They were great men, too—great enough to give frame to a great age. It does not often happen to a nation to raise, at one time, such a number of truly great men. The point from which I am compelled to view them is not, certainly, the most favorable; and yet I cannot contemplate their great deeds with less than admiration. They were statesmen, patriots and heroes, and for the good they did, and the principles they contended for, I will unite with you to honor their memory.

They loved their country better than their own private interests; and, though this is not the highest form of human excellence, all will concede that it is a rare virtue, and that when it is exhibited it ought to command respect. He who will, intelligently, lay down his life for his country is a man whom it is not in human nature to despise. Your fathers staked their lives, their fortunes, and their sacred honor, on the cause of their country. In their admiration of liberty, they lost sight of all other interests.

They were peace men; but they preferred revolution to peaceful submission to bondage. They were quiet men; but they did not shrink from agitating against oppression. They showed forbearance; but that they knew its limits. They believed in order; but not in the order of tyranny. With them, nothing was "settled" that was not right. With them, justice, liberty and humanity were "final"; not slavery and oppression. You may well cherish the memory of such men. They were great in their day and generation. Their solid manhood stands out the more as we contrast it with these degenerate times.

How circumspect, exact and proportionate were all their movements! How unlike the politicians of an hour! Their statesmanship looked beyond the passing moment, and stretched away in strength into the distant future. They seized upon eternal principles, and set a glorious example in their defence. Mark them!

Fully appreciating the hardships to be encountered, firmly believing in the right of their cause, honorably inviting the scrutiny of an on-looking world, reverently appealing to heaven to attest their sincerity, soundly comprehending the solemn responsibility they were about to assume, wisely measuring the terrible odds against them, your fathers, the fathers of this republic, did, most deliberately, under the inspiration of a glorious patriotism, and with a sublime faith in the great principles of justice and freedom, lay deep, the corner-stone of the national super-structure, which has risen and still rises in grandeur around you.

25   Of this fundamental work, this day is the anniversary. Our eyes are met with demonstrations of joyous enthusiasm. Banners and pennants wave exultingly on the breeze. The din of business, too, is hushed. Even mammon seems to have quitted his grasp on this day. The ear-piercing fife and the stirring drum unite their accents with the ascending peal of a thousand church bells. Prayers are made, hymns are sung, and sermons are preached in honor of this day; while the quick martial tramp of a great and multitudinous nation, echoed back by all the hills, valleys and mountains of a vast continent, bespeak the occasion one of thrilling and universal interest—a nation's jubilee.

Friends and citizens, I need not enter further into the causes which led to this anniversary. Many of you understand them better than I do. You could instruct me in regard to them. That is a branch of knowledge in which you feel, perhaps, a much deeper interest than your speaker. The causes which led to the separation of the colonies from the British crown have never lacked for a tongue. They have all been taught in your common schools, narrated at your firesides, unfolded from your pulpits, and thundered from your legislative halls, and are as familiar to you as household words. They form the staple of your national poetry and eloquence.

I remember, also, that, as a people, Americans are remarkably familiar with all facts which make in their own favor. This is esteemed by some as a national trait-perhaps a national weakness. It is a fact, that whatever makes for the wealth or for the reputation of Americans and can be had cheap! will be found by Americans. I shall not be charged with slandering Americans if I say I think the American side of any question may be safely left in American hands.

I leave, therefore, the great deeds of your fathers to other gentlemen whose claim to have been regularly descended will be less likely to be disputed than mine!

My business, if I have any here to-day, is with the present. The accepted time with God and His cause is the ever-living now.

> *Trust no future, however pleasant,*   30
>   *Let the dead past bury its dead;*
> *Act, act in the living present,*
>   *Heart within, and God overhead.*

We have to do with the past only as we can make it useful to the present and to the future. To all inspiring motives, to noble deeds which can be gained from the past, we are welcome. But now is the time, the important time. Your fathers have lived, died, and have done their work, and have done much of it well. You live and must die, and you must do your work. You have no right to enjoy a child's share in the labor of your fathers, unless your children are to be blest by your labors. You have no right to wear out and waste the hard-earned fame of your fathers to cover your indolence. Sydney Smith tells us that men seldom eulogize the wisdom and virtues of their fathers, but to excuse some folly or wickedness of their own. This truth is not a doubtful one. There are illustrations of it near and remote, ancient and modern. It was fashionable, hundreds of years ago, for the children of Jacob to boast, we have "Abraham to our father," when they had long lost Abraham's faith and spirit. That people contented themselves under the shadow of Abraham's great name, while they repudiated the deeds which made his name great. Need I remind you that a similar thing is being done all over this country to-day? Need I tell you that the Jews are not the only people who built the tombs of the prophets, and garnished the sepulchers of the righteous? Washington could not die till he had broken the chains of his slaves. Yet his monument is built up by the price of human blood, and the traders in the bodies and souls of men shout—"We have Washington to *our father*."—Alas! that it should be so; yet it is.

The evil, that men do, lives after them,
The good is oft interred with their bones.

Fellow-citizens, pardon me, allow me to ask, why am I called upon to speak here to-day? What have I, or those I represent, to do with your national independence? Are the great principles of political freedom and of natural justice, embodied in that Declaration of Independence, extended to us? and am I, therefore, called upon to bring our humble offering to the national altar, and to confess the benefits and express devout gratitude for the blessings resulting from your independence to us?

Would to God, both for your sakes and ours, that an affirmative answer could be truthfully returned to these questions! Then would my task be light, and my burden easy and delightful. For *who* is there so cold, that a nation's sympathy could not warm him? Who so obdurate and dead to the claims of gratitude, that would not thankfully acknowledge such priceless benefits? Who so stolid and selfish, that would not give his voice to swell the hallelujahs of a nation's jubilee, when the chains of servitude had been torn from his limbs? I am not that man. In a case like that, the dumb might eloquently speak, and the "lame man leap as an hart."

35   But such is not the state of the case. I say it with a sad sense of the disparity between us. I am not included within the pale of this glorious anniversary! Your high independence only reveals the immeasurable distance between us. The blessings in which you, this day, rejoice, are not enjoyed in common.—The rich inheritance of justice, liberty, prosperity and independence, bequeathed by your fathers, is shared by you, not by me. The sunlight that brought light and healing to you, has brought stripes and death to me. This Fourth July is *yours*, not *mine. You* may rejoice, *I* must mourn. To drag a man in fetters into the grand illuminated temple of liberty, and call upon him to join you in joyous anthems, were inhuman mockery and sacrilegious irony. Do you mean, citizens, to mock me, by asking me to speak to-day? If so, there is a parallel to your conduct. And let me warn you that it is dangerous to copy the example of a nation whose crimes, towering up to heaven, were thrown down by the breath of the Almighty, burying that nation in irrevocable ruin! I can to-day take up the plaintive lament of a peeled and woe-smitten people!

"By the rivers of Babylon, there we sat down. Yea! we wept when we remembered Zion. We hanged our harps upon the willows in the midst thereof. For there, they that carried us away captive, required of us a song; and they who wasted us required of us mirth, saying, Sing us one of the songs of Zion. How can we sing the Lord's song in a strange land? If I forget thee, O Jerusalem, let my right hand forget her cunning. If I do not remember thee, let my tongue cleave to the roof of my mouth."

Fellow-citizens, above your national, tumultuous joy, I hear the mournful wail of millions! whose chains, heavy and grievous yesterday, are, to-day, rendered more intolerable by the jubilee shouts that reach them. If I do forget, if I do not faithfully remember those bleeding children of sorrow this day, "may my right hand forget her cunning, and may my tongue cleave to the roof of my mouth!" To forget them, to pass lightly over their wrongs, and to chime in with the popular theme, would be treason most scandalous and shocking, and would make me a reproach before God and the world. My subject, then, fellow-citizens, is American slavery. I shall see this day and its popular characteristics from the slave's point of view. Standing there identified with the American bondman, making his wrongs mine, I do not hesitate to declare, with all my soul, that the character and conduct of this nation never looked blacker to me than on this 4th of July! Whether we turn to the declarations of the past, or to the professions of the present, the conduct of the nation seems equally hideous and revolting. America is false to the past, false to the present, and solemnly binds herself to be false to the future. Standing with God and the crushed and bleeding slave on this occasion, I will, in the name of humanity which is outraged, in the name of liberty which is fettered, in the name of the constitution and the Bible which are disregarded and trampled upon, dare to call in question and to denounce, with all the emphasis I can command, everything that serves to perpetuate slavery—the great sin and shame of America! "I will not equivocate; I will not excuse"; I will use the severest language I can command; and yet not one word shall escape me that any man, whose judgment is not blinded by prejudice, or who is not at heart a slaveholder, shall not confess to be right and just.

But I fancy I hear some one of my audience say, "It is just in this circumstance that you and your brother abolitionists fail to make a favorable impression on the public mind. Would you argue more, and denounce less; would you persuade more, and rebuke less; your cause would be much more likely to succeed." But, I submit, where all is plain there is nothing to be argued. What point in the anti-slavery creed would you have me argue? On what branch of the subject do the people of this country need light? Must I undertake to prove that the slave is a man? That point is conceded already. Nobody doubts it. The slaveholders themselves acknowledge it in the enactment of laws for their government. They ac knowledge it when they punish disobedience on the part of the slave. There are seventy-two crimes in the State of Virginia which, if committed by a black man (no matter how ignorant he be), subject him to the punishment of death; while only two of the same crimes will subject a white man to the like punishment. What is this but the acknowledgment that the slave is a moral, intellectual, and responsible being? The manhood of the slave is conceded. It is admitted in the fact that Southern statute books are covered with enactments forbidding, under severe fines and penalties, the teaching of the slave to read or to write. When you can point to any such laws in reference to the beasts of the field, then I may consent to argue the manhood of the slave. When the dogs in your streets, when the fowls of the air, when the cattle on your hills, when the fish of the sea, and the reptiles that crawl, shall be unable to distinguish the slave from a brute, then will I argue with you that the slave is a man!

For the present, it is enough to affirm the equal manhood of the Negro race. Is it not astonishing that, while we are ploughing, planting, and reaping, using all kinds of mechanical tools, erecting houses, constructing bridges, building ships, working in metals of brass, iron, copper, silver and gold; that, while we are reading, writing and ciphering, acting as clerks, merchants and secretaries, having among us lawyers, doctors, ministers, poets, authors, editors, orators and teachers; that, while we are engaged in all manner of enterprises common to other men, digging gold in California, capturing the whale in the Pacific, feeding sheep and cattle on the hill-side, living, moving, acting, thinking, planning, living in families as husbands, wives and children, and, above all, confessing and worshipping the Christian's God, and looking hopefully for life and immortality beyond the grave, we are called upon to prove that we are men!

40   Would you have me argue that man is entitled to liberty? that he is the rightful owner of his own body? You have already declared it. Must I argue the wrongfulness of slavery? Is that a question for Republicans? Is it to be settled by the rules of logic and argumentation, as a matter beset with great difficulty, involving a doubtful application of the principle of justice, hard to be understood? How should I look to-day, in the presence of Americans, dividing, and subdividing a discourse, to show that men have a natural right to freedom? speaking of it relatively and positively, negatively and affirmatively. To do so, would be to make myself ridiculous, and to offer an insult to your

understanding.—There is not a man beneath the canopy of heaven that does not know that slavery is wrong *for him*.

What, am I to argue that it is wrong to make men brutes, to rob them of their liberty, to work them without wages, to keep them ignorant of their relations to their fellow men, to beat them with sticks, to flay their flesh with the lash, to load their limbs with irons, to hunt them with dogs, to sell them at auction, to sunder their families, to knock out their teeth, to burn their flesh, to starve them into obedience and submission to their masters? Must I argue that a system thus marked with blood, and stained with pollution, is *wrong*? No! I will not. I have better employment for my time and strength than such arguments would imply.

What, then, remains to be argued? Is it that slavery is not divine; that God did not establish it; that our doctors of divinity are mistaken? There is blasphemy in the thought. That which is inhuman, cannot be divine! *Who* can reason on such a proposition? They that can, may; I cannot. The time for such argument is passed.

At a time like this, scorching irony, not convincing argument, is needed. O! had I the ability, and could reach the nation's ear, I would, to-day, pour out a fiery stream of biting ridicule, blasting reproach, withering sarcasm, and stern rebuke. For it is not light that is needed, but fire; it is not the gentle shower, but thunder. We need the storm, the whirlwind, and the earthquake. The feeling of the nation must be quickened; the conscience of the nation must be roused; the propriety of the nation must be startled; the hypocrisy of the nation must be exposed; and its crimes against God and man must be proclaimed and denounced.

What, to the American slave, is your 4th of July? I answer; a day that reveals to him, more than all other days in the year, the gross injustice and cruelty to which he is the constant victim. To him, your celebration is a sham; your boasted liberty, an unholy license; your national greatness, swelling vanity; your sounds of rejoicing are empty and heartless; your denunciation of tyrants, brass fronted impudence; your shouts of liberty and equality, hollow mockery; your prayers and hymns, your sermons and thanksgivings, with all your religious parade and solemnity, are, to Him, mere bombast, fraud, deception, impiety, and hypocrisy—a thin veil to cover up crimes which would disgrace a nation of savages. There is not a nation on the earth guilty of practices more shocking and bloody than are the people of the United States, at this very hour.

45   Go where you may, search where you will, roam through all the monarchies and despotisms of the Old World, travel through South America, search out every abuse, and when you have found the last, lay your facts by the side of the everyday practices of this nation, and you will say with me, that, for revolting barbarity and shameless hypocrisy, America reigns without a rival.

Take the American slave-trade, which we are told by the papers, is especially prosperous just now. Ex-Senator Benton tells us that the price of men was never higher than now. He mentions the fact to show that slavery is in no danger. This trade is one of the peculiarities of American institutions. It is carried on in all the large towns and cities in one-half of this confederacy; and millions are pocketed every year by dealers in this horrid traffic. In several states this trade is a chief source of wealth. It is called (in contradistinction to the foreign slave-trade) "*the internal slave-trade.*" It is, probably, called so, too, in order to divert from it the horror with which the foreign slave-trade is contemplated. That trade has long since been denounced by this government as piracy. It has been denounced with burning words from the high places of the nation as an execrable traffic. To arrest it, to put an end to it, this nation keeps a squadron, at immense cost, on the coast of Africa. Everywhere, in this country, it is safe to speak of this foreign slave-trade as a most inhuman traffic, opposed alike to the laws of God and of man. The duty to extirpate and destroy it, is admitted even by our doctors of divinity. In order to put an end to it, some of these last have consented that their colored brethren (nominally free) should leave this country, and establish themselves on the western coast of Africa! It is, however, a notable fact that, while so much execration is poured out by Americans upon all those engaged in the foreign slave-trade, the men engaged in the slave-trade between the states pass without condemnation, and their business is deemed honorable.

Behold the practical operation of this internal slave-trade, the American slave-trade, sustained by American politics and American religion. Here you will see men and women reared like swine for the market. You know what is a swine-drover? I will show you a man-drover. They inhabit all our Southern States. They perambulate the country, and crowd the highways of the nation, with droves of human stock. You will see one of these human flesh jobbers, armed with pistol, whip, and bowie-knife, driving a company of a hundred men, women, and children, from the Potomac to the slave market at New Orleans. These wretched people are to be sold singly, or in lots, to suit purchasers. They are food for the cotton-field and the deadly sugar-mill. Mark the sad procession, as it moves wearily along, and the inhuman wretch who drives them. Hear his savage yells and his blood-curdling oaths, as he hurries on his affrighted captives! There, see the old man with locks thinned and gray. Cast one glance, if you please, upon that young mother, whose shoulders are bare to the scorching sun, her briny tears falling on the brow of the babe in her arms. See, too, that girl of thirteen, weeping, *yes!* weeping, as she thinks of the mother from whom she has been torn! The drove moves tardily. Heat and sorrow have nearly consumed their strength; suddenly you hear a quick snap, like the discharge of a rifle; the fetters clank, and the chain rattles simultaneously; your ears are saluted with a scream, that seems to have torn its way to the centre of your soul The crack you heard was the sound of the slave-whip; the scream you heard was from the woman you saw with the babe. Her speed had faltered under the weight of her child and her chains! that gash on her shoulder tells her to move on. Follow this drove to New Orleans. Attend the auction; see men examined like horses; see the forms of women rudely and brutally exposed to the shocking gaze of American slave-buyers. See this drove sold and separated forever; and never forget the deep, sad sobs that arose from that scattered multitude. Tell me, citizens, where, under the sun, you can witness a spectacle more fiendish and shocking. Yet this is but a glance at the American slave-trade, as it exists, at this moment, in the ruling part of the United States.

I was born amid such sights and scenes. To me the American slave-trade is a terrible reality. When a child, my soul was often pierced with a sense of its horrors. I lived on Philpot Street, Fell's Point, Baltimore, and have watched from the wharves the slave ships in the Basin, anchored from the shore, with their cargoes of human flesh, waiting for favorable winds to waft them down the Chesapeake. There was, at that time, a grand slave mart kept at the head of Pratt Street, by Austin Woldfolk. His agents were sent into every town and county in Maryland, announcing their arrival, through the papers, and on flaming "*hand-bills,*" headed cash for Negroes. These men were generally well dressed men, and very captivating in their manners; ever ready to drink, to treat, and to gamble. The fate of many a slave has depended upon the turn of a single card; and many a child has been snatched from the arms of its mother by bargains arranged in a state of brutal drunkenness.

The flesh-mongers gather up their victims by dozens, and drive them, chained, to the general depot at Baltimore. When a sufficient number has been collected here, a ship is chartered for the purpose of conveying the forlorn crew to Mobile, or to New Orleans. From the slave prison to the ship, they are usually driven in the darkness of night; for since the antislavery agitation, a certain caution is observed.

50   In the deep, still darkness of midnight, I have been often aroused by the dead, heavy footsteps, and the piteous cries of the chained gangs that passed our door. The anguish of my boyish heart was intense; and I was often consoled, when speaking to my mistress in the morning, to hear her say that the custom was very wicked; that she hated to hear the rattle of the chains and the heart-rending cries. I was glad to find one who sympathized with me in my horror.

Fellow-citizens, this murderous traffic is, to-day, in active operation in this boasted republic. In the solitude of my spirit I see clouds of dust raised on the highways of the South; I see the bleeding footsteps; I hear the doleful wail of fettered humanity on the way to the slave-markets, where the victims are to be sold like *horses*, *sheep*, and *swine*, knocked off to the highest bidder. There I see the tenderest ties ruthlessly broken, to gratify the lust, caprice and rapacity of the buyers and sellers of men. My soul sickens at the sight.

> *Is this the land your Fathers loved,*
> *The freedom which they toiled to win?*
> *Is this the earth whereon they moved?*
> *Are these the graves they slumber in?*

But a still more inhuman, disgraceful, and scandalous state of things remains to be presented. By an act of the American Congress, not yet two years old, slavery has been nationalized in its most horrible and revolting form. By that act, Mason and Dixon's line has been obliterated; New York has become as Virginia; and the power to hold, hunt, and sell men, women and children, as slaves, remains no longer a mere state institution, but is now an institution of the whole United States. The power is co-extensive with the star-spangled banner, and American Christianity. Where these go, may also go the merciless slave-hunter. Where these are, man is not sacred. He is a bird for the sportsman's gun. By that most foul and fiendish of all human decrees, the liberty and person of every man are put in peril. Your broad republican domain is hunting ground for *men*. *Not* for thieves and robbers, enemies of society, merely, but for men guilty of no crime. Your law-makers have commanded all good citizens to engage in this hellish sport. Your President, your Secretary of State, your *lords*, *nobles*, and ecclesiastics enforce, as a duty you owe to your free and glorious country, and to your God, that you do this accursed thing. Not fewer than forty Americans have, within the past two years, been hunted down and, without a moment's warning, hurried away in chains, and consigned to slavery and excruciating torture. Some of these have had wives and children, dependent on them for bread; but of this, no account was made. The right of the hunter to his prey stands superior to the right of marriage, and to all *rights* in this republic, the rights of God included! For black men there is neither law nor justice, humanity nor religion. The Fugitive Slave *Law* makes mercy to them a crime; and bribes the judge who tries them. An American judge gets ten dollars for every victim he consigns to slavery, and five, when he fails to do so. The oath of any two villains is sufficient, under this hell-black enactment, to send the most pious and exemplary black man into the remorseless jaws of slavery! His own testimony is nothing. He can bring no witnesses for himself. The minister of American justice is bound by the law to hear but *one* side; and *that* side is the side of the oppressor. Let this damning fact be perpetually told. Let it be thundered around the world that in tyrant-killing, king-hating, people-loving, democratic, Christian America the seats of justice are filled with judges who hold their offices under an open and palpable *bribe*, and are bound, in deciding the case of a man's liberty, *to hear only his accusers*!

In glaring violation of justice, in shameless disregard of the forms of administering law, in cunning arrangement to entrap the defenceless, and in diabolical intent this Fugitive Slave Law stands alone in the annals of tyrannical legislation. I doubt if there be another nation on the globe having the brass and the baseness to put such a law on the statute-book. If any man in this assembly thinks differently from me in this matter, and feels able to disprove my statements, I will gladly confront him at any suitable time and place he may select.

I take this law to be one of the grossest infringements of Christian Liberty, and, if the churches and ministers of our country were not stupidly blind, or most wickedly indifferent, they, too, would so regard it.

At the very moment that they are thanking God for the enjoyment 55 of civil and religious liberty, and for the right to worship God according to the dictates of their own consciences, they are utterly silent in respect to a law which robs religion of its chief significance and makes it utterly worthless to a world lying in wickedness. Did this law concern the "*mint, anise, and cummin*"—abridge the right to sing psalms, to partake of the sacrament, or to engage in any of the ceremonies of religion, it would be smitten by the thunder of a thousand pulpits. A general shout would go up from the church demanding *repeal, repeal, instant repeal!*—And it would go hard with that politician who presumed to so licit the votes of the people without inscribing this motto on his banner. Further, if this demand were not complied with, another Scotland would be added to the history of religious liberty, and the stern old covenanters would be thrown into the shade. A John Knox would be seen at every church door and heard from every pulpit, and Fillmore would have no more quarter than was shown by Knox to the beautiful, but treacherous, Queen Mary of Scotland. The fact that the church of our country (with fractional exceptions) does not esteem "the Fugitive Slave Law" as a declaration of war against religious liberty, implies that that church regards religion simply as a form of worship, an empty ceremony, and not a vital principle, requiring active benevolence, justice, love, and good will towards man. It esteems sacrifice above mercy; psalm-singing above right doing; solemn meetings above practical righteousness. A worship that can be conducted by persons who refuse to give shelter to the houseless, to give bread to the hungry, clothing to the naked, and who enjoin obedience to a law forbidding these acts of mercy is a curse, not a blessing to mankind. The Bible addresses all such persons as "scribes, pharisees, hypocrites, who pay tithe of *mint, anise, and cummin,* and have omitted the weightier matters of the law, judgment, mercy, and faith."

But the church of this country is not only indifferent to the wrongs of the slave, it actually takes sides with the oppressors. It has made itself the bulwark of American slavery, and the shield of American slave-hunters. Many of its most eloquent Divines, who stand as the very lights of the church, have shamelessly given the sanction of religion and the Bible to the whole slave system. They have taught that man may, properly, be a slave; that the relation of master and slave is ordained of God; that to send back an escaped bondman to his master is clearly the duty of all the followers of the Lord Jesus Christ; and this horrible blasphemy is palmed off upon the world for Christianity.

For my part, I would say, welcome infidelity! welcome atheism! welcome anything! in preference to the gospel, *as preached by those Divines!* They convert the very name of religion into an engine of tyranny and barbarous cruelty, and serve to confirm more infidels, in this age, than all the infidel writings of Thomas Paine, Voltaire, and Bolingbroke put together have done! These ministers make religion a cold and flinty-hearted thing, having neither principles of right action nor bowels of compassion. They strip the love of God of its beauty and leave the throne of religion a huge, horrible, repulsive form. It is a religion for oppressors, tyrants, man-stealers, and thugs. It is not that *"pure and undefiled religion"* which is from above, and which is *"first pure, then peaceable, easy to be entreated,* full of mercy and good fruits, *without partiality, and without hypocrisy."* But a religion which favors the rich against the poor; which exalts the proud above the humble; which divides mankind into two classes, tyrants and slaves; which says to the man in chains, *stay there*; and to the oppressor, *oppress on*; it is a religion which may be professed and enjoyed by all the robbers and enslavers of mankind; it makes God a respecter of persons, denies his fatherhood of the race, and tramples in the dust the great truth of the brotherhood of man. All this we affirm to be true of the popular church, and the popular worship of our land and nation—a religion, a church, and a worship which, on the authority of inspired wisdom, we pronounce to be an abomination in the sight of God. In the language of Isaiah, the American church might be well addressed, "Bring no more vain oblations; incense is an abomination unto me: the new moons and Sabbaths, the calling of assemblies, I cannot away with; it is iniquity, even the solemn meeting. Your new moons, and your appointed feasts my soul hateth. They are a trouble to me; I am weary to bear them; and when ye spread forth your hands I will hide mine eyes from you. Yea' when ye make many prayers, I will not hear. Your hands are full of blood; cease to do evil, learn to do well; seek judgment; relieve the oppressed; judge for the fatherless; plead for the widow."

The American church is guilty, when viewed in connection with what it is doing to uphold slavery; but it is superlatively guilty when viewed in its connection with its ability to abolish slavery.

The sin of which it is guilty is one of omission as well as of commission. Albert Barnes but uttered what the common sense of every man at all observant of the actual state of the case will receive as truth, when he declared that "There is no power out of the church that could sustain slavery an hour, if it were not sustained in it."

Let the religious press, the pulpit, the Sunday School, the 60 conference meeting, the great ecclesiastical, missionary, Bible and tract associations of the land array their immense powers against slavery, and slave-holding; and the whole system of crime and blood would be scattered to the winds, and that they do not do this involves them in the most awful responsibility of which the mind can conceive.

In prosecuting the anti-slavery enterprise, we have been asked to spare the church, to spare the ministry; but *how*, we ask, could such a thing be done? We are met on the threshold of our efforts for the redemption of the slave, by the church and ministry of the country, in battle arrayed against us; and we are compelled to fight or flee. From *what* quarter, I beg to know, has proceeded a fire so deadly upon our ranks, during the last two years, as from the Northern pulpit? As the champions of oppressors, the chosen men of American theology have appeared—men honored for their so-called piety, and their real learning. The Lords of Buffalo, the Springs of New York, the Lathrops of Auburn, the Coxes and Spencers of Brooklyn, the Gannets and Sharps of Boston, the Deweys of Washington, and other great religious lights of the land have, in utter denial of the authority of *Him* by whom they professed to be called to the ministry, deliberately taught us, against the example of the Hebrews, and against the remonstrance of the Apostles, *that we ought to obey man's law before the law of God.*

My spirit wearies of such blasphemy; and how such men can be supported, as the "standing types and representatives of Jesus Christ," is a mystery which I leave others to penetrate. In speaking of the American church, however, let it be distinctly understood that I mean the *great mass* of the religious organizations of our land. There are exceptions, and I thank God that there are. Noble men may be found, scattered all over these Northern States, of whom Henry Ward Beecher, of Brooklyn; Samuel J. May, of Syracuse; and my esteemed friend (Rev. R. R. Raymond) on the platform, are shining examples; and let me say further, that, upon these men lies the duty to inspire our ranks with high religious faith and zeal, and to cheer us on in the great mission of the slave's redemption from his chains.

One is struck with the difference between the attitude of the American church towards the anti-slavery movement, and that occupied by the churches in Eng land towards a similar movement in that country. There, the church, true to its mission of ameliorating, elevating and improving the condition of mankind, came forward promptly, bound up the wounds of the West Indian slave, and re stored him to his liberty. There, the question of emancipation was a high religious question. It was demanded in the name of humanity, and according to the law of the living God. The Sharps, the Clarksons, the Wilberforces, the Buxtons, the Burchells, and the Knibbs were alike famous for their piety and for their philanthropy. The anti-slavery movement *there* was not an anti-church movement, for the reason that the church took its full share in prosecuting that movement: and the anti-slavery movement in this country will cease to be an anti-church movement, when the church of this country shall assume a favorable instead of a hostile position towards that movement.

Americans! your republican politics, not less than your republican religion, are flagrantly inconsistent. You boast of your love of liberty, your superior civilization, and your pure Christianity, while the whole political power of the nation (as embodied in the two great political parties) is solemnly pledged to support and perpetuate the enslavement of three millions of your countrymen. You hurl your anathemas at the crowned headed tyrants of Russia and Austria and pride yourselves on your Democratic institutions, while you yourselves consent to be the mere *tools* and *body-guards* of the tyrants of Virginia and Carolina. You invite to your shores fugitives of oppression from abroad, honor them with banquets, greet them with ovations, cheer them, toast them, salute them, protect them, and pour out your money to them like water; but the fugitives from oppression in your own land you advertise, hunt, arrest, shoot, and kill. You glory in your refinement and your universal education; yet you maintain a system as barbarous and dreadful as ever stained the character of a nation—a system begun in avarice, supported in pride, and perpetuated in cruelty. You shed tears over fallen Hungary, and make the sad story of her wrongs the theme of your poets, statesmen, and orators, till your gallant sons are ready to fly to arms to vindicate her cause against the oppressor; but, in regard to the ten thousand wrongs of the American slave, you would enforce the strictest silence, and would hail him as an enemy of the nation who dares to make those wrongs the subject of public discourse! You are all on fire at the mention of liberty for France or for Ireland; but are as cold as an iceberg at the thought of liberty for the enslaved of America. You discourse eloquently on the dignity of labor; yet, you sustain a system which, in its very essence, casts a stigma upon labor. You can bare your bosom to the storm of British artillery to throw off a three-penny tax on tea; and yet wring the last hard earned farthing from the grasp of the black laborers of your country. You profess to believe "that, of one blood, God made all nations of men to dwell on the face of all the earth," and hath commanded all men, everywhere, to love one another; yet you notoriously hate (and glory in your hatred) all men whose skins are not colored like your own. You declare before the world, and are understood by the world to declare that you *"hold these truths to be self-evident, that all men are created equal; and are endowed by their Creator with certain in alienable rights; and that among these are, life, liberty, and the pursuit of happiness;*

and yet, you hold securely, in a bondage which, according to your own Thomas Jefferson, "*is worse than ages of that which your fathers rose in rebellion to oppose*," a seventh part of the inhabitants of your country.

65   Fellow-citizens, I will not enlarge further on your national inconsistencies. The existence of slavery in this country brands your republicanism as a sham, your humanity as a base pretense, and your Christianity as a lie. It destroys your moral power abroad: it corrupts your politicians at home. It saps the foundation of religion; it makes your name a hissing and a bye-word to a mocking earth. It is the antagonistic force in your government, the only thing that seriously disturbs and endangers your *Union*. it fetters your progress; it is the enemy of improvement; the deadly foe of education; it fosters pride; it breeds insolence; it promotes vice; it shelters crime; it is a curse to the earth that supports it; and yet you cling to it as if it were the sheet anchor of all your hopes. Oh! be warned! be warned! a horrible reptile is coiled up in your nation's bosom; the venomous creature is nursing at the tender breast of your youthful republic; *for the love of God, tear away*, and fling from you the hideous monster, and *let the weight of twenty millions crush and destroy it forever!*

But it is answered in reply to all this, that precisely what I have now denounced is, in fact, guaranteed and sanctioned by the Constitution of the United States; that, the right to hold, and to hunt slaves is a part of that Constitution framed by the illustrious Fathers of this Republic.

Then, I dare to affirm, notwithstanding all I have said before, your fathers stooped, basely stooped

> *To palter with us in a double sense:*
> *And keep the word of promise to the ear,*
> *But break it to the heart.*

And instead of being the honest men I have before declared them to be, they were the veriest impostors that ever practised on mankind. This is the inevitable conclusion, and from it there is no escape; but I differ from those who charge this baseness on the framers of the Constitution of the United States. It is a slander upon their memory, at least, so I believe. There is not time now to argue the constitutional question at length; nor have I the ability to discuss it as it ought to be discussed. The subject has been handled with masterly power by Lysander Spooner, Esq. by William Goodell, by Samuel E. Sewall, Esq., and last, though not least, by Gerrit Smith, Esq. These gentlemen have, as I think, fully and clearly vindicated the Constitution from any design to support slavery for an hour.

Fellow-citizens! there is no matter in respect to which the people   70 of the North have allowed themselves to be so ruinously imposed upon as that of the pro-slavery character of the Constitution. In that instrument I hold there is neither warrant, license, nor sanction of the hateful thing; but interpreted, as it ought to be interpreted, the Constitution is a glorious liberty document. Read its preamble, consider its purposes. Is slavery among them? Is it at the gate way? or is it in the temple? it is neither. While I do not intend to argue this question on the present occasion, let me ask, if it be not somewhat singular that, if the Constitution were intended to be, by its framers and adopters, a slaveholding instrument, why neither slavery, slaveholding, nor slave can anywhere be found in it. What would be thought of an instrument, drawn up, legally drawn up, for the purpose of entitling the city of Rochester to a tract of land, in which no mention of land was made? Now, there are certain rules of interpretation for the proper understanding of all legal instruments. These rules are well established. They are plain, commonsense rules, such as you and I, and all of us, can understand and apply, without having passed years in the study of law. I scout the idea that the question of the constitutionality, or unconstitutionality of slavery, is not a question for the people. I hold that every American citizen has a right to form an opinion of the constitution, and to propagate that opinion, and to use all honorable means to make his opinion the prevailing one. Without this right, the liberty of an American citizen would be as insecure as that of a Frenchman. Ex-Vice-President Dallas tells us that the constitution is an object to which no American mind can be too attentive, and no American heart too devoted. He further says, the Constitution, in its words, is plain and intelligible, and is meant for the home-bred, unsophisticated understandings of our fellow-citizens. Senator Berrien tells us that the Constitution is the fundamental law, that which controls all others. The charter of our liberties, which every citizen has a personal interest in understanding thoroughly. The testimony of Senator Breese, Lewis Cass, and many others that might be named, who are everywhere esteemed as sound lawyers, so regard the constitution. I take it, therefore, that it is not presumption in a private citizen to form an opinion of that instrument.

Now, take the Constitution according to its plain reading, and I defy the presentation of a single pro-slavery clause in it. On the other hand, it will be found to contain principles and purposes, entirely hostile to the existence of slavery.

I have detained my audience entirely too long already. At some future period I will gladly avail myself of an opportunity to give this subject a full and fair discussion.

Allow me to say, in conclusion, notwithstanding the dark picture I have this day presented, of the state of the nation, I do not despair of this country. There are forces in operation which must inevitably work the downfall of slavery.

"The arm of the Lord is not shortened," and the doom of slavery is certain. I, therefore, leave off where I began, with hope. While drawing encouragement from "the Declaration of Independence," the great principles it contains, and the genius of American Institutions, my spirit is also cheered by the obvious tendencies of the age. Nations do not now stand in the same relation to each other that they did ages ago. No nation can now shut itself up from the surrounding world and trot round in the same old path of its fathers without interference. The time was when such could be done. Long established customs of hurtful character could formerly fence themselves in, and do their evil work with social impunity. Knowledge was then confined and enjoyed by the privileged few, and the multitude walked on in mental darkness. But a change has now come over the affairs of mankind. Walled cities and empires have become unfashionable. The arm of commerce has borne away the gates of the strong city. Intelligence is penetrating the darkest corners of the globe. It makes its pathway over and under the sea, as well as on the earth. Wind, steam, and lightning are its chartered agents. Oceans no longer divide, but link nations together. From Boston to London is now a holiday excursion. Space is comparatively annihilated.—Thoughts expressed on one side of the Atlantic are distinctly heard on the other.

75   The far off and almost fabulous Pacific rolls in grandeur at our feet. The Celestial Empire, the mystery of ages, is being solved. The fiat of the Almighty, "Let there be Light," has not yet spent its force. No abuse, no outrage whether in taste, sport or avarice, can now hide itself from the all-pervading light. The iron shoe, and crippled foot of China must be seen in contrast with nature. Africa must rise and put on her yet unwoven garment. "Ethiopia shall stretch out her hand unto God." In the fervent aspirations of William Lloyd Garrison, I say, and let every heart join in saying it:

God speed the year of jubilee
The wide world o'er!
When from their galling chains set free,
Th' oppress'd shall vilely bend the knee,
And wear the yoke of tyranny
Like brutes no more.
That year will come, and freedom's reign.
To man his plundered rights again
Restore.

God speed the day when human blood
Shall cease to flow!
In every clime be understood,
The claims of human brotherhood,
And each return for evil, good,
Not blow for blow;
That day will come all feuds to end,
And change into a faithful friend
Each foe.

God speed the hour, the glorious hour,
When none on earth
Shall exercise a lordly power;
But to all manhood's stature tower,
By equal birth!
That hour will come, to each, to all,
And from his prison-house, to thrall
Go forth.

Until that year, day, hour, arrive,
With head, and heart, and hand I'll strive,
To break the rod, and rend the gyve,
The spoiler of his prey deprive—
So witness Heaven!
And never from my chosen post,
Whate'er the peril of the cost,
Be driven.

How It Feels to Be Colored Me

Zora Neale Hurston

Zora Neale Hurston (1891-1960)

Zora Neale Hurston was born in Alabama to a Baptist preacher father and teacher mother. Hurston's childhood was marked by frequent moves and upheaval, and after expulsion from boarding school for a failure to pay tuition, she took on odd jobs. In 1917, at age 26, Hurston claimed 1901 as her birth year in order to attend Morgan Academy, the high school offshoot of Baltimore's historically black Morgan College. After graduating in 1918, she entered Howard University, earning an Associate's Degree in 1920. In 1925, she received a scholarship to Barnard College and in 1927 obtained a B.A. in anthropology, she followed this accomplishment with graduate study at Columbia University. Hurston's literary career began in New York City just as the Harlem Renaissance was in full swing. Her first work, the play *Color Struck* (1925) appeared during the period and reflected many of the themes of the movement. Some of Hurston's major works, like *Mules and Men* (1935), were non-fiction, based upon her studies and travels throughout the Caribbean and American South as a cultural anthropologist and folklorist. This research heavily informed her fiction, including 1937's *Their Eyes Were Watching God*. After the 1940s, Hurston fell into obscurity for a period, with her work considered to be less politically-focused than that of contemporaries like Ralph Ellison, and her use of dialect to represent speech patterns somewhat controversial. A decade after her death, Hurston's work was revived in the 1970s by Alice Walker, as black female authors such as Walker and Toni Morrison, who wrote with similar emphases to Hurston's, rose to prominence.

1 I am colored but I offer nothing in the way of extenuating circumstances except the fact that I am the only Negro in the United States whose grandfather on the mother's side was *not* an Indian chief.

I remember the very day that I became colored. Up to my thirteenth year I lived in the little Negro town of Eatonville, Florida. It is exclusively a colored town. The only white people I knew passed through the town going to or coming from Orlando. The native whites rode dusty horses, the Northern tourists chugged down the sandy village road in automobiles. The town knew the Southerners and never stopped cane chewing when they passed. But the Northerners were something else again. They were peered at cautiously from behind curtains by the timid. The more venturesome would come out on the porch to watch them go past and got just as much pleasure out of the tourists as the tourists got out of the village.

The front porch might seem a daring place for the rest of the town, but it was a gallery seat for me. My favorite place was atop the gate-post. Proscenium box for a born first-nighter. Not only did I enjoy the show, but I didn't mind the actors knowing that I liked it. I usually spoke to them in passing. I'd wave at them and when they returned my salute, I would say something like this: "Howdy-do-well-I-thank-you-where-you-goin'?" Usually the automobile or the horse paused at this, and after a queer exchange of compliments, I would probably "go a piece of the way" with them, as we say in farthest Florida. If one of my family happened to come to the front in time to see me, of course negotiations would be rudely broken off. But even so, it is clear that I was the first "welcome-to-our-state" Floridian, and I hope the Miami Chamber of Commerce will please take notice.

During this period, white people differed from colored to me only in that they rode through town and never lived there. They liked to hear me "speak pieces" and sing and wanted to see me dance the parse-me-la, and gave me generously of their small silver for doing these things, which seemed strange to me for I wanted to do them so much that I needed bribing to stop. Only they didn't know it. The colored people gave no dimes. They deplored any joyful tendencies in me, but I was their Zora nevertheless. I belonged to them, to the nearby hotels, to the county— everybody's Zora.

But changes came in the family when I was thirteen, and I was sent   5 to school in Jacksonville. I left Eatonville, the town of the oleanders, as Zora. When I disembarked from the river-boat at Jacksonville, she was no more. It seemed that I had suffered a sea change. I was not Zora of Orange County any more, I was now a little colored girl. I found it out in certain ways. In my heart as well as in the mirror, I became a fast brown—warranted not to rub nor run.

But I am not tragically colored. There is no great sorrow dammed up in my soul, nor lurking behind my eyes. I do not mind at all. I do not belong to the sobbing school of Negrohood who hold that nature somehow has given them a lowdown dirty deal and whose feelings are all hurt about it. Even in the helter-skelter skirmish that is my life, I have seen that the world is to the strong regardless of a little pigmentation more or less. No, I do not weep at the world—I am too busy sharpening my oyster knife.

Someone is always at my elbow reminding me that I am the granddaughter of slaves. It fails to register depression with me. Slavery is sixty years in the past. The operation was successful and the patient is doing well, thank you. The terrible struggle that made me an American out of a potential slave said "On the line!" The Reconstruction said "Get set!"; and the generation before said "Go!" I am off to a flying start and I must not halt in the stretch to look behind and weep. Slavery is the price I paid for civilization, and the choice was not with me. It is a bully adventure and worth all that I have paid through my ancestors for it. No one on earth ever had a greater chance for glory. The world to be won and nothing to be lost. It is thrilling to think—to know that for any act of mine, I shall get twice as much praise or twice as much blame. It is quite exciting to hold the center of the national stage, with the spectators not knowing whether to laugh or weep.

The position of my white neighbor is much more difficult. No brown specter pulls up a chair beside me when I sit down to eat. No dark ghost thrusts its leg against mine in bed. The game of keeping what one has is never so exciting as the game of getting.

I do not always feel colored. Even now I often achieve the unconscious Zora of Eatonville before the Hegira. I feel most colored when I am thrown against a sharp white background.

10   For instance at Barnard. "Beside the waters of the Hudson" I feel my race. Among the thousand white persons, I am a dark rock surged upon, overswept by a creamy sea. I am surged upon and overswept, but through it all, I remain myself. When covered by the waters, I am; and the ebb but reveals me again.

Sometimes it is the other way around. A white person is set down in our midst, but the contrast is just as sharp for me. For instance, when I sit in the drafty basement that is The New World Cabaret with a white person, my color comes. We enter chatting about any little nothing that we have in common and are seated by the jazz waiters. In the abrupt way that jazz orchestras have, this one plunges into a number. It loses no time in circumlocutions, but gets right down to business. It constricts the thorax and splits the heart with its tempo and narcotic harmonies. This orchestra grows rambunctious, rears on its hind legs and attacks the tonal veil with primitive fury, rending it, clawing it until it breaks through to the jungle beyond. I follow those heathen—follow them exultingly. I dance wildly inside myself; I yell within, I whoop; I shake my assegai above my head, I hurl it true to the mark *yeeeeooww!* I am in the jungle and living in the jungle way. My face is painted red and yellow and my body is painted blue. My pulse is throbbing like a war drum. I want to slaughter something— give pain, give death to what, I do not know. But the piece ends. The men of the orchestra wipe their lips and rest their fingers. I creep back slowly to the veneer we call civilization with the last tone and find the white friend sitting motionless in his seat, smoking calmly.

"Good music they have here," he remarks, drumming the table with his fingertips.

Music! The great blobs of purple and red emotion have not touched him. He has only heard what I felt. He is far away and I see him but dimly across the ocean and the continent that have fallen between us. He is so pale with his whiteness then and I am *so* colored.

At certain times I have no race, I am *me*. When I set my hat at a certain angle and saunter down Seventh Avenue, Harlem City, feeling as snooty as the lions in front of the Forty-Second Street Library, for instance. So far as my feelings are concerned, Peggy Hopkins Joyce on the Boule Mich with her gorgeous raiment, stately carriage, knees knocking together in a most aristocratic manner, has nothing on me. The cosmic Zora emerges. I belong to no race nor time. I am the eternal feminine with its string of beads.

I have no separate feeling about being an American citizen and 15 colored. I am merely a fragment of the Great Soul that surges within the boundaries. My country, right or wrong.

Sometimes, I feel discriminated against, but it does not make me angry. It merely astonishes me. How *can* any deny themselves the pleasure of my company? It's beyond me.

But in the main, I feel like a brown bag of miscellany propped against a wall. Against a wall in company with other bags, white, red and yellow. Pour out the contents, and there is discovered a jumble of small things priceless and worthless. A first-water diamond, an empty spool, bits of broken glass, lengths of string, a key to a door long since crumbled away, a rusty knife-blade, old shoes saved for a road that never was and never will be, a nail bent under the weight of things too heavy for any nail, a dried flower or two, still a little fragrant. In your hand is the brown bag. On the ground before you is the jumble it held—so much like the jumble in the bags, could they be emptied, that all might be dumped in a single heap and the bags refilled without altering the content of any greatly. A bit of colored glass more or less would not matter. Perhaps that is how the Great Stuffer of Bags filled them in the first place—who knows?

From *The World Tomorrow* (May, 1928). Copyright © 1929 by Zora Neale Hurston, renewed 1956 by John C. Hurston

◆

SIZE 6: THE WESTERN WOMEN'S HAREM

Fatema Mernissi

FATEMA MERNISSI (1940-)

Fatema Mernissi was born in Fes, Morocco in 1940. She first studied at the Mohammed V University in Rabat before entering the Sorbonne in 1957, studying political science and later earning her doctorate in the same field at Brandeis University in Massachusetts. Mernissi's first and perhaps most influential work, *Beyond the Veil*, was published in 1975. She is primarily known for her work as an Islamic feminist writer, a label enforced by texts including *The Veil and the Male Elite: A Feminist Interpretation of Islam* (1987) and *Doing Daily Battle: Interviews with Moroccan Women* (1991). Her memoirs are recounted in 1995's *Dreams of Trespass: Tales of a Harem Girlhood* and 2001's *Scheherazade Goes West*. In 2003, Mernissi won Spain's Prince of Asturias Award, which recognizes those who have made a notable contribution in the arts, sciences, or humanities. Since 1974, Mernissi has been a lecturer at the Mohammed V University, and is also a research scholar at Rabat's University Institute for Scientific Research.

It was during my unsuccessful attempt to buy a cotton skirt in an   1
American department store that I was told my hips were too large
to fit into a size 6. That distressing experience made me realize how
the image of beauty in the West can hurt and humiliate a woman as
much as the veil does when enforced by the state police in extremist
nations such as Iran, Afghanistan, or Saudi Arabia. Yes, that day I
stumbled onto one of the keys to the enigma of passive beauty in
Western harem fantasies. The elegant saleslady in the American store
looked at me without moving from her desk and said that she had
no skirt my size. "In this whole big store, there is no skirt for me?" I
said. "You are joking." I felt very suspicious and thought that she just
might be too tired to help me. I could understand that. But then the
saleswoman added a condescending judgment, which sounded to me
like an imam's fatwa. It left no room for discussion:

"You are too big!" she said.

"I am too big compared to what?" I asked, looking at her intently, because I realized that I was facing a critical cultural gap here.

"Compared to a size 6," came the saleslady's reply.

5   Her voice had a clear-cut edge to it that is typical of those who enforce religious laws. "Size 4 and 6 are the norm," she went on, encouraged by my bewildered look. "Deviant sizes such as the one you need can be bought in special stores."

That was the first time that I had ever heard such nonsense about my size. In the Moroccan streets, men's flattering comments regarding my particularly generous hips have for decades led me to believe that the entire planet shared their convictions. It is true that with advancing age, I have been hearing fewer and fewer flattering comments when walking in the medina, and sometimes the silence around me in the bazaars is deafening. But since my face has never met with the local beauty standards, and I have often had to defend myself against remarks such as *zirafa* (giraffe), because of my long neck, I learned long ago not to rely too much on the outside world for my sense of self-worth. In fact, paradoxically, as I discovered when I went to Rabat as a student, it was the self-reliance that I had developed to protect myself against "beauty blackmail" that made me attractive to others. My male fellow students could not believe that I did not give a damn about what they thought about my body. "You know, my dear," I would say in response to one of them, "all I need to survive is bread, olives, and sardines. That you think my neck is too long is your problem, not mine."

In any case, when it comes to beauty and compliments, nothing is too serious or definite in the medina, where everything can be negotiated. But things seemed to be different in that American department store. In fact, I have to confess that I lost my usual self-confidence in that New York environment. Not that I am always sure of myself, but I don't walk around the Moroccan streets or down the university corridors wondering what people are thinking about me.

Of course, when I hear a compliment, my ego expands like a cheese soufflé, but on the whole, I don't expect to hear much from others. Some mornings, I feel ugly because I am sick or tired; others, I feel wonderful because it is sunny out or I have written a good paragraph. But suddenly, in that peaceful American store that I had entered so triumphantly, as a sovereign consumer ready to spend money, I felt savagely attacked. My hips, until then the sign of a relaxed and uninhibited maturity, were suddenly being condemned as a deformity....

"And who says that everyone must be a size 6?" I joked to the saleslady that day, deliberately neglecting to mention size 4, which is the size of my skinny twelve-year-old niece.

At that point, the saleslady suddenly gave me an anxious look.   10 "The norm is everywhere, my dear," she said. "It's all over, in the magazines, on television, in the ads. You can't escape it. There is Calvin Klein, Ralph Lauren, Gianni Versace, Giorgio Armani, Mario Valentino, Salvatore Ferragamo, Christian Dior, Yves Saint-Laurent, Christian Lacroix, and Jean-Paul Gaultier. Big department stores go by the norm." She paused and then concluded, "If they sold size 14 or 16, which is probably what you need, they would go bankrupt."

She stopped for a minute and then stared at me, intrigued. "Where on earth do you come from? I am sorry I can't help you. Really, I am." And she looked it too. She seemed, all of a sudden, interested, and brushed off another woman who was seeking her attention with a cutting, "Get someone else to help you, I'm busy." Only then did I notice that she was probably my age, in her late fifties. But unlike me, she had the thin body of an adolescent girl. Her knee-length, navy blue, Chanel dress had a white silk collar reminiscent of the subdued elegance of aristocratic French Catholic schoolgirls at the turn of the century. A pearl-studded belt emphasized the slimness of her waist. With her meticulously styled short hair and sophisticated makeup, she looked half my age at first glance.

"I come from a country where there is no size for women's clothes," I told her. "I buy my own material and the neighborhood seamstress of craftsman makes me the silk or leather skirt I want. They just take my measurements each time I see them. Neither the seamstress nor I know exactly what size my new skirt is. We discover it together in the making. No one cares about my size in Morocco as long as I pay taxes on time. Actually, I don't know what my size is, to tell you the truth."

The saleswoman laughed merrily and said that I should advertise my country as a paradise for stressed working women. "You mean you don't watch your weight?" she inquired, with a tinge of disbelief in her voice. And then, after a brief moment of silence, she added in a lower register, as if talking to herself: "Many women working in highly paid fashion-related jobs could lose their positions if they didn't keep to a strict diet."

Her words sounded so simple, but the threat they implied was so cruel that I realized for the first time that maybe "size 6" is a more violent restriction imposed on women than is the Muslim veil. Quickly I said good-bye so as not to make any more demands on the saleslady's time or involve her in any more unwelcome, confidential exchanges about age-discriminating salary cuts. A surveillance camera was probably watching us both.

15   Yes, I thought as I wandered off, I have finally found the answer to my harem enigma. Unlike the Muslim man, who uses space to establish male domination by excluding women from the public arena, the Western man manipulates time and light. He declares that in order to be beautiful, a woman must look fourteen years old. If she dares to look fifty, or worse, sixty, she is beyond the pale. By putting the spotlight on the female child and framing her as the ideal of beauty, he condemns the mature woman to invisibility. In fact, the modern Western man enforces Immanuel Kant's nineteenth-century theories: To be beautiful, women have to appear childish and brainless. When a woman looks mature and self-assertive, or allows her hips to expand, she is condemned as ugly. Thus, the walls of the European harem separate youthful beauty from ugly maturity.

These Western attitudes, I thought, are even more dangerous and cunning than the Muslim ones because the weapon used against women is time. Time is less visible, more fluid than space. The Western man uses images and spotlights to freeze female beauty within an idealized childhood, and forces women to perceive aging— that normal unfolding of the years—as a shameful devaluation. "Here I am, transformed into a dinosaur," I caught myself saying aloud as I went up and down the rows of skirts in the store, hoping to prove the saleslady wrong—to no avail. This Western time-defined veil is even crazier than the space-defined one enforced by the ayatollahs.

The violence embodied in the Western harem is less visible than in the Eastern harem because aging is not attacked directly, but rather masked as an aesthetic choice. Yes, I suddenly felt not only very ugly but also quite useless in that store, where, if you had big hips, you were simply out of the picture. You drifted into the fringes of nothingness. By putting the spotlight on the prepubescent female, the Western man veils the older, more mature woman, wrapping her in shrouds of ugliness. This idea gives me the chills because it tattoos the invisible harem directly onto a woman's skin. Chinese foot-binding worked the same way: Men declared beautiful only those women who had small, child-like feet. Chinese men did not force women to bandage their feet to keep them from developing normally—all they did was to define the beauty ideal. In feudal China, a beautiful woman was the one who voluntarily sacrificed her right to unhindered physical movement by mutilating her own feet, and thereby proving that her main goal in life was to please men. Similarly, in the Western world, I was expected to shrink my hips into a size 6 if I wanted to find a decent skirt tailored for a beautiful woman. We Muslim women have only one month of fasting, Ramadan, but the poor Western woman who diets has to fast twelve months out of the year. "*Quelle horreur*," I kept repeating to myself, while looking around at the American women shopping. All those my age looked like youthful teenagers....

Now, at last, the mystery of my Western harem made sense. Framing youth as beauty and condemning maturity is the weapon used against women in the West just as limiting access to public space is the weapon used in the East. The objective remains identical in both cultures: to make women feel unwelcome, inadequate, and ugly. The power of the Western man resides in dictating what women should wear and how they should look. He controls the whole fashion industry, from cosmetics to underwear. The West, I realized, was the only part of the world where women's fashion is a man's business. In places like Morocco, where you design your own clothes and discuss them with craftsmen and women, fashion is your own business. Not so in the West....

But how does the system function? I wondered. Why do women accept it?

Of all the possible explanations, I like that of the French sociologist   20 Pierre Bourdieu the best. In his latest book, *La Domination Masculine*, he proposes something he calls "*la violence symbolique*": "Symbolic violence is a form of power which is hammered directly on the body, and as if by magic, without any apparent physical constraint. But this magic operates only because it activates the codes pounded in the deepest layers of the body." Reading Bourdieu, I had the impression that I finally understood Western man's psyche better. The cosmetic and fashion industries are only the tip of the iceberg, he states, which is why women are so ready to adhere to their dictates. Something else is going on on a far deeper level. Otherwise, why would women belittle themselves spontaneously? Why, argues Bourdieu, would women make their lives more difficult, for example, by preferring men who are taller or older than they are? "The majority of French women wish to have a husband who is older and also, which seems consistent, bigger as far as size is concerned," writes Bourdieu. Caught in the enchanted submission characteristic of the symbolic violence inscribed in the mysterious layers of the flesh, women relinquish what he calls "les signes ordinaires de la hiérarchie sexuelle," the ordinary signs of sexual hierarchy, such as old age and a larger body.

By so doing, explains Bourdieu, women spontaneously accept the subservient position. It is this spontaneity Bourdieu describes as magic enchantment.

Once I understood how this magic submission worked, I became very happy that the conservative ayatollahs do not know about it yet. If they did, they would readily switch to its sophisticated methods, because they are so much more effective. To deprive me of food is definitely the best way to paralyze my thinking capabilities....

"I thank you, Allah, for sparing me the tyranny of the 'size 6 harem,'" I repeatedly said to myself while seated on the Paris-Casablanca flight, on my way back home at last. "I am so happy that the conservative male elite does not know about it. Imagine the fundamentalists switching from the veil to forcing women to fit size 6."

How can you stage a credible political demonstration and shout in the streets that your human rights have been violated when you cannot find the right skirt?

EXCERPT FROM ON SEEING ENGLAND FOR THE FIRST TIME

Jamaica Kincaid

❖

JAMAICA KINCAID (1949-)

Jamaica Kincaid was born Elaine Cynthia Potter Richardson, in St. John's on Antigua. She was sent to the United States at age 17 to become an au pair, but she instead found herself adopting a series of odd jobs and studying at community college. When she began writing for magazines, she adopted her new name as a measure to conceal her identity from those at home. Kincaid began work at the New Yorker in 1976, quickly becoming a featured columnist, and it was here that her first short story, "*Girl*," was published in 1978. It also appeared in her first book, 1983's story collection *At the Bottom of the River*, which was nominated for the PEN/Faulkner Award for Fiction. Kincaid's work is often informed by her personal experiences in the Caribbean and abroad, with additional books including novels *Annie John* (1985) and *Lucy* (1990), as well as memoir *A Small Place* (1988). Her latest work is 2013's *See Now Then*. Kincaid currently teaches at Claremont McKenna College in California.

When I saw England for the first time, I was a child in school sitting [1] at a desk. The England I was looking at was laid out on a map gently, beautifully, delicately, a very special jewel; it lay on a bed of sky blue— the background of the map—its yellow form mysterious, because though it looked like a leg of mutton, it could not really look like anything so familiar as a leg of mutton because it was England—with shadings of pink and green unlike any shadings of pink and green I had seen before, squiggly veins of red running in every direction. England was a special jewel all right, and only special people got to wear it. The people who got to wear England were English people.

They wore it well and they wore it everywhere: in jungles, in deserts, on plains, on top of the highest mountains, on all the oceans, on all the seas, in places where they were not welcome, in places they should not have been. When my teacher had pinned this map up on the blackboard, she said, "This is England"—and she said it with authority, seriousness, and adoration, and we all sat up. It was as if she had said, "This is Jerusalem, the place you will go to when you die but only if you have been good." We understood then—we were meant to understand then—that England was to be our source myth and the source from which we got our sense of reality, our sense of what was meaningful, our sense of what was meaningless—and much about our own lives and much about the very idea of us headed that last list.

At the time I was a child sitting at my desk seeing England for the first time, I was already very familiar with the greatness of it. Each morning before I left for school, I ate a breakfast of half a grapefruit, an egg, bread and butter and a slice of cheese, and a cup of cocoa; or half a grapefruit, a bowl of oat porridge, bread and butter and a slice of cheese, and a cup of cocoa. The can of cocoa was often left on the table in front of me. It had written on it the name of the company, the year the company was established, and the words, "Made in England." Those words, "Made in England," were written on the box the oats came in too. They would also have been written on the box the shoes I was wearing came in; a bolt of gray linen cloth lying on the shelf of a store from which my mother had brought three yards to make the uniform that I was wearing had written along its edge those three words. The shoes I wore were made in England; so were my socks and cotton undergarments and the satin ribbons I wore tied at the end of two plaits of my hair. My father, who might have sat next to me at breakfast, was a carpenter and a cabinet maker. The shoes he wore to work would have been made in England, as were his khaki shirt and trousers, his underpants and undershirt, his socks and brown felt hat. Felt was not the proper material from which a hat that was expected to provide shade from the hot sun should be made, but my father must have seen and admired a picture of an Englishman wearing such a hat in England, and this picture that he saw must have been so compelling that it caused him to wear the wrong hat for a hot climate most of his long life. And this hat—a brown felt hat—became so central to his character that it was the first thing he put on in the morning as he stepped out of bed and the last thing he took off before he stepped back into bed at night. As we sat at breakfast a car might go by. The car, a Hillman or a Zephyr, was made in England. The very idea of the meal itself, of breakfast, and its substantial quality and quantity was an idea from England; we somehow knew that in England they began the day with this meal called breakfast and a proper breakfast was a big breakfast. No one I knew liked eating so much food so early in the day; it made us feel sleepy, tired. But this breakfast business was Made in England like almost everything else that surrounded us, the exceptions being the sea, the sky, and the air we breathed.

At the time I saw this map—seeing England for the first time—I did not say to myself, "Ah, so that's what it looks like," because there was no longing in me to put a shape to those three words that ran through every part of my life, no matter how small; for me to have had such a longing would have meant that I lived in a certain atmosphere, an atmosphere in which those three words were felt as a burden. But I did not live in such an atmosphere. My father's brown felt hat would develop a hole in its crown, the lining would separate from the hat itself, and six weeks before he thought that he could not be seen wearing it—he was a very vain man—he would order another hat from England. And my mother taught me to eat my food in the English way: the knife in the right had, the fork in the left, my elbows still held close to my side, the food carefully balanced on my fork and then brought up to my mouth. When I had finally mastered it, I overheard her saying to a friend, "Did you see how nicely she can eat?" But I knew then that I enjoyed my food more when I ate it with my bare hands, and I continued to do so when she wasn't looking. And when my teacher showed us the map, she asked us to study it carefully, because no test we would ever take would be complete without this statement: "Draw a map of England."

I did not know then that the statement "Draw a map of England" was something far worse than a declaration of war, for in fact, a flat-out declaration of war would have put me on alert, and again in fact, there was no need for war—I had long ago been conquered. I did not know then that this statement was part of a process that would result in my erasure, not my physical erasure, but my erasure all the same. I did not know then that this statement was meant to make me feel in awe and small whenever I heard the word "England": awe at its existence, small because I was not from it. I did not know very much of anything then— certainly not what a blessing it was that I was unable to draw a map of England correctly.

Excerpt from *"On Seeing England for the First Time,"* by Jamaica Kincaid, 1981, Wylie Aitken, and Stone.

CLASS IN AMERICA—2006

Gregory Mantsios

◈

GREGORY MANTSIOS

Gregory Mantsios is Director of the City University of New York's Joseph F. Murphy Institute for Worker Education and Labor Studies. Previously, he was director of the Center for Worker Studies at Queens College, the forerunner to the Institute, which he founded in 1984. His writings include "*Media Magic: Making Class Invisible*," which appeared in 1995's *Race, Class, and Gender in the United States: An Integrated Study*. He has edited or contributed to a number of books, including *A New Labor Movement for the New Century* (1998). He is also the founder and publisher of the journal New Labor Forum.

1 People in the United States don't like to talk about class. Or so it would seem. We don't speak about class privileges, or class oppression, or the class nature of society. These terms are not part of our everyday vocabulary, and in most circles they are associated with the language of the rhetorical fringe. Unlike people in most other parts of the world, we shrink from using words that classify along economic lines or that point to class distinctions: phrases like "working class," "upper class," and "ruling class" are rarely uttered by Americans.

For the most part, avoidance of class-laden vocabulary crosses class boundaries. There are few among the poor who speak of themselves as lower class; instead, they refer to their race, ethnic group, or geographic location. Workers are more likely to identify with their employer, industry, or occupational group than with other workers, or with the working class.[1]

Neither are those at the other end of the economic spectrum likely to use the word "class." In her study of thirty-eight wealthy and socially prominent women, Susan Ostrander asked participants if they considered themselves members of the upper class. One participant responded, "I hate to use the word 'class.' We are responsible, fortunate people, old families, the people who have something."

Another said, "I hate [the term] upper class. It is so non-upper class to use it. I just call it 'all of us,' those who are wellborn."[2]

It is not that Americans, rich or poor, aren't keenly aware of class   5
differences—those quoted above obviously are; it is that class is not in the domain of public discourse. Class is not discussed or debated in public because class identity has been stripped from popular culture. The institutions that shape mass culture and define the parameters of public debate have avoided class issues. In politics, in primary and secondary education, and in the mass media, formulating issues in terms of class is unacceptable, perhaps even un-American. See my paper, "Media Magic: Making Class Invisible."

There are, however, two notable exceptions to this phenomenon. First, it is acceptable in the United States to talk about "the middle class." Interestingly enough, such references appear to be acceptable precisely because they mute class differences. References to the middle class by politicians, for example, are designed to encompass and attract the broadest possible constituency. Not only do references to the middle class gloss over differences, but these references also avoid any suggestion of conflict or injustice.

This leads us to the second exception to the class-avoidance phenomenon. We are, on occasion, presented with glimpses of the upper class and the lower class (the language used is "the wealthy" and "the poor"). In the media, these presentations are designed to satisfy some real or imagined voyeuristic need of "the ordinary person." As curiosities, the ground-level view of street life and the inside look at the rich and the famous serve as unique models, one to avoid and one to aspire to. In either case, the two models are presented without causal relation to each other: one is not rich because the other is poor.

Similarly, when social commentators or liberal politicians draw attention to the plight of the poor, they do so in a manner that obscures the class structure and denies any sense of exploitation. Wealth and poverty are viewed as one of several natural and inevitable states of being: differences are only differences. One may even say differences are the American way, a reflection of American social diversity.

We are left with one of two possibilities: either talking about class and recognizing class distinctions are not relevant to U.S. society, or we mistakenly hold a set of beliefs that obscure the reality of class differences and their impact on people's lives.

Let us look at four common, albeit contradictory, beliefs about the   10
United States.

Myth 1: The United States is fundamentally a classless society. Class distinctions are largely irrelevant today, and whatever differences do exist in economic standing, they are—for the most part— insignificant. Rich or poor, we are all equal in the eyes of the law, and such basic needs as health care and education are provided to all regardless of economic standing.

Myth 2: We are, essentially, a middle-class nation. Despite some variations in economic status, most Americans have achieved relative affluence in what is widely recognized as a consumer society.

Myth 3: We are all getting richer. The American public as a whole is steadily moving up the economic ladder, and each generation propels itself to greater economic well-being. Despite some fluctuations, the U.S. position in the global economy has brought previously unknown prosperity to most, if not all, Americans.

Myth 4: Everyone has an equal chance to succeed. Success in the United States requires no more than hard work, sacrifice, and perseverance: "In America, anyone can become a millionaire; it's just a matter of being in the right place at the right time."

15   In trying to assess the legitimacy of these beliefs, we want to ask several important questions. Are there significant class differences among Americans? If these differences do exist, are they getting bigger or smaller, and do these differences have a significant impact on the way we live? Finally, does everyone in the United States really have an equal opportunity to succeed?

The Economic Spectrum

Let's begin by looking at difference. An examination of available data reveals that variations in economic well-being are, in fact, immense. Consider the following:

- The wealthiest 1 percent of the American population holds 34 percent of the total national wealth. That is, they own over one-third of all the consumer durables (such as houses, cars, and stereos) and financial assets (such as stocks, bonds, property, and savings accounts). The richest 20 percent of Americans hold nearly 85 percent of the total household wealth in the country.[3]

- Approximately 183,000 Americans, or approximately three-quarters of 1 percent of the adult population, earn more than $1 million *annually*.[4] There are nearly 400 billionaires in the

U.S. today, more than three dozen of them worth more than $10 billion each. It would take the average American (earning $35,672 and spending absolutely nothing at all) a total of 28,033 years (or approximately 400 lifetimes) to earn just $1 billion.

Affluence and prosperity are clearly alive and well in certain segments of the U.S. population. However, this abundance is in contrast to the poverty and despair that is also prevalent in the United States. At the other end of the spectrum:

- Approximately 13 percent of the American population—that is, nearly one of every eight people in this country—live below the official poverty line (calculated in 2004 at $9,645 for an individual and $19,307 for a family of four).[5] An estimated 3.5 million people—of whom nearly 1.4 million are children—experience homelessness in any given year.[6]

- Approximately one out of every five children (4.4 million) in the United States under the age of six lives in poverty.[7]

20

The contrast between rich and poor is sharp, and with nearly one-third of the American population living at one extreme or the other, it is difficult to argue that we live in a classless society. Big-pay-off reality shows, celebrity salaries, and multimillion dollar lotteries notwithstanding, evidence suggests that the level of inequality in the United States is getting higher. Census data show the gap between the rich and the poor to be the widest since the government began collecting information in 1947[8] and that this gap is continuing to grow. In 2004 alone, the average real income of 99 percent of the U.S. population grew by little more than 1 percent, while the real income of the richest 1 percent saw their income rise by 12 percent in the same year.[9]

Nor is such a gap between rich and poor representative of the rest of the industrialized world. In fact, the United States has by far the most unequal distribution of household income.[10] The income gap between rich and poor in the United States (measured as the percentage of total income held by the wealthiest 20 percent of the population versus the poorest 20 percent) is approximately 12 to 1, one of the highest ratios in the industrialized world. The ratio in Japan and Germany, by contrast, is 4 to 1.[11]

Reality 1: There are enormous differences in the economic standing of American citizens. A sizable proportion of the U.S. population occupies opposite ends of the economic spectrum. In the middle range of the economic spectrum:

25

- Sixty percent of the American population holds less than 6 percent of the nation's wealth.[12]

- While the real income of the top 1 percent of U.S. families skyrocketed by more than 180 percent between 1979 and 2000, the income of the middle fifth of the population grew only slightly (12.4 percent over that same 21-year period) and its share of income (15 percent of the total compared to 48 percent of the total for the wealthiest fifth) actually declined during this period.[13]

- Regressive changes in governmental tax policies and the weakening of labor unions over the last quarter century have led to a significant rise in the level of inequality between the rich and the middle class. Between 1979 and 2000, the gap in household income between the top fifth and middle fifth of the population rose by 31 percent.[14] During the economic boom of the 1990s, the top fifth of the nation's population saw their share of net worth increase (from 59 to 63 percent) while four out of five Americans saw their share of net worth decline.[15] One prominent economist described economic growth in the United States as a "spectator sport for the majority of American families."[16] Economic decline, on the other hand, is much more "inclusive," with layoffs impacting hardest on middle-and-lower-income families—those with fewer resources to fall back on.

The level of inequality is sometimes difficult to comprehend fully by looking at dollar figures and percentages. To help his students visualize the distribution of income, the well-known economist Paul Samuelson asked them to picture an income pyramid made of children's blocks, with each layer of blocks representing $1,000. If we were to construct Samuelson's pyramid today, the peak of the pyramid would be much higher than the Eiffel Tower, yet almost all of us would be within six feet of the ground.[17] In other words, the distribution of income is heavily skewed; a small minority of families take the lion's share of national income, and the remaining income is distributed among the vast majority of middle-income and low-income families.

Keep in mind that Samuelson's pyramid represents the distribution of income, not wealth. The distribution of wealth is skewed even further.

Reality 2: The middle class in the United States holds a very small share of the nation's wealth and that share is declining steadily. The gap between rich and poor and between rich and the middle class is larger than it has ever been.

American Life-styles

At last count, nearly 37 million Americans across the nation lived in unrelenting poverty.[18] Yet, as political scientist Michael Harrington once commented, "America has the best dressed poverty the world has ever known."[19] Clothing disguises much of the poverty in the United States, and this may explain, in part, its middle-class image. With increased mass marketing of "designer" clothing and with shifts in the nation's economy from blue-collar (and often better-paying) manufacturing jobs to white-collar and pink-collar jobs in the service sector, it is becoming increasingly difficult to distinguish class differences based on appearance.[20] The dress-down environment prevalent in the high-tech industry (what one author refers to as the "no-collars movement") has reduced superficial distinctions even further.[21]

Beneath the surface, there is another reality. Let's look at some "typical" and not-so-typical life-styles.

American Profile

Name:	Harold S. Browning
Father:	manufacturer, industrialist
Mother:	prominent social figure in the community
Principal child-rearer:	governess
Primary education:	an exclusive private school on Manhattan's Upper East Side
Note:	a small, well-respected primary school where teachers and administrators have a reputation for nurturing student creativity and for providing the finest educational preparation
Ambition:	"to become President"
Supplemental tutoring:	tutors in French and mathematics
Summer camp:	sleep-away camp in northern Connecticut

Note:	camp provides instruction in the creative arts, athletics, and the natural sciences
Secondary education:	a prestigious preparatory school in Westchester County
Note:	classmates included the sons of ambassadors, doctors, attorneys, television personalities, and well-known business leaders
Supplemental education:	private SAT tutor
After-school activities:	private riding lessons
Ambition:	"to take over my father's business"
High-school graduation gift:	BMW
Family activities:	theater, recitals, museums, summer vacations in Europe, occasional winter trips to the Caribbean
Note:	as members of and donors to the local art museum, the Brownings and their children attend private receptions and exhibit openings at the invitation of the museum director
Higher education:	an Ivy League liberal arts college in Massachusetts
Major:	economics and political science
After-class activities:	debating club, college newspaper, swim team
Ambition:	"to become a leader in business"
First full-time job	(age 23): assistant manager of operations, Browning Tool and Die, Inc. (family enterprise)
Subsequent employment:	*3 years*—executive assistant to the president, Browning Tool and Die
Responsibilities included:	purchasing (materials and equipment), personnel, and distribution networks
	4 years—advertising manager, Lackheed Manufacturing (home appliances)
	3 years—director of marketing and sales, Comerex, Inc. (business machines)

Present employment	(age 38): executive vice president, SmithBond and Co. (digital instruments)
Typical daily activities:	review financial reports and computer printouts, dictate memoranda, lunch with clients, initiate conference calls, meet with assistants, plan business trips, meet with associates
Transportation to and from work:	chauffeured company limousine
Annual salary:	$324,000
Ambition:	"to become chief executive officer of the firm, or one like it, within the next five to ten years"
Present residence:	eighteenth-floor condominium on Manhattan's Upper West Side, eleven rooms, including five spacious bedrooms and terrace overlooking river
Interior:	professionally decorated and accented with elegant furnishings, valuable antiques, and expensive artwork
Note:	building management provides doorman and elevator attendant; family employs au pair for children and maid for other domestic chores
Second residence:	farm in northwestern Connecticut, used for weekend retreats and for horse breeding (investment/hobby)
Note:	to maintain the farm and cater to the family when they are there, the Brownings employ a part-time maid, groundskeeper, and horse breeder

Harold Browning was born into a world of nurses, maids, and governesses. His world today is one of airplanes and limousines, five-star restaurants, and luxurious living accommodations. The life and life-style of Harold Browning is in sharp contrast to that of Bob Farrell.

American Profile

Name:	Bob Farrell
Father:	machinist
Mother:	retail clerk
Principal child-rearer:	mother and sitter
Primary education:	a medium-size public school in Queens, New York, characterized by large class size, outmoded physical facilities, and an educational philosophy emphasizing basic skills and student discipline
Ambition:	"to become President"
Supplemental tutoring:	none
Summer camp:	YMCA day camp
Note:	emphasis on team sports, arts and crafts
Secondary education:	large regional high school in Queens
Note:	classmates included the sons and daughters of carpenters, postal clerks, teachers, nurses, shopkeepers, mechanics, bus drivers, police officers, salespersons
Supplemental education:	SAT prep course offered by national chain
After-school activities:	basketball and handball in school park
Ambition:	"to make it through college"
High-school graduation gift:	$500 savings bond
Family activities:	family gatherings around television set, softball, an occasional trip to the movie theater, summer Sundays at the public beach

Higher education:	a two-year community college with a technical orientation
Major:	electrical technology
After-class activities:	employed as a part-time bagger in local supermarket
Ambition:	"to become an electrical engineer"
First full-time job	(age 19): service-station attendant
Note:	continued to take college classes in the evening
Subsequent employment:	mail clerk at large insurance firm; manager trainee, large retail chain
Present employment	(age 38): assistant sales manager, building supply firm
Typical daily activities:	demonstrate products, write up product orders, handle customer complaints, check inventory
Transportation to and from work:	city subway
Annual salary:	$45,261
Ambition:	"to open up my own business"
Additional income:	$6,100 in commissions from evening and weekend work as salesman in local men's clothing store
Present residence:	the Farrells own their own home in a working-class neighborhood in Queens, New York

Bob Farrell and Harold Browning live very differently: the life-style of one is very privileged; that of the other is not so privileged. The differences are class differences, and these differences have a profound impact on the way they live. They are differences between playing a game of handball in the park and taking riding lessons at a private stable; watching a movie on television and going to the theater; and taking the subway to work and being driven in a limousine. More important, the difference in class determines where they live, who their friends are, how well they are educated, what they do for a living, and what they come to expect from life.

Yet, as dissimilar as their life-styles are, Harold Browning and Bob Farrell have some things in common: they live in the same city, they work long hours, and they are highly motivated. More important, they are both white males.

35   Let's look at someone else who works long and hard and is highly motivated. This person, however, is black and female.

American Profile

Name:	Cheryl Mitchell
Father:	janitor
Mother:	waitress
Principal child-rearer:	grandmother
Primary education:	large public school in Ocean Hill-Brownsville, Brooklyn, New York
Note:	rote teaching of basic skills and emphasis on conveying the importance of good attendance, good manners, and good work habits; school patrolled by security guards
Ambition:	"to be a teacher"
Supplemental tutoring:	none
Summer camp:	none
Secondary education:	large public school in Ocean Hill-Brownsville
Note:	classmates included the sons and daughters of hairdressers, groundskeepers, painters, dressmakers, dishwashers, domestics
Supplemental education:	none
After-school activities:	domestic chores, part-time employment as babysitter and housekeeper

Ambition:	"to be a social worker"
High-school graduation gift:	corsage
Family activities:	church-sponsored socials
Higher education:	one semester of local community college
Note:	dropped out of school for financial reasons
First full-time job	(age 17): counter clerk, local bakery
Subsequent employment:	file clerk with temporary-service agency, supermarket checker
Present employment	(age 38): nurse's aide at a municipal hospital
Typical daily activities:	make up hospital beds, clean out bedpans, weigh patients and assist them to the bathroom, take temperature readings, pass out and collect food trays, feed patients who need help, bathe patients, and change dressings
Annual salary:	$15,820
Ambition:	"to get out of the ghetto"
Present residence:	three-room apartment in the South Bronx, needs painting, has poor ventilation, is in a high-crime area
Note:	Cheryl Mitchell lives with her four-year-old son and her elderly mother

When we look at the lives of Cheryl Mitchell, Bob Farrell, and Harold Browning, we see life-styles that are very different. We are not looking, however, at economic extremes. Cheryl Mitchell's income as a nurse's aide puts her above the government's official poverty line.[22] Below her on the income pyramid are 37 million poverty-stricken Americans. Far from being poor, Bob Farrell has an annual income as an assistant sales manager that puts him well above the median income level—that is, more than 50 percent of the U.S. population earns less money than Bob Farrell.[23] And while Harold Browning's income puts him in a high-income bracket, he stands only a fraction of the way up Samuelson's income pyramid. Well above him are the 183,000 individuals whose annual salary exceeds $1 million. Yet Harold Browning spends more money on his horses than Cheryl Mitchell earns in a year.

Reality 3: Even ignoring the extreme poles of the economic spectrum, we find enormous class differences in the life-styles among the haves, the have-nots, and the have-littles.

Class affects more than life-style and material well-being. It has a significant impact on our physical and mental well-being as well.

Researchers have found an inverse relationship between social class and health. Lower-class standing is correlated to higher rates of infant mortality, eye and ear disease, arthritis, physical disability, diabetes, nutritional deficiency, respiratory disease, mental illness, and heart disease.[24] In all areas of health, poor people do not share the same life chances as those in the social class above them. Furthermore, lower-class standing is correlated with a lower quality of treatment for illness and disease. The results of poor health and poor treatment are borne out in the life expectancy rates within each class. Researchers have found that the higher your class standing, the higher your life expectancy. Conversely, they have also found that within each age group, the lower one's class standing, the higher the death rate; in some age groups, the figures are as much as two and three times as high.[25]

40   **Reality 4:** From cradle to grave, class standing has a significant impact on our chances for survival.

The lower one's class standing, the more difficult it is to secure appropriate housing, the more time is spent on the routine tasks of everyday life, the greater is the percentage of income that goes to pay for food and other basic necessities, and the greater is the likelihood of crime victimization.[26] Class can accurately predict chances for both survival and success.

Class and Educational Attainment

School performance (grades and test scores) and educational attainment (level of schooling completed) also correlate strongly with economic class. Furthermore, despite some efforts to make testing fairer and schooling more accessible, current data suggests that the level of inequity is staying the same or getting worse.

In his study for the Carnegie Council on Children nearly thirty years ago, Richard De Lone examined the test scores of over half a million students who took the College Board exams (SATs). His findings were consistent with earlier studies that showed a relationship between class and scores on standardized tests; his conclusion: "the higher the student's social status, the higher the probability that he or she will get higher grades."[27] Almost thirty years after the release of the Carnegie report, College Board surveys reveal data that are no different: test scores still correlate strongly with family income.

Average Combined Score by Income
(400 to 1600 scale)[28]

Family Income	Median Score
More than $100,000	1119
$80,000 to $100,000	1063
$70,000 to $80,000	1039
$60,000 to $70,000	1026
$50,000 to $60,000	1014
$40,000 to $50,000	996
$30,000 to $40,000	967
$20,000 to $30,000	937
$10,000 to $20,000	906
less than $10,000	884

These figures are based on the test results of 987,584 SAT takers in 2005.

A little more than thirty years ago, researcher William Sewell showed a positive correlation between class and overall educational achievement. In comparing the top quartile (25 percent) of his sample to the bottom quartile, he found that students from upper-class families were twice as likely to obtain training beyond high school and four times as likely to attain a postgraduate degree. Sewell concluded: "Socioeconomic background...operates independently of academic ability at every stage in the process of educational attainment."[29]

Today, the pattern persists. There are, however, two significant changes. On the one hand, the odds of getting into college have improved for the bottom quartile of the population, although they still remain relatively low compared to the top. On the other hand, the chances of completing a college degree have deteriorated markedly for the bottom quartile. Researchers estimate the chances of completing a four-year college degree (by age 24) to be nineteen times as great for the top 25 percent of the population as it is for the bottom 25 percent.[30]

Reality 5: Class standing has a significant impact on chances for educational achievement.

Class standing, and consequently life chances, are largely determined at birth. Although examples of individuals who have gone from rags to riches abound in the mass media, statistics on class mobility show these leaps to be extremely rare. In fact, dramatic advances in class standing are relatively infrequent. One study showed that fewer than one in five men surpass the economic status of their fathers.[31] For those whose annual income is in six figures, economic success is due in large part to the wealth and privileges bestowed on them at birth. Over 66 percent of the consumer units with incomes of $100,000 or more have inherited assets. Of these units, over 86 percent reported that inheritances constituted a substantial portion of their total assets.[32]

Economist Harold Wachtel likens inheritance to a series of Monopoly games in which the winner of the first game refuses to relinquish his or her cash and commercial property for the second game. "After all," argues the winner, "I accumulated my wealth and income by my own wits." With such an arrangement, it is not difficult to predict the outcome of subsequent games.[33]

Reality 6: All Americans do not have an equal opportunity to succeed. Inheritance laws ensure a greater likelihood of success for the offspring of the wealthy.

Spheres of Power and Oppression

50   When we look at society and try to determine what it is that keeps most people down—what holds them back from realizing their potential as healthy, creative, productive individuals—we find institutional forces that are largely beyond individual control. Class domination is one of these forces. People do not choose to be poor or working class; instead, they are limited and confined by the opportunities afforded or denied them by a social and economic system. The class structure in the United States is a function of its economic system: capitalism, a system that is based on private rather than public ownership and control of commercial enterprises. Under capitalism, these enterprises are governed by the need to produce a profit for the owners, rather

than to fulfill societal needs. Class divisions arise from the differences between those who own and control corporate enterprise and those who do not.

Racial and gender domination are other forces that hold people down. Although there are significant differences in the way capitalism, racism, and sexism affect our lives, there are also a multitude of parallels. And although class, race, and gender act independently of each other, they are at the same time very much interrelated.

On the one hand, issues of race and gender cut across class lines. Women experience the effects of sexism whether they are well-paid professionals or poorly paid clerks. As women, they are not only subjected to catcalls and stereotyping, but face discrimination and are denied opportunities and privileges that men have. Similarly, a wealthy black man faces racial oppression, is subjected to racial slurs, and is denied opportunities because of his color. Regardless of their class standing, women and members of minority races are constantly dealing with institutional forces that are holding them down precisely because of their gender, the color of their skin, or both.

On the other hand, the experiences of women and minorities are differentiated along class lines. Although they are in subordinate positions vis-à-vis white men, the particular issues that confront women and people of color may be quite different depending on their position in the class structure.

Power is incremental, and class privileges can accrue to individual women and to individual members of a racial minority. While power is incremental, oppression is cumulative, and those who are poor, black, and female are often subject to all of the forces of class, race, and gender discrimination simultaneously. This cumulative situation is what is meant by the double and triple jeopardy of women and minorities.

Furthermore, oppression in one sphere is related to the likelihood 55 of oppression in another. If you are black and female, for example, you are much more likely to be poor or working class than you would be as a white male. Census figures show that the incidence of poverty varies greatly by race and gender.

Chances of Being Poor in America[34]

White male/ female	White female head*	Hispanic male/ female	Hispanic female head*	Black male/ female	Black female head*
1 in 10	1 in 5	1 in 5	1 in 3	1 in 4	1 in 3

*Persons in families with female householder, no husband present.

In other words, being female and being nonwhite are attributes in our society that increase the chances of poverty and of lower-class standing.

Reality 7: Racism and sexism significantly compound the effects of class in society.

None of this makes for a very pretty picture of our country. Despite what we like to think about ourselves as a nation, the truth is that opportunity for success and life itself are highly circumscribed by our race, our gender, and the class we are born into. As individuals, we feel hurt and anger when someone is treating us unfairly; yet as a society we tolerate unconscionable injustice. A more just society will require a radical redistribution of wealth and power. We can start by reversing the current trends that further polarize us as a people and adapt policies and practices that narrow the gaps in income, wealth, and privilege.

End Notes

1. See Jay McLeod, *Ain't No Makin' It: Aspirations and Attainment in a Lower-Income Neighborhood* (Boulder, CO: Westview Press, 1995); Benjamin DeMott, *The Imperial Middle* (New York: Morrow, 1990); Ira Katznelson, *City Trenches: Urban Politics and Patterning of Class in the United States* (New York: Pantheon Books, 1981); Charles W. Tucker, "A Comparative Analysis of Subjective Social Class: 1945-1963," *Social Forces*, no. 46, June 1968, pp. 508-514; Robert Nisbet, "The Decline and Fall of Social Class," *Pacific Sociological Review*, vol. 2, Spring 1959, pp. 11-17; and Oscar Glantz, "Class Consciousness and Political Solidarity," *American Sociological Review*, vol. 23, August 1958, pp. 375-382.

2. Susan Ostrander, "Upper-Class Women: Class Consciousness as Conduct and Meaning," in G. William Domhoff, *Power Structure Research* (Beverly Hills, CA: Sage Publications, 1980), pp. 78-79. Also see Stephen Birmingham, *America's Secret Aristocracy* (Boston: Little Brown, 1987).

3. Lawrence Mishel, Jared Bernstein, and Sylvia Allegretto, *The State of Working America: 2004-2005* (Ithaca: ILR Press, Cornell University Press, 2005), p. 282.

4. The number of individuals filing tax returns showing a gross adjusted income of $1 million or more in 2003 was 182,932 (Tax Stats at a Glance, Internal Revenue Service, U.S. Treasury Department, available at http://www.irs.gov/taxstats/ article/0,,id=102886,00.html).

5. Carmen DeNavas-Walt, Bernadette D. Proctor, and Cheryl Hill Lee, U.S. Census Bureau, Current Population Reports, P60-229, *Income, Poverty, and Health Insurance in the United States: 2004* (Washington, DC: U.S. Government Printing Office, 2005), pp. 9, 45.

6. National Coalition for the Homeless "How many people experience homelessness?" NCH Fact Sheet #2 (June 2006), citing a 2004 National Law Center on Homelessness and Poverty Study. Available at http://www.nationalhomeless.org/publications/facts/How_Many.pdf.

7. Mishel et al., op. cit., pp. 318-319.

8. Lawrence Mishel, Jared Bernstein, and Heather Boushey, *The State of Working America: 2002-2003* (Ithaca: ILR Press, Cornell University Press, 2003), p. 53.

9. Paul Krugman, "Left Behind Economics" *New York Times*, July 14, 2006.

10. Based on a comparison of 19 industrialized states: Mishel et al., *2004-2005*, pp. 399-401.

11. Mishel et al., ibid, p. 64.

12. Derived from Mishel et al., *2002-2003*, p. 281.

13. Mishel et al., *2004-2005*, ibid, pp. 62-63.

14. Mishel et al., *2002-2003*, ibid, p. 70.

15. Mishel et al., ibid, p. 280.

16. Alan Blinder, quoted by Paul Krugman, in "Disparity and Despair," *U.S. News and World Report*, March 23, 1992, p. 54.

17. Paul Samuelson, *Economics,* 10th ed. (New York: McGraw-Hill, 1976), p. 84.

18. DeNavas-Walt et al., op. cit., p. 9.

19. Michael Harrington, *The Other America* (New York: MacMillan, 1962), pp. 12-13.

20. Stuart Ewen and Elizabeth Ewen, *Channels of Desire: Mass Images and the Shaping of American Consciousness* (New York: McGraw-Hill, 1982).

21. Andrew Ross, *No-Collar: The Humane Work Place and Its Hidden Costs* (New York: Basic Books, 2002).

22. Based on a poverty threshold for a three-person household in 2004 of $15,205. DeNavas-Walt et al., op. cit., p. 45.

23. The median income in 2004 was $40,798 for men, $31,223 for women, and $44,389 for households. DeNavas-Walt et al., op. cit., pp. 3-5.

24. E. Pamuk, D. Makuc, K. Heck, C. Reuben, and K. Lochner, *Socioeconomic Status and Health Chartbook, Health, United States, 1998* (Hyattsville, MD: National Center for Health Statistics, 1998), pp. 145-159; Vincente Navarro "Class, Race, and Health Care in the United States," in Bersh Berberoglu, *Critical Perspectives in Sociology,* 2nd ed. (Dubuque, IA: Kendall/Hunt, 1993), pp. 148-156; Melvin Krasner, *Poverty and Health in New York City* (New York: United Hospital Fund of New York, 1989). See also U.S. Dept. of Health and Human Services, *Health Status of Minorities and Low Income Groups,* 1985; and Dan Hughes, Kay Johnson, Sara Rosenbaum, Elizabeth Butler, and Janet Simons, *The Health of America's Children* (The Children's Defense Fund, 1988).

25. E. Pamuk et al., op. cit.; Kenneth Neubeck and Davita Glassberg, *Sociology: A Critical Approach* (New York: McGraw-Hill, 1996), pp. 436-438; Aaron Antonovsky, "Social Class, Life Expectancy, and Overall Mortality," in *The Impact of Social Class* (New York: Thomas Crowell, 1972), pp. 467-491. See also Harriet Duleep, "Measuring the Effect of Income on Adult Mortality Using Longitudinal Administrative Record Data," *Journal of Human Resources,* vol. 21, no. 2, Spring 1986. See also Paul Farmer, *Pathologies of Power: Health, Human Rights, and the New War on the Poor,* (Berkeley: University of California Press, 2005).

26. E. Pamuk et al., op. cit., fig. 20; Dennis W. Roncek, "Dangerous Places: Crime and Residential Environment," *Social Forces,* vol. 60, no. 1, September 1981, pp. 74-96.

27. Richard De Lone, *Small Futures* (New York: Harcourt Brace Jovanovich, 1978), pp. 14-19.

28. Derived from "2005 College-Bound Seniors, Total Group Profile," *College Board*, p. 7, available at http://www.collegeboard.com/prod_downloads/about/ news_info/cbsenior/yr2005/2005-college-bound-seniors.pdf.

29. William H. Sewell, "Inequality of Opportunity for Higher Education," *American Sociological Review*, vol. 36, no. 5, 1971, pp. 793-809.

30. The Mortenson Report on Public Policy Analysis of Opportunity for Postsecondary Education, "Postsecondary Education Opportunity" (Iowa City, IA: September 1993, no. 16).

31. De Lone, op. cit., pp. 14-19.

32. Howard Tuchman, *Economics of the Rich* (New York: Random House, 1973), p. 15. For more information on inheritance see, Sam Bowles and Herbert Gintis, "The Inheritance of Inequality," *The Journal of Economic Perspectives*, vol. 16, no. 3 (summer, 2002) pp. 2-30 and Tom Hertz, *Understanding Mobility in America*, Center for American Progress, http://www.americanprogress.org/site/ pp.asp?c=biJRJ8OVF&b=1579981.

33. Howard Wachtel, *Labor and the Economy* (Orlando, FL: Academic Press, 1984), pp. 161-162.

34. Derived from DeNavas-Walt et al., op. cit., pp. 46-51.

❖

THE HUMAN COST OF AN ILLITERATE SOCIETY

Jonathan Kozol

JONATHAN KOZOL (1936-)

A native of Boston, Jonathan Kozol graduated from Harvard University in 1958 with a B.A. in English literature. After a period spent in Paris to focus on writing, Kozol became a teacher in the Boston and neighboring Newton public school systems. His first book, *Death at an Early Age* (1967), which recounts his first year as a teacher, won a National Book Award. Other award-winning works include *Savage Inequalities: Children in America's Schools* (1991) and *Amazing Grace: The Lives of Children and the Conscience of a Nation* (1995). Kozol is the founder of the Cambridge Institute for Public Education and Education Action! which organizes and supports teachers working in underfunded schools. Kozol's most recent book is Letters to a Young Teacher (2007).

PRECAUTIONS. READ BEFORE USING.

Poison: Contains sodium hydroxide (caustic soda-lye).

Corrosive: Causes severe eye and skin damage, may cause blindness. Harmful or fatal if swallowed.

If swallowed, give large quantities of milk or water.

Do not induce vomiting.

Important: Keep water out of can at all times to prevent contents from violently erupting...

—warning on a can of Drano

1 Questions of literacy, in Socrates' belief, must at length be judged as matters of morality. Socrates could not have had in mind the moral compromise peculiar to a nation like our own. Some of our Founding Fathers did, however, have this question in their minds. One of the wisest of the Founding Fathers (one who may not have been most

compassionate but surely was more prescient than some of his peers) recognized the special dangers that illiteracy would pose to basic equity in the political construction that he helped to shape.

"A people who mean to be their own governors," James Madison wrote, "must arm themselves with the power knowledge gives. A popular government without popular information or the means of acquiring it, is but a prologue to a farce or a tragedy, or perhaps both."

Tragedy looms larger than farce in the United States today. Illiterate citizens seldom vote. Those who do are forced to cast a vote of questionable worth. They cannot make informed decisions based on serious print information. Sometimes they can be alerted to their interests by aggressive voter education. More frequently, they vote for a face, a smile, or a style, not for a mind or character or body of beliefs.

The number of illiterate adults exceeds by 16 million the entire vote cast for the winner in the 1980 presidential contest. If even one third of all illiterates could vote, and read enough and do sufficient math to vote in their self-interest, Ronald Reagan would not likely have been chosen president. There is, of course, no way to know for sure. We do know this: Democracy is a mendacious term when used by those who are prepared to countenance the forced exclusion of one third of our electorate. So long as 60 million people are denied significant participation, the government is neither of, nor for, nor by, the people. It is a government, at best, of those two thirds whose wealth, skin color, or parental privilege allows them opportunity to profit from the provocation and instruction of the written word.

The undermining of democracy in the United States is one   5
"expense" that sensitive Americans can easily deplore because it represents a contradiction that endangers citizens of all political positions. The human price is not so obvious at first.

Since I first immersed myself within this work I have often had the following dream: I find that I am in a railroad station or a large department store within a city that is utterly unknown to me and where I cannot understand the printed words. None of the signs or symbols is familiar. Everything looks strange: like mirror writing of some kind. Gradually I understand that I am in the Soviet Union. All the letters on the walls around me are Cyrillic. I look for my pocket dictionary but I find that it has been mislaid. Where have I left it? Then I recall that I forgot to bring it with me when I packed my bags in Boston. I struggle to remember the name of my hotel. I try to ask somebody for directions. One person stops and looks at me in a peculiar way. I lose the nerve to ask. At last I reach into my wallet for an ID card.

The card is missing. Have I lost it? Then I remember that my card was confiscated for some reason, many years before. Around this point, I wake up in a panic.

This panic is not so different from the misery that millions of adult illiterates experience each day within the course of their routine existence in the U.S.A.

Illiterates cannot read the menu in a restaurant.

They cannot read the cost of items on the menu in the *window* of the restaurant before they enter.

10   Illiterates cannot read the letters that their children bring home from their teachers. They cannot study school department circulars that tell them of the courses that their children must be taking if they hope to pass the SAT exams. They cannot help with homework. They cannot write a letter to the teacher. They are afraid to visit in the classroom. They do not want to humiliate their child or themselves.

Illiterates cannot read instructions on a bottle of prescription medicine. They cannot find out when a medicine is past the year of safe consumption; nor can they read of allergenic risks, warnings to diabetics, or the potential sedative effect of certain kinds of nonprescription pills. They cannot observe preventive health care admonitions. They cannot read about "the seven warning signs of cancer" or the indications of blood-sugar fluctuations or the risks of eating certain foods that aggravate the likelihood of cardiac arrest.

Illiterates live, in more than literal ways, an uninsured existence. They cannot understand the written details on a health insurance form. They cannot read the waivers that they sign preceding surgical procedures. Several women I have known in Boston have entered a slum hospital with the intention of obtaining a tubal ligation and have emerged a few days later having been subjected to a hysterectomy. Unaware of their rights, incognizant of jargon, intimidated by the unfamiliar air of fear and atmosphere of ether that so many of us find oppressive in the confines even of the most attractive and expensive medical facilities, they have signed their names to documents they could not read and which nobody, in the hectic situation that prevails so often in those overcrowded hospitals that serve the urban poor, had even bothered to explain.

Childbirth might seem to be the last inalienable right of any female citizen within a civilized society. Illiterate mothers, as we shall see, already have been cheated of the power to protect their progeny against the likelihood of demolition in deficient public schools and, as a result, against the verbal servitude within which they themselves exist. Surgical denial of the right to bear that child in the first place represents an ultimate denial, an unspeakable metaphor, a final darkness that denies even the twilight gleamings of our own humanity. What greater violation of our biological, our biblical, our spiritual humanity could possibly exist than that which takes place nightly, perhaps hourly these days, within such over-burdened and benighted institutions as the Boston City Hospital? Illiteracy has many costs; few are so irreversible as this.

Even the roof above one's head, the gas or other fuel for heating that protects the residents of northern city slums against the threat of illness in the winter months become uncertain guarantees. Illiterates cannot read the lease that they must sign to live in an apartment which, too often, they cannot afford. They cannot manage check accounts and therefore seldom pay for anything by mail. Hours and entire days of difficult travel (and the cost of bus or other public transit) must be added to the real cost of whatever they consume. Loss of interest on the check accounts they do not have, and could not manage if they did, must be regarded as another of the excess costs paid by the citizen who is excluded from the common instruments of commerce in a numerate society.

"I couldn't understand the bills," a woman in Washington, D.C., 15 reports, "and then I couldn't write the checks to pay them. We signed things we didn't know what they were."

Illiterates cannot read the notices that they receive from welfare offices or from the IRS. They must depend on word-of-mouth instruction from the welfare worker—or from other persons whom they have good reason to mistrust. They do not know what rights they have, what deadlines and requirements they face, what options they might choose to exercise. They are half-citizens. Their rights exist in print but not in fact.

Illiterates cannot look up numbers in a telephone directory. Even if they can find the names of friends, few possess the sorting skills to make use of the yellow pages; categories are bewildering and trade names are beyond decoding capabilities for millions of nonreaders. Even the emergency numbers listed on the first page of the phone book—"Ambulance," "Police," and "Fire"—are too frequently beyond the recognition of nonreaders.

Many illiterates cannot read the admonition on a pack of cigarettes. Neither the Surgeon General's warning nor its reproduction on the package can alert them to the risks. Although most people learn by word of mouth that smoking is related to a number of grave physical disorders, they do not get the chance to read the detailed stories which can document this danger with the vividness that turns concern into determination to resist. They can see the handsome cowboy or the slim Virginia lady lighting up a filter cigarette; they cannot heed the words that tell them that this product is (not "may be") dangerous to their health. Sixty million men and women are condemned to be the unalerted, high-risk candidates for cancer.

Illiterates do not buy "no-name" products in the supermarkets. They must depend on photographs or the familiar logos that are printed on the packages of brand-name groceries. The poorest people, therefore, are denied the benefits of the least costly products.

20   Illiterates depend almost entirely upon label recognition. Many labels, however, are not easy to distinguish. Dozens of different kinds of Campbell's soup appear identical to the nonreaders. The purchaser who cannot read and does not dare to ask for help, out of the fear of being stigmatized (a fear which is unfortunately realistic), frequently comes home with something which she never wanted and her family never tasted.

Illiterates cannot read instructions on a pack of frozen food. Packages sometimes provide an illustration to explain the cooking preparations; but illustrations are of little help to someone who must "boil water, drop the food—*within* its plastic wrapper—in the boiling water, wait for it to simmer, instantly remove."

Even when labels are seemingly clear, they may be easily mistaken. A woman in Detroit brought home a gallon of Crisco for her children's dinner. She thought that she had bought the chicken that was pictured on the label. She had enough Crisco now to last a year—but no more money to go back and buy the food for dinner.

Recipes provided on the packages of certain staples sometimes tempt a semiliterate person to prepare a meal her children have not tasted. The longing to vary the uniform and often starchy content of low-budget meals provided to the family that relies on food stamps commonly leads to ruinous results. Scarce funds have been wasted and the food must be thrown out. The same applies to distribution of food-surplus produce in emergency conditions. Government inducements to poor people to "explore the ways" by which to make a tasty meal from tasteless noodles, surplus cheese, and powdered milk are useless to nonreaders. Intended as benevolent advice, such recommendations mock reality and foster deeper feelings of resentment and of inability to cope. (Those, on the other hand, who cautiously refrain from "innovative" recipes in preparation of their children's meals must suffer the opprobrium of "laziness," "lack of imagination....")

Illiterates cannot travel freely. When they attempt to do so, they encounter risks that few of us can dream of. They cannot read traffic signs and, while they often learn to recognize and to decipher symbols, they cannot manage street names which they haven't seen before. The same is true for bus and subway stops. While ingenuity can sometimes help a man or woman to discern directions from familiar landmarks, buildings, cemeteries, churches, and the like, most illiterates are virtually immobilized. They seldom wander past the streets and neighborhoods they know. Geographical paralysis becomes a bitter metaphor for their entire existence. They are immobilized in almost every sense we can imagine. They can't move up. They can't move out. They cannot see beyond. Illiterates may take an oral test for drivers' permits in most sections of America. It is a questionable concession. Where will they go? How will they get there? How will they get home? Could it be that some of us might like it better if they stayed where they belong?

Travel is only one of many instances of circumscribed existence.   25
Choice, in almost all of its facets, is diminished in the life of an illiterate adult. Even the printed TV schedule, which provides most people with the luxury of preselection, does not belong with the arsenal of options in illiterate existence. One consequence is that the viewer watches only what appears at moments when he happens to have time to turn the switch. Another consequence, a lot more common, is that the TV set remains in operation night and day. Whatever the program offered at the hour when he walks into the room will be the nutriment that he accepts and swallows. Thus, to passivity, is added frequency—indeed, almost uninterrupted continuity. Freedom to select is no more possible here than in the choice of home or surgery or food.

"You don't choose," said one illiterate woman. "You take your wishes from somebody else." Whether in perusal of a menu, selection of highways, purchase of groceries, or determination of affordable enjoyment, illiterate Americans must trust somebody else: a friend, a relative, a stranger on the street, a grocery clerk, a TV copywriter.

"All of our mail we get, it's hard for her to read. Settin' down and writing a letter, she can't do it. Like if we get a bill...we take it over to my sister-in-law...My sister-in-law reads it."

Billing agencies harass poor people for the payment of the bills for purchases that might have taken place six months before. Utility companies offer an agreement for a staggered payment schedule on a bill past due. "You have to trust them," one man said. Precisely for this reason, you end up by trusting no one and suspecting everyone of possible deceit. A submerged sense of distrust becomes the corollary to a constant need to trust. "They are cheating me...I have been tricked...I do not know..."

Not knowing: This is a familiar theme. Not knowing the right word for the right thing at the right time is one form of subjugation. Not knowing the world that lies concealed behind those words is a more terrifying feeling. The longitude and latitude of one's existence are beyond all easy apprehension. Even the hard, cold stars within the firmament above one's head begin to mock the possibilities for self-location. Where am I? Where did I come from? Where will I go?

30   "I've lost a lot of jobs," one man explains. "Today, even if you're a janitor, there's still reading and writing...They leave a note saying, 'Go to room so-and-so...' You can't do it. You can't read it. You don't know."

"The hardest thing about it is that I've been places where I didn't know where I was. You don't know where you are...You're lost."

"Like I said: I have two kids. What do I do if one of my kids starts choking? I go running to the phone...I can't look up the hospital phone number. That's if we're at home. Out on the street, I can't read the sign. I get to a pay phone. 'Okay, tell us where you are. We'll send an ambulance.' I look at the street sign. Right there, I can't tell you what it says. I'd have to spell it out, letter for letter. By that time, one of my kids would be dead...These are the kinds of fears you go with, every single day..."

"Reading directions, I suffer with. I work with chemicals...That's scary to begin with..."

"You sit down. They throw the menu in front of you. Where do you go from there? Nine times out of ten you say, 'Go ahead. Pick out something for the both of us.' I've eaten some weird things, let me tell you!"

35   Menus. Chemicals. A child choking while his mother searches for a word she does not know to find assistance that will come too late. Another mother speaks about the inability to help out her kids to read: "I can't read to them. Of course that's leaving them out of something they should have. Oh, it matters. You believe it matters! I ordered all these books. The kids belong to a book club. Donny wanted me to read a book to him. I told Donny: 'I can't read.' He said: 'Mommy, you sit down. I'll read it to you.' I tried it one day, reading from the

pictures. Donny looked at me. He said, 'Mommy, that's not right.' He's only five. He knew I couldn't read…"

A landlord tells a woman that her lease allows him to evict her if her baby cries and causes inconvenience to her neighbors. The consequence of challenging his words conveys a danger which appears, unlikely as it seems, even more alarming than the danger of eviction. Once she admits that she can't read, in the desire to maneuver for the time in which to call a friend, she will have defined herself in terms of an explicit impotence that she cannot endure. Capitulation in this case is preferable to self-humiliation. Resisting the definition of oneself in terms of what one cannot do, what others take for granted, represents a need so great that other imperatives (even one so urgent as the need to keep one's home in winter's cold) evaporate and fall away in face of fear. Even the loss of home and shelter, in this case, is not so terrifying as the loss of self.

"I come out of school. I was sixteen. They had their meetings. The directors meet. They said that I was wasting their school paper. I was wasting pencils…"

Another illiterate, looking back, believes she was not worthy of her teacher's time. She believes that it was wrong of her to take up space within her school. She believes that it was right to leave in order that somebody more deserving could receive her place.

Children choke. Their mother chokes another way: on more than chicken bones.

People eat what others order, know what others tell them, struggle   40 not to see themselves as they believe the world perceives them. A man in California speaks about his own loss of identity, of self-location, definition:

"I stood at the bottom of the ramp. My car had broke down on the freeway. There was a phone. I asked for the police. They was nice. They said to tell them where I was. I looked up at the signs. There was one that I had seen before. I read it to them: ONE WAY STREET. They thought it was a joke. I told them I couldn't read. There was other signs above the ramp. They told me to try. I looked around for somebody to help. All the cars was going by real fast. I couldn't make them understand that I was lost. The cop was nice. He told me: 'Try once more,' I did my best. I couldn't read. I only knew the sign above my head. The cop was trying to be nice. He knew that I was trapped. 'I can't send out a car to you if you can't tell me where you are.' I felt afraid. I nearly cried. I'm forty-eight years old. I only said: 'I'm on a one-way street…'"

The legal problems and the courtroom complications that confront illiterate adults have been discussed above. The anguish that may underlie such matters was brought home to me this year while I was working on this book. I have spoken, in the introduction, of a sudden phone call from one of my former students, now in prison for a criminal offense. Stephen is not a boy today. He is twenty-eight years old. He called to ask me to assist him in his trial, which comes up next fall. He will be on trial for murder. He has just knifed and killed a man who first enticed him to his home, then cheated him, and then insulted him—as "an illiterate subhuman."

Stephen now faces twenty years to life. Stephen's mother was illiterate. His grandparents were illiterate as well. What parental curse did not destroy was killed off finally by the schools. Silent violence is repaid with interest. It will cost us $25,000 yearly to maintain this broken soul in prison. But what is the price that has been paid by Stephen's victim? What is the price that will be paid by Stephen?

Perhaps we might slow down a moment here and look at the realities described above. This is the nation that we live in. This is a society that most of us did not create but which our President and other leaders have been willing to sustain by virtue of malign neglect. Do we possess the character and courage to address a problem which so many nations, poorer than our own, have found it natural to correct?

45   The answers to these questions represent a reasonable test of our belief in the democracy to which we have been asked in public school to swear allegiance.

◈

AMBIVALENT COMMUNITIES: HOW AMERICANS UNDERSTAND THEIR LOCALITIES

Claude S. Fischer

+

CLAUDE S. FISCHER (1948-)

Born in Paris, France Claude S. Fischer moved with his family to the United States at the age of four in 1952. He obtained a B.A. in sociology from UCLA in 1968, and subsequently received both his M.A. and Ph.D. in sociology from Harvard University. Fischer joined the faculty of the University of California, Berkeley in 1972. His scholarly work, including books such as *To Dwell Among Friends* (1982) and *America Calling* (1992), has focused primarily on social networks and urban sociology. Fischer was also the founding editor of Contexts, the American Sociological Association's magazine aimed at a general readership, where he also served as executive editor until 2004. In 1996, he received the Robert and Helen Lind Award from the American Sociological Association, honoring his lifetime achievement contribution to community and urban sociology. Fischer's most recent work is *Made in America: A Social History of American Culture and Character* (2010).

Americans of the Left and of the Right esteem the local community. [1] It rests in the pantheon of American civil religion paradoxically close to that supreme value, individualism. In our ideology, the locality is, following the family, the premier locus for "community," in the fullest sense of solidarity, commitment, and intimacy. Thus, activists of all political hues seek to restore, empower, and mobilize the locality... Over the years, Americans have become more committed, in practical ways, to their localities, even while enjoying access to ever-widening social horizons. This localism has served most individual American families well, but the political role of the locality exacts severe costs to the national community.

Contrasting Visions of Community

Americans' affections for "community" are ironic, for much of American history and ideology undercut traditional local solidarity. Unlike Europe, the United States lacks the feudal experience of closed, corporate communities; its founders resisted hierarchy; marketplace liberalism undergirds its economics and politics; its settlers were linguistically, religiously, and culturally diverse; its people have always been mobile; its once-dominant farmers usually lived in isolated homesteads; and in all, unlike Europe, Americans have been, consensus has it, intensely individualistic.[1]

In spite—or perhaps because—of these conditions, Americans have glorified and sought the local community. From before Tocqueville to beyond Riesman, observers have described us as inveterate joiners, people in quest of fellowship. The quest has been for the locally based association as much as or more than any other. Although American culture esteems the wilderness as an escape from society, as for Thoreau, it simultaneously values the small, rural community as the locus of intimate society, as in Brook Farm. Most Americans believe that small communities preserve morality. Politicians' rhetoric celebrates the virtues of the small, local community. (Recall Geraldine Ferraro's claim in 1984 that her corner of Queens, New York City, was *really* just a small town—like Mondale's Elmore, Minnesota, and Reagan's Dixon, Illinois—and by being that, entitled her to the same halo of grassroots innocence that the others claimed.) And local political autonomy has long been entrenched in strong home rule, dispersed authority, and checks against central government. Americans continue to subscribe to "community ideologies," beliefs about the inherent connection between place and *persona*, theories that where we live partly determines who we are, and most often that the best people are to be found in the smallest, most localized places.

This contradiction between individualism and the pursuit of fellowship has yielded paradoxical forms of "voluntary community" in the United States. The classic old-world village, nowadays viewed through pastel prisms, was a place of constraint. Confined together by barriers of geography, poverty, illness, ignorance, law, prejudice, and custom, most old-world people lived out their lives in a small group, shared a common fate, and knew one another intimately. This familiarity, by the way, did not necessarily mean affection. In contrast, Americans have more typically found their fellowship in voluntary associations, be it clubs, churches, or neighborhoods. They have also joined or left those associations as each individual deemed appropriate.[2] We can see this voluntarism in the American approach to caring for the unfortunate, well expressed in George Bush's "thousand points of light" rhetoric. And so with our neighborhoods. They are, as Morris Janowitz termed them, "communities of limited liability," associations in which we invest our families, wealth, and concern— but we guiltlessly leave them for larger houses, more rewarding jobs, or finer amenities.[3]

With minor exceptions, Americans founded their towns as business   5 ventures. Developers platted the land and advertised its bountiful future. Settlers came and then left in search of a higher standard of living. Indeed, they left in vast numbers, making for a great churning of population in nineteenth-century America, through the big cities and small towns alike. Despite sentiment, then, we have for the most part long treated our residential communities as "easy come, easy go," rather than as social worlds that envelop us.

Is Ours a "Rootless" Society?

How has the connection of Americans to their localities changed over the years? Many believe that ours has become an ever more "rootless" society; sage commentators diagnose "placelessness" as the source of modern America's ills. The facts are more complex. In several ways, Americans have become more "rooted" to their localities, and in several ways, less rooted. To simplify these complexities, I will argue that, in net, several historical changes have *increased* Americans' commitments to their localities, *decreased* their dependence on the locality for sociability, but *increased* their political—and thus, social— significance.

We cannot directly judge how people of earlier periods felt about their localities and compare them to people of today, but we can examine several changes that, logically, should have affected Americans' attachments to place. Several historical changes probably increased how much Americans care about and invest themselves in their localities.

Reduced residential mobility is one such change. Americans are more mobile than other Western peoples, and they have always been highly mobile. But this mobility has been declining. Historians, by comparing lists of town residents from one year to another, have found that Americans in the nineteenth century were at least as geographically mobile and perhaps twice as much so as contemporary Americans. Since World War II, Census Bureau evidence shows the total rate of moving from one house to another generally dropped.... Among those who moved, proportionately more crossed county lines recently, a change attributable to suburbanization and thus implying that these movers remained in the same urban area. The year-to-year fluctuations can be tied to oscillations in the job and housing markets. But the general picture is one of modestly increasing residential *stability*.

In cross-national perspective, however, Americans remain notably more footloose than Europeans, although only a little more so than the other continental Anglophone countries, Canada and Australia.[4] The reasons are probably structural (our many dispersed metropolises), historical (our open-door immigration until 1924), and cultural (our famed individualism). What has probably changed over the years is a modest shift from "push" to "pull" mobility. Some pushes on the nineteenth-century Americans to move—such as land shortages, job losses, disasters, and poverty—weakened in the twentieth century, while pulls—such as retirement communities, climate, college, and job opportunities—expanded.

10   Americans' greater residential stability has probably increased their attachment to their localities. Studies have repeatedly shown that the longer people live in a place the stronger their emotional and social commitments to it.

Another secular change that, in net, probably increased local commitment is the dispersal of the urban population. Despite the popular image of the ever more crowded city, over the last century, American metropolises have been spreading and thinning out. As a result, proportionately more Americans live in suburban single-family houses, located in small, autonomous, suburban municipalities. For about a generation now more Americans have lived in suburbs than in either center cities or non-metropolitan areas. These, low-density housing and suburban governments, in turn, tend to encourage local commitments.

(What about the great migration from farm to city in this century? In that area, one of rural Americans' chronic problems was their difficulty in forming communities—in organizing associations, mobilizing politically, or seeing one another socially. For former homesteaders, the move to town probably increased local involvement.)

A third change, one connected to the growth of urban sprawl, has been the evolution of class-homogeneous neighborhoods. At least until the early streetcar era in the 1880s, all but the affluent lived close to their jobs. The elite had their suburban enclaves but different classes mixed in city neighborhoods, although residents were sometimes well separated by ethnicity. Today, neighborhoods are less segregated by ethnicity—greatly excepting black ghettos—but more finely differentiated by income level. Greater local homogeneity also reinforces neighboring and attachment to the neighborhood.

The great exception of the black ghettos in fact gives emphasis to the general increase in local homogeneity. During the twentieth century, blacks, at least those in the North, became more segregated from whites, even as white ethnic groups, and for that matter Asians and Hispanics, became less segregated from one another. This racial divide has provided to whites neighborhoods devoid of what many find to be the unsettling presence of blacks. It has largely confined blacks, including many in the middle class, to districts with other blacks, including the very poor. Analyses by Douglas Massey and his colleagues suggest that there may have been some small breaches in racial walls recently, but for poor blacks, geographic isolation increased through the 1970s.

A fourth trend is increasing home ownership. Over the century, most American families came to own their homes, with the fastest increase occurring between 1940 and 1960.... The most dramatic change was among the young. In the 1940s the median age of male homeowner was forty-one, but in 1970 it was 28.[5] Home ownership has stagnated in the last fifteen to twenty years of housing inflation and economic doldrums, but remained historically high. (These data do not consider any increase in homelessness.)

Although Americans have long vested their dwellings with important moral qualities—a proper house both reflects and nurtures noble values—in the nineteenth century, Americans did not esteem ownership as they do now. Many middle-class families were content to be renters. The connection between property and propriety apparently arose around the turn of the century, when increasing affordability, suburbanization, and ideologies of domesticity combined to make ownership easier and socially correct. Then, in the twentieth century, rising affluence, new mortgage instruments, government subsidies, tax breaks, and in the 1950s the family boom spurred home ownership to its current levels.

Today, home ownership, preferably of a single, detached house, is the American ideal, despite the financial hurdles involved. In a 1985 poll, for example, 76 percent of respondents agreed that people who do not own their homes are "missing out on an important part of the

American dream."[6] Being a renter is stigmatizing unless the person is in a transitional stage, a young single, or elderly.

Growth in home ownership has slowed and even declined slightly in the late 1980s. A sense of crisis about middle-class housing arose. In historical perspective, still, the decline has been mild. Demographic changes in the last thirty years—aging of the baby-boomers, more divorce, delayed marriage and child rearing—should have led to home ownership sagging much more than it did. The big drop in ownership during the 1980s was precisely among Americans under thirty, who were increasingly putting off marriage and childbearing. Still, income losses, housing speculation, and financing changes strained many families, forcing some to rely on two incomes when they would have preferred one, and pushing some home-seekers out of the market. Other would-be owners turned to condominiums or, in rural areas, mobile homes.[7] The proportion of available housing that is single detached units has dropped since the 1960s.[8] This shift to condos or trailers also contributes to a sense of crisis, since the American dream is so closely tied to the single-family house. Altogether, much of the concern arises from a comparison to the late 1960s, when, with boom times, owning a detached house was easier than now and seemed so normal.

Despite fluctuations owing to changes in demographics and economics, the general increase in home ownership during the twentieth century is unlikely to be soon reversed.

20   These conditions—urban sprawl, segregation, and home ownership—distinguish America from most European societies. David Popenoe credits them for creating a higher level of neighborhood involvement in the United States than he observed in either Sweden or the United Kingdom.[9] Changes in these conditions over the last few generations, along with declining mobility, would all seem to have helped Americans further attach themselves to their neighborhoods and towns. Besides, most Americans have enjoyed increasing freedom of choice in where they live. Freedom can mean lack of commitment and transiency; but it seems here to have made it easier for most people to find and stay in places they most prefer.

Yet, other changes in the twentieth century may have reduced commitment to the locality. One such change has been the increasing separation of home and workplace. Although some commentators have exaggerated the extent to which home and work were entwined in the past—most people in days gone by were *not* independent craftsmen working in their homes—the distance between where people live and where they work expanded, particularly with the coming of streetcars in the 1880s. Working outside one's home area probably detracts not only from the time people spend in the neighborhood but also from their subjective feeling of commitment to it.

A second such change is the increasing participation of married women in the labor force. In 1900, 6 percent of married women worked for pay; by 1987, 56 percent did. (The rates for divorced women, a growing fraction of all women, were much higher.)[10] Though married women's employment has typically been part-time, it does mean that fewer American households have a "traditional" homemaker at home all day, the same homemaker who critically connected the family to the neighborhood.

Third, households shrank. With the virtual disappearance of servants, boarders, and lodgers, with later marriage, more divorce, and fewer children, the size of the median American household shrank from 4.8 people in 1900 to 2.7 in 1987.[11] We can assume that, generally, the fewer people at home, the less attached the household is to the locality.

Thus, in the complex weave of twentieth-century social changes, some drew Americans closer to and some pulled them from their neighborhoods and towns. As it stands, the changes that more tightly bound people to places probably outweighed those that weakened the bonds, and the best estimate is that, contrary to convention, Americans are more "rooted," practically and sentimentally, to their communities than ever before.

The Fate of Local Ties

On another dimension, however, Americans have probably become less rooted to their residential communities: social ties. Although this evidence is also indirect, probably fewer of Americans' relatives, friends, and associates live near them than was true in earlier generations. (I am not referring here to "neighboring," defined as casual interaction with people living nearby. Americans are often "neighborly" but rarely socially close to their neighbors.) In one study, fewer than a third of respondents' important relations were with people living within a five-minute drive. This dispersion was even greater for the middle class. The neighborhood provides proportionately few of middle-class Americans' important ties.

The best guess is that there has been a historical change, that Americans' social ties are today less localized than they were a century ago. The more striking conclusion, however, is that the change may not have been as great as we imagine.

The Place of Place

Peter Rossi has pointed out that "the world has become increasingly cosmopolitan, but the daily lives of most people are contained within local communities."[12] Place still matters. The variations in house prices between and within regions, for example, mock economists' models and futurists' projections that the nation is leveling out into a uniform, placeless realm. How important place will be in the future we can only speculate. Will "cocooning," a media buzzword of the 1980s, typify the next decades, or will there be increasing cosmopolitanism? Much will depend on economic changes and demographic shifts. Unless the economy fails, American wealth should help sustain residential stability and home ownership. As baby-boomers move beyond child rearing and then retire, they will increase geographical mobility, but they will also release more single-family housing for their grandchildren. Spots of inner-city gentrification notwithstanding, the sprawling of the metropolises continues, augmenting suburbanization and "exurbanization" beyond the suburbs. That trend suggests yet more homogeneity, low-density housing, and autonomous political localities.

Most Americans would, in all likelihood, applaud those trends. Raising a family in a detached house, in a homogeneously middle-class, suburban locality, governed by people much like oneself, seems almost ideal. As with other equity issues, even Americans who lack this privilege would preserve it. Experts may criticize localism for its "collective irrationalities" costly to residents themselves—traffic congestion, governmental paralysis, unbalanced growth, domination by business interests, and so on—and for its "externalities" costly to the wider community—ghettoization of the poor, abandonment of the great cities, unjust tax burdens, and so on. No matter. In America, the free pursuit of the private good is the public good. Localism is, as much as ever an instrument to that good.

Herein lies a seeming contradiction: an inconsistency between the locality's communal role and its role as a vehicle for individual interest. American ideologies of community paint the locality, especially the small one, as a site for fellowship, in contrast to the atomism of the wider, especially the urban, world. Many Americans value and enjoy the congeniality of a local community. They often resist that same local community, yet, when it constrains their interests, be they constraints in taxes, behavioral codes, or infringements of private property. Neighborhood organizations, for example, typically awaken when outsiders threaten residents' safety or wealth. Otherwise, the energy that drives them usually rests dormant. Neighborhood groups rarely act as local governments. Other evidence of the priority of the individual comes in negotiations within condominium complexes, where collective needs and rules run up against assertions of home owners' rights. While Americans value the locality as solidarity, it takes second place to individual freedom.

.... The reality is that Americans generally resist government at all   30
levels, but give more grudging preference to local rule by like-minded neighbors as the lesser evil.

National action, piecemeal as it is, also occurs in response to translocal coalitions. That was one lesson, for example, of the Civil Rights struggle, which as movement and as legislation ran roughshod over local autonomy. The environmental movement is a more complex example. In some ways, it too imposed national concerns over local ones, for example, threatening local jobs for old trees or peculiar fish. (In other ways, though, it reinforced the NIMBY pattern of localism, legitimating a "draw up the drawbridge" style of conservatism.) Although local events—Love Canal, for one—dramatized the environmental agenda, the movement's power still appears to rest on coalitions of interests that are translocal.

A strategy to move the nation in a progressive direction would in a similar way involve rethinking the ideology of locality, an ideology really more attuned to privilege than to reform. Thomas Bender has pointed out the dangers of confusing values attached to "community" with the needs of the public, political sphere. To insist, for example, on personal knowledge of political candidates may mean selecting the lesser rather than the better candidate. Or, to cry for "local control" for a community wealthier in needs than in resources may end by perpetuating disadvantage.[13] It is important to look clear-eyed at the consequences of America's localism, not with romanticized nostalgia.

End Notes

1. The notable exceptions to many of these descriptions are the early puritan villages, which only goes to show how atypical they were, their ideological legacy notwithstanding.

2. This pattern is the sort of thing treated by Robert N. Bellah and his colleagues in *Habits of the Heart* (Berkeley and Los Angeles: University of California Press, 1985).

3. Janowitz, M. (1967). *The community press in an urban setting.* (2nd ed). Chicago: University of Chicago Press.

4. Long & Boertlein, *Geographical mobility;* Long, *Migration and residential mobility*, 253-282.

5. Chevan, A. (1989) The growth of home ownership: 1940-1980. *Demography, 26,* 255.

6. *New York Times* (1985, February 28), 17.

7. Chevan, Growth of home ownership; Home Ownership, *New York Times;* Adams, *Housing America.*

8. U.S. Bureau of the Census. (1975). *Historical statistics of the United States, colonial times to 1970.* Washington, DC: Government Printing Office, 639, 683.

9. Popenoe, D. (1985). *Private pleasure, public plight: American metropolitan community life in comparative perspective.* New Brunswick, NJ: Transaction.

10. U.S. Bureau of the Census, *Historical Statistics,* 133; idem., *Statistical Abstract: 1988,* 374.

11. U.S. Bureau of the Census, *Historical Statistics,* 41; idem., *Statistical Abstract: 1988,* 43.

12. Rossi, P. (1972). Community social indicators. In A. Campbell & P.E. Converse (Eds.), *The human meaning of social change* (p. 87). New York: Russell Sage Foundation. Bender, *Community and social change,* chapter 5.

Reprinted from *America at Century's End*, edited by Alan Wolfe (1991), by permission of the University of California.

VII

RESOLUTIONS

THE CRITO

Plato

❖

PLATO (C. 428-347 B.C.)

Plato, the ancient Greek philosopher, writer and mathematician was born
c. 428 B.C. in Athens. He is best known as Socrates' (c. 469 B.C. – 399
B.C.) student and for the series of Socratic dialogues he wrote featuring
his teacher as the central character. These dialogues demonstrate a
style of argument that is now known as the Socratic Method and also
introduce what have become some of the most elemental philosophies
of Western thought. Plato would, in turn, teach another foundational
philosopher: Aristotle. Plato founded the Academy in Athens around
387 B.C., the first large institution of higher learning in the West. Plato
wrote extensively on political philosophy; *The Republic* is his most famous
work on the subject. Some other key writings include *the Apology* and *the
Phaedo* (which follow the trial and death of Socrates); *the Crito* (on the
themes of justice and injustice); and Symposium (on the nature of love).

---

1   *Socrates*: Why have you come at this hour, Crito? It must be
quite early?

Crito: Yes, certainly.

Socrates: What is the exact time?

Crito: The dawn is breaking.

5   *Socrates*: I wonder that the keeper of the prison would let
you in.

Crito: He knows me because I often come, Socrates;
moreover, I have done him a kindness.

Socrates: And are you only just arrived?

Crito: No, I came some time ago.

Socrates: Then why did you sit and say nothing, instead of awakening me at once?

Crito: Why, indeed, Socrates, I myself would rather not have   10
all this sleeplessness and sorrow. But I have been wondering at your peaceful slumbers, and that was the reason why I did not awaken you, because I wanted you to be out of pain. I have always thought you happy in the calmness of your temperament; but never did I see the like of the easy, cheerful way in which you bear this calamity.

Socrates: Why, Crito, when a man has reached my age he ought not to be repining at the prospect of death.

Crito: And yet other old men find themselves in similar misfortunes, and age does not prevent them from repining.

Socrates: That may be. But you have not told me why you come at this early hour.

Crito: I come to bring you a message which is sad and painful; not, as I believe, to yourself but to all of us who are your friends, and saddest of all to me.

Socrates: What! I suppose that the ship has come from Delos, on   15
the arrival of which I am to die?

Crito: No, the ship has not actually arrived, but she will probably be here today, as persons who have come from Sunium tell me that they have left her there; and therefore tomorrow, Socrates, will be the last day of your life.

Socrates: Very well, Crito; if such is the will of God, I am willing; but my belief is that there will be a delay of a day.

Crito: Why do you say this?

Socrates: I will tell you. I am to die on the day after the arrival of the ship.

20   *Crito*: Yes; that is what the authorities say.

Socrates: But I do not think that the ship will be here until tomorrow; this I gather from a vision which I had last night, or rather only just now, when you fortunately allowed me to sleep.

Crito: And what was the nature of the vision?

Socrates: There came to me the likeness of a woman, fair and comely, clothed in white raiment, who called to me and said: O Socrates, *"The third day hence, to Phthia shalt thou go."*

Crito: What a singular dream, Socrates!

25   *Socrates*: There can be no doubt about the meaning, Crito, I think.

Crito: Yes; the meaning is only too clear. But, oh! my beloved Socrates, let me entreat you once more to take my advice and escape. For if you die I shall not only lose a friend who can never be replaced, but there is another evil: people who do not know you and me will believe that I might have saved you if I had been willing to give money, but that I did not care. Now, can there be a worse disgrace than this— that I should be thought to value money more than the life of a friend? For the many will not be persuaded that I wanted you to escape, and that you refused.

Socrates: But why, my dear Crito, should we care about the opinion of the many? Good men, and they are the only persons who are worth considering, will think of these things truly as they happened.

Crito: But do you see, Socrates, that the opinion of the many must be regarded, as is evident in your own case, because they can do the very greatest evil to anyone who has lost their good opinion.

Socrates: I only wish, Crito, that they could; for then they could also do the greatest good, and that would be well. But the truth is, that they can do neither good nor evil: they cannot make a man wise or make him foolish; and whatever they do is the result of chance.

Crito: Well, I will not dispute about that; but please to tell me, 30 Socrates, whether you are not acting out of regard to me and your other friends: Are you not afraid that, if you escape, hence we may get into trouble with the informers for having stolen you away and lose either the whole or a great part of our property; or that even a worse evil may happen to us? Now, if this is your fear, be at ease; for in order to save you, we ought surely to run this or even a greater risk; be persuaded, then, and do as I say.

Socrates: Yes, Crito, that is one fear which you mention, but by no means the only one.

Crito: Fear not. There are persons who at no great cost are willing to save you and bring you out of prison; and as for the informers, you may observe that they are far from being exorbitant in their demands—a little money will satisfy them. My means, which, as I am sure, are ample, are at your service; and if you have a scruple about spending all mine, here are strangers who will give you the use of theirs; and one of them, Simmias the Theban, has brought a sum of money for this very purpose; and Cebes and many others are willing to spend their money too. I say, therefore, do not on that account hesitate about making your escape, and do not say, as you did in the court, that you will have a difficulty in knowing what to do with yourself if you escape. For men will love you in other places to which you may go, and not in Athens only; there are friends of mine in Thessaly, if you like to go to them, who will value and protect you, and no Thessalian will give you any trouble. Nor can I think that you are justified, Socrates, in betraying your own life when you might be saved; this is playing into the hands of your enemies and destroyers; and moreover I should say that you were betraying your children; for you might bring them up and educate them; instead of which you go away and leave them, and they will have to take their chance; and if they do not meet with the usual fate of orphans, there will be small thanks to you. No man should bring children into the world who is unwilling to persevere to the end in their nurture and education. But you are choosing the easier part, as I think, not the better and manlier, which would rather have become one who professes virtue in all his actions, like yourself. And, indeed, I am ashamed not only of you, but of us who are your friends, when I reflect that this entire business of yours will be attributed to our want of courage. The trial need never have come on, or might have been brought to another issue; and the end of all, which is the crowning absurdity, will seem to have been permitted by us, through cowardice and baseness, who might have saved you, as you might have saved yourself, if we had been good for anything (for there was no difficulty in escaping); and we did not see how disgraceful, Socrates, and also miserable all this will be to us as well as to you. Make your mind up then, or rather have your mind already made up, for the time of deliberation is over, and there is only one thing to be done, which must be done, if at all, this very night, and which any delay will render all but impossible; I beseech you therefore, Socrates, to be persuaded by me, and to do as I say.

Socrates: Dear Crito, your zeal is invaluable, if a right one; but if wrong, the greater the zeal the greater the evil; and therefore we ought to consider whether these things shall be done or not. For I am and always have been one of those natures who must be guided by reason, whatever the reason may be which upon reflection appears to me to be the best; and now that this fortune has come upon me, I cannot put away the reasons which I have before given: the principles which I have hitherto honored and revered I still honor, and unless we can find other and better principles on the instant, I am certain not to agree with you; no, not even if the power of the multitude could inflict many more imprisonments, confiscations, deaths, frightening us like children with hobgoblin terrors. But what will be the fairest way of considering the question? Shall I return to your old argument about the opinions of men, some of which are to be regarded, and others, as we were saying, are not to be regarded? Now were we right in maintaining this before I was condemned? And has the argument which was once good now proved to be talk for the sake of talking; in fact an amusement only, and altogether vanity? That is what I want to consider with your help, Crito: whether, under my present circumstances, the argument appears to be in any way different or not; and is to be allowed by me or disallowed. That argument, which, as I believe, is maintained by many who assume to be authorities, was to the effect, as I was saying, that the opinions of some men are to be regarded, and of other men not to be regarded. Now you, Crito, are a disinterested person who are not going to die tomorrow—at least, there is no human probability of this, and you are therefore not liable to be deceived by the circumstances in which you are placed. Tell me, then, whether I am right in saying that some opinions, and the opinions of some men only, are to be valued, and other opinions, and the opinions of other men, are not to be valued. I ask you whether I was right in maintaining this?

Crito: Certainly.

Socrates: The good are to be regarded, and not the bad?   35

Crito: Yes.

Socrates: And the opinions of the wise are good, and the opinions of the unwise are evil?

Crito: Certainly.

Socrates: And what was said about another matter? Was the disciple in gymnastics supposed to attend to the praise and blame and opinion of every man, or of one man only—his physician or trainer, whoever that was?

Crito: Of one man only.   40

Socrates: And he ought to fear the censure and welcome the praise of that one only, and not of the many?

Crito: That is clear.

Socrates: And he ought to live and train, and eat and drink in the way which seems good to his single master who has understanding, rather than according to the opinion of all other men put together?

Crito: True.

Socrates: And if he disobeys and disregards the opinion and   45 approval of the one, and regards the opinion of the many who have no understanding, will he not suffer evil?

Crito: Certainly he will.

Socrates: And what will the evil be, whither tending and what affecting, in the disobedient person?

Crito: Clearly, affecting the body; that is what is destroyed by the evil.

Socrates: Very good; and is not this true, Crito, of other things which we need not separately enumerate? In the matter of just and unjust, fair and foul, good and evil, which are the subjects of our present consultation, ought we to follow the opinion of the many and to fear them; or the opinion of the one man who has understanding, and whom we ought to fear and reverence more than all the rest of the world: and whom deserting we shall destroy and injure that principle in us which may be assumed to be improved by justice and deteriorated by injustice; is there not such a principle?

50   *Crito*: Certainly there is, Socrates.

Socrates: Take a parallel instance; if, acting under the advice of men who have no understanding, we destroy that which is improvable by health and deteriorated by disease—when that has been destroyed, I say, would life be worth having? And that is—the body?

Crito: Yes.

Socrates: Could we live, having an evil and corrupted body?

Crito: Certainly not.

55   *Socrates*: And will life be worth having, if that higher part of man be depraved, which is improved by justice and deteriorated by injustice? Do we suppose that principle, whatever it may be in man, which has to do with justice and injustice, to be inferior to the body?

Crito: Certainly not.

Socrates: More honored, then?

Crito: Far more honored.

Socrates: Then, my friend, we must not regard what the many say of us: but what he, the one man who has understanding of just and unjust, will say, and what the truth will say. And therefore you begin in error when you suggest that we should regard the opinion of the many about just and unjust, good and evil, honorable and dishonorable. Well, someone will say, "But the many can kill us."

Crito: Yes, Socrates; that will clearly be the answer.   60

Socrates: That is true; but still I find with surprise that the old argument is, as I conceive, unshaken as ever. And I should like to know whether I may say the same of another proposition—that not life, but a good life, is to be chiefly valued?

Crito: Yes, that also remains.

Socrates: And a good life is equivalent to a just and honorable one—that holds also?

Crito: Yes, that holds.

Socrates: From these premises I proceed to argue the question   65 whether I ought or ought not to try to escape without the consent of the Athenians: and if I am clearly right in escaping, then I will make the attempt; but if not, I will abstain. The other considerations which you mention, of money and loss of character, and the duty of educating children, are, I fear, only the doctrines of the multitude, who would be as ready to call people to life, if they were able, as they are to put them to death—and with as little reason. But now, since the argument has thus far prevailed, the only question which remains to be considered is, whether we shall do rightly either in escaping or in suffering others to aid in our escape and paying them in money and thanks, or whether we shall not do rightly; and if the latter, then death or any other calamity which may ensue on my remaining here must not be allowed to enter into the calculation.

Crito: I think that you are right, Socrates; how then shall we proceed?

Socrates: Let us consider the matter together, and do you either refute me if you can, and I will be convinced; or else cease, my dear friend, from repeating to me that I ought to escape against the wishes of the Athenians: for I am extremely desirous to be persuaded by you, but not against my own better judgment. And now please to consider my first position, and do your best to answer me.

Crito: I will do my best.

Socrates: Are we to say that we are never intentionally to do wrong, or that in one way we ought and in another way we ought not do wrong, or is doing wrong always evil and dishonorable, as I was just now saying, and as has been already acknowledged by us? Are all our former admissions which were made within a few days to be thrown away? And have we, at our age, been earnestly discoursing with one another all our life long only to discover that we are no better than children? Or are we to rest assured, in spite of the opinion of the many, and in spite of consequences whether better or worse, of the truth of what was then said, that injustice is always an evil and dishonor to him who acts unjustly? Shall we affirm that?

70   **Crito**: Yes.

Socrates: Then we must do no wrong?

Crito: Certainly not.

Socrates: Nor when injured injure in return, as the many imagine; for we must injure no one at all?

Crito: Clearly not.

75   **Socrates**: Again, Crito, may we do evil?

Crito: Surely not, Socrates.

Socrates: And what of doing evil in return for evil, which is the morality of the many—is that just or not?

Crito: Not just.

Socrates: For doing evil to another is the same as injuring him?

80   **Crito**: Very true.

Socrates: Then we ought not to retaliate or render evil for evil to anyone, whatever evil we may have suffered from him. But I would have you consider, Crito, whether you really mean what you are saying. For this opinion has never been held, and never will be held, by any considerable number of persons; and those who are agreed and those who are not agreed upon this point have no common ground, and can only despise one another, when they see how widely they differ. Tell me, then, whether you agree with and assent to my first principle, that neither injury nor retaliation nor warding off evil by evil is ever right. And shall that be the premise of our agreement? Or do you decline and dissent from this? For this has been of old and is still my opinion; but, if you are of another opinion, let me hear what you have to say. If, however, you remain of the same mind as formerly, I will proceed to the next step.

Crito: You may proceed, for I have not changed my mind.

Socrates: Then I will proceed to the next step, which may be put in the form of a question: Ought a man to do what he admits to be right, or ought he to betray the right?

Crito: He ought to do what he thinks right.

Socrates: But if this is true, what is the application? In leaving the   85
prison against the will of the Athenians, do I wrong any? or rather do I not wrong those whom I ought least to wrong? Do I not desert the principles which were acknowledged by us to be just? What do you say?

Crito: I cannot tell, Socrates, for I do not know.

Socrates: Then consider the matter in this way: Imagine that I am about to play truant (you may call the proceeding by any name which you like), and the laws and the government come and interrogate me: "Tell us, Socrates," they say; "what are you about? Are you going by an act of yours to overturn us—the laws and the whole State, as far as in you lies? Do you imagine that a State can subsist and not be overthrown, in which the decisions of law have no power, but are set aside and overthrown by individuals?" What will be our answer, Crito, to these and the like words? Anyone, and especially a clever rhetorician, will have a good deal to urge about the evil of setting aside the law which requires a sentence to be carried out; and we might reply, "Yes; but the State has injured us and given an unjust sentence." Suppose I say that?

Crito: Very good, Socrates.

Socrates: "And was that our agreement with you?" the law would say, "or were you to abide by the sentence of the State?" And if I were to express astonishment at their saying this, the law would probably add: "Answer, Socrates, instead of opening your eyes: you are in the habit of asking and answering questions. Tell us what complaint you have to make against us which justifies you in attempting to destroy us and the State? In the first place did we not bring you into existence? Your father married your mother by our aid and begat you. Say whether you have any objection to urge against those of us who regulate marriage?" None, I should reply. "Or against those of us who regulate the system of nurture and education of children in which you were trained? Were not the laws, who have the charge of this, right in commanding your father to train you in music and gymnastic?" Right, I should reply. "Well, then, since you were brought into the world and nurtured and educated by us, can you deny in the first place that you are our child and slave, as your fathers were before you? And if this is true you are not on equal terms with us; nor can you think that you have a right to do to us what we are doing to you. Would you have any right to strike or revile or do any other evil to a father or to your master, if you had one, when you have been struck or reviled by him, or received some other evil at his hands?—you would not say this? And because we think right to destroy you, do you think that you have any right to destroy us in return, and your country as far as in you lies? And will you, O professor of true virtue, say that you are justified in this? Has a philosopher like you failed to discover that our country is more to be valued and higher and holier far than mother or father or any ancestor, and more to be regarded in the eyes of the gods and of men of understanding? Also to be soothed, and gently and reverently entreated when angry, even more than a father, and if not persuaded, obeyed? And when we are punished by her, whether with imprisonment or stripes, the punishment is to be endured in silence; and if she leads us to wounds or death in battle, thither we follow as is right; neither may anyone yield or retreat or leave his rank, but whether in battle or in a court of law, or in any other place, he must do what his city and his country order him; or he must change their view of what is just: and if he may do no violence to his father or mother, much less may he do violence to his country." What answer shall we make to this, Crito? Do the laws speak truly, or do they not?

Crito: I think that they do.

Socrates: Then the laws will say: "Consider, Socrates, if this is true, that in your present attempt you are going to do us wrong. For, after having brought you into the world, and nurtured and educated you, and given you and every other citizen a share in every good that we had to give, we further proclaim and give the right to every Athenian, that if he does not like us when he has come of age and has seen the ways of the city, and made our acquaintance, he may go where he pleases and take his goods with him; and none of us laws will forbid him or interfere with him. Any of you who does not like us and the city, and who wants to go to a colony or to any other city, may go where he likes, and take his goods with him. But he who has experience of the manner in which we order justice and administer the State, and still remains, has entered into an implied contract that he will do as we command him. And he who disobeys us is, as we maintain, thrice wrong: first, because in disobeying us he is disobeying his parents; secondly, because we are the authors of his education; thirdly, because he has made an agreement with us that he will duly obey our commands; and he neither obeys them nor convinces us that our commands are wrong; and we do not rudely impose them, but give him the alternative of obeying or convincing us; that is what we offer and he does neither. These are the sort of accusations to which, as we were saying, you, Socrates, will be exposed if you accomplish your intentions; you, above all other Athenians." Suppose I ask, why is this? They will justly retort upon me that I above all other men have acknowledged the agreement. "There is clear proof," they will say, "Socrates, that we and the city were not displeasing to you. Of all Athenians you have been the most constant resident in the city, which, as you never leave, you may be supposed to love. For you never went out of the city either to see the games, except once when you went to the Isthmus, or to any other place unless when you were on military service; nor did you travel as other men do. Nor had you any curiosity to know other States or their laws: your affections did not go beyond us and our State; we were your especial favorites, and you acquiesced in our government of you; and this is the State in which you begat your children, which is a proof of your satisfaction. Moreover, you might, if you had liked, have fixed the penalty at banishment in the course of the trial—the State which refuses to let you go now would have let you go then. But you pretended that you preferred death to exile, and that you were not grieved at death. And now you have forgotten these fine sentiments, and pay no respect to us, the laws, of whom you are the destroyer; and are doing what only a miserable slave would do, running away and turning your back upon the compacts and agreements which you made as a citizen. And first of all answer this very question: Are we right in saying that you agreed to be governed according to us in deed, and not in word only? Is that true or not?" How shall we answer that, Crito? Must we not agree?

Crito: There is no help, Socrates.

Socrates: Then will they not say: "You, Socrates, are breaking the covenants and agreements which you made with us at your leisure, not in any haste or under any compulsion or deception, but having had seventy years to think of them, during which time you were at liberty to leave the city, if we were not to your mind, or if our covenants appeared to you to be unfair. You had your choice, and might have gone either to Lacedaemon or Crete, which you often praise for their good government, or to some other Hellenic or foreign State. Whereas you, above all other Athenians, seemed to be so fond of the State, or, in other words, of us her laws (for who would like a State that has no laws?), that you never stirred out of her: the halt, the blind, the maimed, were not more stationary in her than you were. And now you run away and forsake your agreements. Not so, Socrates, if you will take our advice; do not make yourself ridiculous by escaping out of the city.

"For just consider, if you transgress and err in this sort of way, what good will you do, either to yourself or to your friends? That your friends will be driven into exile and deprived of citizenship, or will lose their property, is tolerably certain; and you yourself, if you fly to one of the neighboring cities, as, for example, Thebes or Megara, both of which are well-governed cities, will come to them as an enemy, Socrates, and their government will be against you, and all patriotic citizens will cast an evil eye upon you as a subverter of the laws, and you will confirm in the minds of the judges the justice of their own condemnation of you. For he who is a corrupter of the laws is more than likely to be corrupter of the young and foolish portion of mankind. Will you then flee from well-ordered cities and virtuous men? and is existence worth having on these terms? Or will you go to them without shame, and talk to them, Socrates? And what will you say to them? What you say here about virtue and justice and institutions and laws being the best things among men? Would that be decent of you? Surely not. But if you go away from well-governed States to Crito's friends in Thessaly, where there is great disorder and license, they will be charmed to have the tale of your escape from prison, set off with ludicrous particulars of the manner in which you were wrapped in a goatskin or some other disguise, and metamorphosed as the fashion of runaways is—that is very likely; but will there be no one to remind you that in your old age you violated the most sacred laws from a miserable desire of a little more life? Perhaps not, if you keep them in a good temper; but if they are out of temper you will hear many degrading things; you will live, but how?—as the flatterer of all men, and the servant of all men; and doing what?—eating and drinking in Thessaly, having gone abroad in order that you may get a dinner. And where will be your fine sentiments about justice and virtue then? Say that you wish to live for the sake of your children, that you may bring them up and educate them— will you take them into Thessaly and deprive them of Athenian citizenship? Is that the benefit which you would confer upon them? Or are you under the impression that they will be better cared for and educated here if you are still alive, although absent from them; for that your friends will take care of them? Do you fancy that if you are an inhabitant of Thessaly they will take care of them, and if you are an inhabitant of the other world they will not take care of them? Nay; but if they who call themselves friends are truly friends, they surely will.

"Listen, then, Socrates, to us who have brought you up. Think not   95 of life and children first, and of justice afterwards, but of justice first, that you may be justified before the princes of the world below. For neither will you nor any that belong to you be happier or holier or juster in this life, or happier in another, if you do as Crito bids. Now you depart in innocence, a sufferer and not a doer of evil; a victim, not of the laws, but of men. But if you go forth, returning evil for evil, and injury for injury, breaking the covenants and agreements which you have made with us, and wronging those whom you ought least to wrong, that is to say, yourself, your friends, your country, and us, we shall be angry with you while you live, and our brethren, the laws in the world below, will receive you as an enemy; for they will know that you have done your best to destroy us. Listen, then, to us and not to Crito."

This is the voice which I seem to hear murmuring in my ears, like the sound of the flute in the ears of the mystic; that voice, I say, is humming in my ears, and prevents me from hearing any other. And I know that anything more which you will say will be in vain. Yet speak, if you have anything to say.

Crito: I have nothing to say, Socrates.

Socrates: Then let me follow the intimations of the will of God.

THE ETHIC OF COMPASSION

The Dalai Lama

THE DALAI LAMA (1935-)

The fourteenth Dalai Lama, Tenzin Gyatso, was born Lhamo Dondrub in 1935 to a farming family in the small village of Taktser in the province of Qinghai on the Chinese border. After a succession of omens, in 1937 the two-year-old was determined to be the reincarnation of the thirteenth Dalai Lama, and was taken to Tibet. Here he was educated, and formally enthroned at the age of 15 in 1950. The Dalai Lama fled to India during the Tibetan uprising of 1959, there establishing a Tibetan government in exile at Dharamshala. In the decades since, the Dalai Lama has advocated widely on behalf of Tibet, speaking before the United Nations and the Congressional Human Rights Caucus, and obtaining humanitarian support for the Tibetan people. These efforts contributed to his being honored with the Nobel Peace Prize in 1989. The Dalai Lama has gained international renown for his popular teaching, lecturing, and writing on issues of religion, morality, ethics, and politics. His books include *Freedom in Exile: The Autobiography of the Dalai Lama* (1990), *The Art of Happiness* (1998), *The Universe in a Single Atom: The Convergence of Science and Spirituality* (2006), and most recently, *Beyond Religion: Ethics for a Whole World* (2011).

We noted earlier that all the world's major religions stress the importance   1
of cultivating love and compassion. In the Buddhist philosophical tradition, different levels of attainment are described. At a basic level, compassion (*nying je*) is understood mainly in terms of empathy—our ability to enter into and, to some extent, share others' suffering. But Buddhists—and perhaps others—believe that this can be developed to such a degree that not only does our compassion arise without any effort, but it is unconditional, undifferentiated, and universal in scope. A feeling of intimacy toward all other sentient beings, including of course those who would harm us, is generated, which is likened in the literature to the love a mother has for her only child.

But this sense of equanimity toward all others is not seen as an end in itself. Rather, it is seen as the springboard to a love still greater. Because our capacity for empathy is innate, and because the ability to reason is also an innate faculty, compassion shares the characteristics of consciousness itself. The potential we have to develop it is therefore stable and continuous. It is not a resource which can be used up—as water is used up when we boil it. And though it can be described in terms of activity, it is not like a physical activity which we train for, like jumping, where once we reach a certain height we can go no further. On the contrary, when we enhance our sensitivity toward others' suffering through deliberately opening ourselves up to it, it is believed that we can gradually extend our compassion to the point where the individual feels so moved by even the subtlest suffering of others that they come to have an overwhelming sense of responsibility toward those others. This causes the one who is compassionate to dedicate themselves entirely to helping others overcome both their suffering and the causes of their suffering. In Tibetan, this ultimate level of attainment is called *nying je chenmo,* literally "great compassion."

Now I am not suggesting that each individual must attain these advanced states of spiritual development in order to lead an ethically wholesome life. I have described *nying je chenmo* not because it is a precondition of ethical conduct but rather because I believe that pushing the logic of compassion to the highest level can act as a powerful inspiration. If we can just keep the aspiration to develop *nying je chenmo,* or great compassion, as an ideal, it will naturally have a significant impact on our outlook. Based on the simple recognition that, just as I do, so do all others desire to be happy and not to suffer, it will serve as a constant reminder against selfishness and partiality. It will remind us that if we reserve ethical conduct for those whom we feel close to, the danger is that we will neglect our responsibilities toward those outside this circle. It will remind us that there is little to be gained from being kind and generous because we hope to win something in return. It will remind us that actions motivated by the desire to create a good name for ourselves are still selfish, however much they may appear to be acts of kindness. It will also remind us that there is nothing exceptional about acts of charity toward those we already feel close to. And it will help us to recognize that the bias we naturally feel toward our families and friends is actually a highly unreliable thing on which to base ethical conduct.

Why is this? So long as the individuals in question continue to meet our expectations, all is well. But should they fail to do so, someone we consider a dear friend one day can become our sworn enemy the next. As we saw earlier, we have a tendency to react badly to all who threaten fulfillment of our cherished desires, though they may be our closest relations. For this reason, compassion and mutual respect offer a much more solid basis for our relations with others. This is also true of partnerships. Likewise, if our love for someone is based largely on attraction, whether it be their looks or some other superficial characteristic, our feelings for that person are liable, over time, to evaporate. When they lose the quality we found alluring, or when we find ourselves no longer satisfied by it, the situation can change completely, this despite their being the same person. This is why relationships based purely on attraction are almost always unstable. On the other hand, when we begin to perfect our compassion, neither the other's appearance nor their behavior affects our underlying attitude.

Consider, too, that habitually our feelings toward others depend very much on their circumstances. Most people, when they see someone who is handicapped, feel sympathetic toward that person. But then when they see others who are wealthier, or better educated, or better placed socially, they immediately feel envious and competitive toward them. Our negative feelings prevent us from seeing the sameness of ourselves and all others. We forget that just like us, whether fortunate or unfortunate, distant or near, they desire to be happy and not to suffer.

The struggle is thus to overcome these feelings of partiality. 5 Certainly, developing genuine compassion for our loved ones is the obvious and appropriate place to start. The impact our actions have on our close ones will generally be much greater than on others, and therefore our responsibilities toward them are greater. Yet we need to recognize that, ultimately, there are no grounds for discriminating in their favor. In this sense, we are all in the same position as a doctor confronted by ten patients suffering the same serious illness. They are each equally deserving of treatment. The reader should not suppose that what is being advocated here is a state of detached indifference, however. The further essential challenge, as we begin to extend our compassion toward all others, is to maintain the same level of intimacy as we feel toward those closest to us. In other words, what is being suggested is that we need to strive for even-handedness in our approach toward all others, a level ground into which we can plant the seed of *nying je chenmo*, of great love and compassion.

If we can begin to relate to others on the basis of such equanimity, our compassion will not depend on the fact that so and so is my husband, my wife, my relative, my friend. Rather, a feeling of closeness toward all others can be developed based on the simple recognition that, just like myself, all wish to be happy and to avoid suffering. In other words, we will start to relate to others on the basis of their sentient nature. Again, we can think of this in terms of an ideal, one which it is immensely difficult to attain. But, for myself, I find it one which is profoundly inspiring and helpful.

Let us now consider the role of compassionate love and kind-heartedness in our daily lives. Does the ideal of developing it to the point where it is unconditional mean that we must abandon our own interests entirely? Not at all. In fact, it is the best way of serving them—indeed, it could even be said to constitute the wisest course for fulfilling self-interest. For if it is correct that those qualities such as love, patience, tolerance, and forgiveness are what happiness consists in, and if it is also correct that *nying je*, or compassion, as I have defined it, is both the source and the fruit of these qualities, then the more we are compassionate, the more we provide for our own happiness. Thus, any idea that concern for others, though a noble quality, is a matter for our private lives only, is simply shortsighted. Compassion belongs to every sphere of activity, including, of course, the workplace.

Here, though, I must acknowledge the existence of a perception—shared by many, it seems—that compassion is, if not actually an impediment, at least irrelevant to professional life. Personally, I would argue that not only is it relevant, but that when compassion is lacking, our activities are in danger of becoming destructive. This is because when we ignore the question of the impact our actions have on others' well-being, inevitably we end up hurting them. The ethic of compassion helps provide the necessary foundation and motivation for both restraint and the cultivation of virtue. When we begin to develop a genuine appreciation of the value of compassion, our outlook on others begins automatically to change. This alone can serve as a powerful influence on the conduct of our lives. When, for example, the temptation to deceive others arises, our compassion for them will prevent us from entertaining the idea. And when we realize that our work itself is in danger of being exploited to the detriment of others, compassion will cause us to disengage from it. So to take an imaginary case of a scientist whose research seems likely to be a source of suffering, they will recognize this and act accordingly, even if this means abandoning the project.

I do not deny that genuine problems can arise when we dedicate ourselves to the ideal of compassion. In the case of a scientist who felt unable to continue in the direction their work was taking them, this could have profound consequences both for themselves and for their families. Likewise, those engaged in the caring profession—in medicine, counseling, social work, and so on—or even those looking after someone at home may sometimes become so exhausted by their duties that they feel overwhelmed. Constant exposure to suffering, coupled occasionally with a feeling of being taken for granted, can induce feelings of helplessness and even despair. Or it can happen that individuals may find themselves performing outwardly generous actions merely for the sake of it—simply going through the motions, as it were. Of course this is better than nothing. But when left unchecked, this can lead to insensitivity toward others' suffering. If this starts to happen, it is best to disengage for a short while and make a deliberate effort to reawaken that sensitivity. In this it can be helpful to remember that despair is never a solution. It is, rather, the ultimate failure. Therefore, as the Tibetan expression has it, even if the rope breaks nine times, we must splice it back together a tenth time. In this way, even if ultimately we do fail, at least there will be no feelings of regret. And when we combine this insight with a clear appreciation of our potential to benefit others, we find that we can begin to restore our hope and confidence.

Some people may object to this ideal on the grounds that by 10 entering into others' suffering, we bring suffering on ourselves. To an extent, this is true. But I suggest that there is an important qualitative distinction to be made between experiencing one's own suffering and experiencing suffering in the course of sharing in others'. In the case of one's own suffering, given that it is involuntary, there is a sense of oppression: it seems to come from outside us. By contrast, sharing in someone else's suffering must at some level involve a degree of voluntariness, which itself is indicative of a certain inner strength. For this reason, the disturbance it may cause is considerably less likely to paralyze us than our own suffering.

Of course, even as an ideal, the notion of developing unconditional compassion is daunting. Most people, including myself, must struggle even to reach the point where putting others' interests on a par with our own becomes easy. We should not allow this to put us off, however. And while undoubtedly there will be obstacles on the way to developing a genuinely warm heart, there is the deep consolation of knowing that in doing so we are creating the conditions for our own happiness. As I mentioned earlier, the more we truly desire to benefit others, the greater the strength and confidence we develop and the greater the peace and happiness we experience. If this still seems unlikely, it is worth asking ourselves how else we are to do so. With violence and aggression? Of course not. With money? Perhaps up to a point, but no further. But with love, by sharing in others' suffering, by recognizing ourselves clearly in all others—especially those who are disadvantaged and those whose rights are not respected—by helping them to be happy: yes. Through love, through kindness, through compassion we establish understanding between ourselves and others. This is how we forge unity and harmony.

Compassion and love are not mere luxuries. As the source both of inner and external peace, they are fundamental to the continued survival of our species. On the one hand, they constitute non-violence in action. On the other, they are the source of all spiritual qualities: of forgiveness, tolerance, and all the virtues. Moreover, they are the very thing that gives meaning to our activities and makes them constructive. There is nothing amazing about being highly educated; there is nothing amazing being rich. Only when the individual has a warm heart do these attributes become worthwhile.

So to those who say that the Dalai Lama is being unrealistic in advocating this ideal of unconditional love, I urge them to experiment with it nonetheless. They will discover that when we reach beyond the confines of narrow self-interest, our hearts become filled with strength. Peace and joy become our constant companion. It breaks down barriers of every kind and in the end destroys the notion of my interest as independent from others' interest. But most important, so far as ethics is concerned, where love of one's neighbor, affection, kindness, and compassion live, we find that ethical conduct is automatic. Ethically wholesome actions arise naturally in the context of compassion.

LETTER FROM BIRMINGHAM JAIL

Martin Luther King, Jr.

MARTIN LUTHER KING, JR. (1929-1968)

Martin Luther King, Jr., was born in Atlanta, Georgia in 1929 to the Rev. Martin Luther King, Sr., a Baptist minister, and Alberta Williams King. After skipping two grades in high school, King entered Atlanta's Morehouse College at the age of 15, graduating in 1948 with a B.A. in sociology. He subsequently entered Crozer Theological Seminary in Pennsylvania, receiving a Bachelor of Divinity degree in 1951, and ultimately obtaining a Ph.D. in systemic theology from Boston University in 1955. In this same period King married Coretta Scott, and in 1954 became pastor of Montgomery's Dexter Avenue Baptist Church. King first rose to notice in the civil rights movement for his leadership in the Montgomery Bus Boycott of 1955, during which time he was arrested and faced threats of violence. King then co-founded the Southern Christian Leadership Conference, which organized churches in non-violent methods of civil rights activism. King's visibility as a civil rights activist continued to grow, reaching new heights with his delivery of the "I Have a Dream" speech at the 1963 March on Washington. While in Birmingham, Alabama, to organize a non-violent campaign against segregation in that same year, King was arrested and incarcerated for his planned actions, and it was here that he wrote "Letter from Birmingham Jail." In 1964, King's work was recognized with a Nobel Peace Prize. King's work as a civil rights leader continued throughout the 1960s, seeing both great successes and serious challenges. On April 4, 1968, while in Memphis on a campaign to support black public works employees, King was assassinated. It was his efforts in life, however, that led to the passage of the Civil Rights Act of 1968 just a few days later; so lasting was the importance of his work that he was posthumously awarded both the Presidential Medal of Freedom (1977) and the Congressional Gold Medal (2004). Though better known as an orator, King published a number of books, including 1964's *Why We Can't Wait and The Measure of a Man* (1959) and *Strength to Love* (1963), which collected some of his sermons.

Public Statement by Eight Alabama Clergymen

April 12, 1963

1   We the undersigned clergymen are among those who, in January, issued "An Appeal for Law and Order and Common Sense," in dealing with racial problems in Alabama. We expressed understanding that honest convictions in racial matters could properly be pursued in the courts, but urged that decisions of those courts should in the meantime be peacefully obeyed.

Since that time, there had been some evidence of increased forbearance and willingness to face facts. Responsible citizens have undertaken to work on various problems which cause racial friction and unrest. In Birmingham, recent public events have given indication that we all have opportunity for a new constructive and realistic approach to racial problems.

However, we are now confronted by a series of demonstrations by some of our Negro citizens, directed and led in part by outsiders. We recognize the natural impatience of people who feel that their hopes are slow in being realized. But we are convinced that these demonstrations are unwise and untimely.

We agree rather with certain local Negro leadership which has called for honest and open negotiation of racial issues in our area. And we believe this kind of facing of issues can best be accomplished by citizens of our own metropolitan area, white and Negro, meeting with their knowledge and experience of the local situation. All of us need to face that responsibility and find proper channels for its accomplishment.

5   Just as we formerly pointed out that "hatred and violence have no sanction in our religious and political traditions," we also point out that such actions as incite to hatred and violence, however technically peaceful those actions may be, have not contributed to the resolution of our local problems. We do not believe that these days of new hope are days when extreme measures are justified in Birmingham.

We commend the community as a whole, and the local news media and law enforcement officials in particular, on the calm manner in which these demonstrations have been handled. We urge the public to continue to show restraint should the demonstrations continue, and the law enforcement officials to remain calm and continue to protect our city from violence.

We further strongly urge our own Negro community to withdraw support from these demonstrations, and to unite locally in working peacefully for a better Birmingham. When rights are consistently denied, a cause should be pressed in the courts and in the negotiations among local leaders, and not in the streets. We appeal to both our white and Negro citizenry to observe the principles of law and order and common sense.

Signed by:

C.C.J. Carpenter, D.D., L.L.D., *Bishop of Alabama*

Joseph A. Durick, D.D., *Auxiliary Bishop, Diocese of Mobile, Birmingham*

Rabbi Milton L. Grafman, *Temple Emau-El, Birmingham, Alabama*

Bishop Paul Hardin, *Bishop of the Alabama-West Florida Conference of the Methodist Church*

Bishop Nolan B. Harmon, *Bishop of the North Alabama Conference of the Methodist Church*

George M. Murray, D.D., L.L.D., *Bishop Coadjutor, Episcopal Diocese of Alabama*

Edward V. Ramage, *Moderator, Synod of the Alabama Presbyterian Church in the United States*

Earl Stallings, Pastor, *First Baptist Church, Birmingham, Alabama*

Letter from Birmingham Jail

Martin Luther King, Jr.

April 16, 1963

My Dear Fellow Clergymen:

1   While confined here in the Birmingham City Jail, I came across your recent statement calling our present activities "unwise and untimely." Seldom, if ever, do I pause to answer criticism of my work and ideas. If I sought to answer all the criticisms that cross my desk, my secretaries would be engaged in little else in the course of the day and I would have no time for constructive work. But since I feel that you are men of genuine goodwill and your criticisms are sincerely set forth, I would like to answer your statement in what I hope will be patient and reasonable terms.

I think I should give the reason for my being in Birmingham, since you have been influenced by the argument of "outsiders coming in." I have the honor of serving as president of the Southern Christian Leadership Conference, an organization operating in every Southern state with headquarters in Atlanta, Georgia. We have some eighty-five affiliate organizations all across the South—one being the Alabama Christian Movement for Human Rights. Whenever necessary and possible we share staff, educational, and financial resources with our affiliates. Several months ago our local affiliate here in Birmingham invited us to be on call to engage in a nonviolent direct action program if such were deemed necessary. We readily consented and when the hour came we lived up to our promises. So I am here, along with several members of my staff, because we were invited here. I am here because I have basic organizational ties here.

Beyond this, I am in Birmingham because injustice is here. Just as the eighth century prophets left their little villages and carried their "thus saith the Lord" far beyond the boundaries of their home town, and just as the Apostle Paul left his little village of Tarsus and carried the gospel of Jesus Christ to practically every hamlet and city of the Greco-Roman world, I too am compelled to carry the gospel of freedom beyond my particular home town. Like Paul, I must constantly respond to the Macedonian call for aid.

Moreover, I am cognizant of the interrelatedness of all communities and states. I cannot sit idly by in Atlanta and not be concerned about what happens in Birmingham. Injustice anywhere is a threat to justice everywhere. We are caught in an inescapable network of mutuality tied in a single garment of destiny. Whatever affects one directly affects all indirectly. Never again can we afford to live with the narrow, provincial "outside agitator" idea. Anyone who lives inside the United States can never be considered an outsider anywhere in this country.

You deplore the demonstrations that are presently taking place   5 in Birmingham. But I am sorry that your statement did not express a similar concern for the conditions that brought the demonstrations into being. I am sure that each of you would want to go beyond the superficial social analyst who looks merely at effects, and does not grapple with underlying causes. I would not hesitate to say that it is unfortunate that so-called demonstrations are taking place in Birmingham at this time, but I would say in more emphatic terms that it is even more unfortunate that the white power structure of this city left the Negro community with no other alternative.

In any nonviolent campaign there are four basic steps: (1) collection of the facts to determine whether injustices are alive; (2) negotiation; (3) self-purification; and (4) direct action. We have gone through all of these steps in Birmingham. There can be no gainsaying of the fact that racial injustice engulfs this community. Birmingham is probably the most thoroughly segregated city in the United States. Its ugly record of police brutality is known in every section of this country. Its unjust treatment of Negroes in the courts is a notorious reality. There have been more unsolved bombings of Negro homes and churches in Birmingham than any city in this nation. These are the hard, brutal, and unbelievable facts. On the basis of these conditions Negro leaders sought to negotiate with the city fathers. But the political leaders consistently refused to engage in good faith negotiation.

Then came the opportunity last September to talk with some of the leaders of the economic community. In these negotiating sessions certain promises were made by the merchants—such as the promise to remove the humiliating racial signs from the stores. On the basis of these promises Rev. Shuttlesworth and the leaders of the Alabama Christian Movement for Human Rights agreed to call a moratorium on any type of demonstrations. As the weeks and months unfolded we realized that we were the victims of a broken promise. The signs remained. As in so many experiences of the past we were confronted with blasted hopes, and the dark shadow of a deep disappointment settled upon us. So we had no alternative except that of preparing for direct action, whereby we would present our very bodies as a means of laying our case before the conscience of the local and national community. We were not unmindful of the difficulties involved. So we decided to go through a process of self-purification. We started having workshops on nonviolence and repeatedly asked ourselves the questions, "Are you able to accept blows without retaliating?" "Are you able to endure the ordeals of jail?"

We decided to set our direct-action program around the Easter season, realizing that with the exception of Christmas, this was the largest shopping period of the year. Knowing that a strong economic withdrawal program would be the by-product of direct action, we felt that this was the best time to bring pressure on the merchants for the needed changes. Then it occurred to us that the March election was ahead, and so we speedily decided to postpone action until after election day. When we discovered that Mr. Connor was in the run-off, we decided again to postpone action so that the demonstrations could not be used to cloud the issues. At this time we agreed to begin our nonviolent witness the day after the run-off.

This reveals that we did not move irresponsibly into direct action. We too wanted to see Mr. Connor defeated; so we went through postponement after postponement to aid in this community need. After this we felt that direct action could be delayed no longer.

10   You may well ask, "Why direct action? Why sit-ins, marches, etc.? Isn't negotiation a better path?" You are exactly right in your call for negotiation. Indeed, this is the purpose of direct action. Nonviolent direct action seeks to create such a crisis and establish such creative tension that a community that has constantly refused to negotiate is forced to confront the issue. It seeks so to dramatize the issue that it can no longer be ignored. I just referred to the creation of tension as a part of the work of the nonviolent resister. This may sound rather shocking. But I must confess that I am not afraid of the word tension. I have earnestly worked and preached against violent tension, but there is a type of constructive nonviolent tension that is necessary for growth. Just as Socrates felt that it was necessary to create a tension in the mind so that individuals could rise from the bondage of myths and half-truths to the unfettered realm of creative analysis and objective appraisal, we must see the need of having nonviolent gadflies to create the kind of tension in society that will help men rise

from the dark depths of prejudice and racism to the majestic heights of understanding and brotherhood. So the purpose of the direct action is to create a situation so crisis-packed that it will inevitably open the door to negotiation. We, therefore, concur with you in your call for negotiation. Too long has our beloved Southland been bogged down in the tragic attempt to live in monologue rather than dialogue.

One of the basic points in your statement is that our acts are untimely. Some have asked, "Why didn't you give the new administration time to act?" The only answer that I can give to this inquiry is that the new administration must be prodded about as much as the outgoing one before it acts. We will be sadly mistaken if we feel that the election of Mr. Boutwell will bring the millennium to Birmingham. While Mr. Boutwell is much more articulate and gentle than Mr. Connor, they are both segregationists dedicated to the task of maintaining the status quo. The hope I see in Mr. Boutwell is that he will be reasonable enough to see the futility of massive resistance to desegregation. But he will not see this without pressure from the devotees of civil rights. My friends, I must say to you that we have not made a single gain in civil rights without determined legal and nonviolent pressure. History is the long and tragic story of the fact that privileged groups seldom give up their privileges voluntarily. Individuals may see the moral light and voluntarily give up their unjust posture; but as Reinhold Niebuhr has reminded us, groups are more immoral than individuals.

We know through painful experience that freedom is never voluntarily given by the oppressor; it must be demanded by the oppressed. Frankly I have never yet engaged in a direct action movement that was "well timed," according to the timetable of those who have not suffered unduly from the disease of segregation. For years now I have heard the word "Wait!" It rings in the ear of every Negro with a piercing familiarity. This "wait" has almost always meant "never." It has been a tranquilizing thalidomide, relieving the emotional stress for a moment, only to give birth to an ill-formed infant of frustration. We must come to see with the distinguished jurist of yesterday that "justice too long delayed is justice denied." We have waited for more than three hundred and forty years for our constitutional and God-given rights. The nations of Asia and Africa are moving with jet-like speed toward the goal of political independence, and we still creep at horse and buggy pace toward the gaining of a cup of coffee at a lunch counter.

I guess it is easy for those who have never felt the stinging darts of segregation to say wait. But when you have seen vicious mobs lynch your mothers and fathers at will and drown your sisters and brothers at whim; when you have seen hate filled policemen curse, kick, brutalize, and even kill your black brothers and sisters with impunity; when you see the vast majority of your twenty million Negro brothers smothering in an air-tight cage of poverty in the midst of an affluent society; when you suddenly find your tongue twisted and your speech stammering as you seek to explain to your six-year-old daughter why she can't go to the public amusement park that has just been advertised on television, and see tears welling up in her little eyes when she is told that Funtown is closed to colored children, and see the depressing clouds of inferiority begin to form in her little mental sky, and see her begin to distort her little personality by unconsciously developing a bitterness toward white people; when you have to concoct an answer for a five-year-old son asking in agonizing pathos: "Daddy, why do white people treat colored people so mean?"; when you take a cross-country drive and find it necessary to sleep night after night in the uncomfortable corners of your automobile because no motel will accept you; when you are humiliated day in and day out by nagging signs reading "white" men and "colored"; when your first name becomes "nigger" and your middle name becomes "boy" (however old you are) and your last name becomes "John," and when your wife and mother are never given the respected title "Mrs."; when you are harried by day and haunted by night by the fact that you are a Negro, living constantly at tip-toe stance never quite knowing what to expect next, and plagued with inner fears and outer resentments; when you are forever fighting a degenerating sense of "nobodiness"— then you will understand why we find it difficult to wait. There comes a time when the cup of endurance runs over, and men are no longer willing to be plunged into an abyss of injustice where they experience the bleakness of corroding despair. I hope, sirs, you can understand our legitimate and unavoidable impatience.

You express a great deal of anxiety over our willingness to break laws. This is certainly a legitimate concern. Since we so diligently urge people to obey the Supreme Court's decision of 1954 outlawing segregation in the public schools, it is rather strange and paradoxical to find us consciously breaking laws. One may well ask: "How can you advocate breaking some laws and obeying others?" The answer is found in the fact that there are two types of laws: There are *just* laws and there are *unjust* laws. I would be the first to advocate obeying just laws. One has not only a legal but moral responsibility to obey just laws. Conversely, one has a moral responsibility to disobey unjust laws. I would agree with Saint Augustine that "An unjust law is no law at all."

Now what is the difference between the two? How does one determine when a law is just or unjust? A just law is a man-made code that squares with the moral law or the law of God. An unjust law is a code that is out of harmony with the moral law. To put it in the terms of Saint Thomas Aquinas, an unjust law is a human law that is not rooted in eternal and natural law. Any law that uplifts human personality is just. Any law that degrades human personality is unjust. All segregation statutes are unjust because segregation distorts the soul and damages the personality. It gives the segregator a false sense of superiority and the segregated a false sense of inferiority. To use the words of Martin Buber, the great Jewish philosopher, segregation substitutes an "I-it" relationship for an "I-thou" relationship, and ends up relegating persons to the status of things. So segregation is not only politically, economically, and sociologically unsound, but it is morally wrong and sinful. Paul Tillich has said that sin is separation. Isn't segregation an existential expression of man's tragic separation, an expression of his awful estrangement, his terrible sinfulness? So I can urge men to obey the1954 decision of the Supreme Court because it is morally right, and I can urge them to disobey segregation ordinances because they are morally wrong.

Let us turn to a more concrete example of just and unjust laws. An unjust law is a code that a majority inflicts on a minority that is not binding on itself. This is *difference* made legal. On the other hand a just law is a code that a majority compels a minority to follow that it is willing to follow itself. This is sameness made legal.

Let me give another explanation. An unjust law is a code inflicted upon a minority which that minority had no part in enacting or creating because they did not have the unhampered right to vote. Who can say that the legislature of Alabama which set up the segregation laws was democratically elected? Throughout the state of Alabama all types of conniving methods are used to prevent Negroes from becoming registered voters and there are some counties without a single Negro registered to vote despite the fact that the Negro constitutes a majority of the population. Can any law set up in such a state be considered democratically structured?

These are just a few examples of unjust and just laws. There are some instances when a law is just on its face but unjust in its application. For instance, I was arrested Friday on a charge of parading without a permit. Now there is nothing wrong with an ordinance which requires

15

a permit for a parade, but when the ordinance is used to preserve segregation and to deny citizens the First Amendment privilege of peaceful assembly and peaceful protest, then it becomes unjust.

I hope you can see the distinction I am trying to point out. In no sense do I advocate evading or defying the law as the rabid segregationist would do. This would lead to anarchy. One who breaks an unjust law must do it *openly, lovingly* (not hatefully as the white mothers did in New Orleans when they were seen on television screaming "nigger, nigger, nigger") and with a willingness to accept the penalty. I submit that an individual who breaks a law that conscience tells him is unjust, and willingly accepts the penalty by staying in jail to arouse the conscience of the community over its injustice, is in reality expressing the very highest respect for law.

20   Of course there is nothing new about this kind of civil disobedience. It was seen sublimely in the refusal of Shadrach, Meshach, and Abednego to obey the laws of Nebuchadnezzar because a higher moral law was involved. It was practiced superbly by the early Christians who were willing to face hungry lions and the excruciating pain of chopping blocks, before submitting to certain unjust laws of the Roman Empire. To a degree academic freedom is a reality today because Socrates practiced civil disobedience.

We can never forget that everything Hitler did in Germany was "legal" and everything the Hungarian freedom fighters did in Hungary was "illegal." It was "illegal" to aid and comfort a Jew in Hitler's Germany. But I am sure that, if I had lived in Germany during that time, I would have aided and comforted my Jewish brothers even though it was illegal. If I lived in a communist country today where certain principles dear to the Christian faith are suppressed, I believe I would openly advocate disobeying these anti-religious laws.

I must make two honest confessions to you, my Christian and Jewish brothers. First, I must confess that over the last few years I have been gravely disappointed with the white moderate. I have almost reached the regrettable conclusion that the Negroes' great stumbling block in the stride toward freedom is not the White Citizen's "Counciler" or the Ku Klux Klanner, but the white moderate who is more devoted to "order" than to justice; who prefers a negative peace which is the absence of tension to a positive peace which is the presence of justice; who constantly says "I agree with you in the goal you seek, but I can't agree with your methods of direct action"; who paternalistically feels that he can set the timetable for another man's freedom; who lives by the myth of time and who constantly advises the Negro to wait until a "more convenient season." Shallow understanding from people of good will is more frustrating than absolute misunderstanding from people of ill will. Lukewarm acceptance is much more bewildering than outright rejection.

I had hoped that the white moderate would understand that law and order exist for the purpose of establishing justice, and that when they fail to do this they become dangerously structured dams that block the flow of social progress. I had hoped that the white moderate would understand that the present tension in the South is merely a necessary phase of the transition from an obnoxious negative peace, where the Negro passively accepted his unjust plight, to a substance-filled positive peace, where all men will respect the dignity and worth of human personality. Actually, we who engage in nonviolent direct action are not the creators of tension. We merely bring to the surface the hidden tension that is already alive. We bring it out in the open where it can be seen and dealt with. Like a boil that can never be cured as long as it is covered up but must be opened with all its pus-flowing ugliness to the natural medicines of air and light, injustice must likewise be exposed, with all of the tension its exposing creates, to the light of human conscience and the air of national opinion before it can be cured.

In your statement you asserted that our actions, even though peaceful, must be condemned because they precipitate violence. But can this assertion be logically made? Isn't this like condemning the robbed man because his possession of money precipitated the evil act of robbery? Isn't this like condemning Socrates because his unswerving commitment to truth and his philosophical delvings precipitated the misguided popular mind to make him drink the hemlock? Isn't this like condemning Jesus because His unique God consciousness and never-ceasing devotion to His will precipitated the evil act of crucifixion? We must come to see, as federal courts have consistently affirmed, that it is immoral to urge an individual to withdraw his efforts to gain his basic constitutional rights because the quest precipitates violence. Society must protect the robbed and punish the robber.

I had also hoped that the white moderate would reject the myth of time. I received a letter this morning from a white brother in Texas which said: "All Christians know that the colored people will receive equal rights eventually, but is it possible that you are in too great of a religious hurry? It has taken Christianity almost 2,000 years to accomplish what it has. The teachings of Christ take time to come to earth." All that is said here grows out of a tragic misconception of time. 25

It is the strangely irrational notion that there is something in the very flow of time that will inevitably cure all ills. Actually time is neutral. It can be used either destructively or constructively. I am coming to feel that the people of ill will have used time much more effectively than the people of good will. We will have to repent in this generation not merely for the vitriolic words and actions of the bad people, but for the appalling silence of the good people. We must come to see that human progress never rolls in on wheels of inevitability. It comes through the tireless efforts and persistent work of men willing to be co-workers with God, and without this hard work time itself becomes an ally of the forces of social stagnation.

We must use time creatively, and forever realize that the time is always ripe to do right. Now is the time to make real the promise of democracy, and transform our pending national elegy into a creative psalm of brotherhood. Now is the time to lift our national policy from the quicksand of racial injustice to the solid rock of human dignity.

You spoke of our activity in Birmingham as extreme. At first I was rather disappointed that fellow clergymen would see my nonviolent efforts as those of the extremist. I started thinking about the fact that I stand in the middle of two opposing forces in the Negro community. One is a force of complacency made up of Negroes who, as a result of long years of oppression, have been so completely drained of self-respect and a sense of "somebodiness" that they have adjusted to segregation, and of a few Negroes in the middle class who, because of a degree of academic and economic security, and because at points they profit by segregation, have unconsciously become insensitive to the problems of the masses. The other force is one of bitterness and hatred and comes perilously close to advocating violence. It is expressed in the various black nationalist groups that are springing up over the nation, the largest and best known being Elijah Muhammad's Muslim movement. This movement is nourished by the contemporary frustration over the continued existence of racial discrimination. It is made up of people who have lost faith in America, who have absolutely repudiated Christianity, and who have concluded that the white man is an incurable "devil." I have tried to stand between these two forces saying that we need not follow the "do-nothingism" of the complacent or the hatred and despair of the black nationalist. There is the more excellent way of love and nonviolent protest. I'm grateful to God that, through the Negro church, the dimension of nonviolence entered our struggle. If this philosophy had not emerged I am convinced that by now many streets of the South would be flowing with floods of blood.

And I am further convinced that if our white brothers dismiss us as "rabble rousers" and "outside agitators"—those of us who are working through the channels of nonviolent direct action—and refuse to support our nonviolent efforts, millions of Negroes, out of frustration and despair, will seek solace and security in black-nationalist ideologies, a development that will lead inevitably to a frightening racial nightmare.

Oppressed people cannot remain oppressed forever. The urge for freedom will eventually come. This is what has happened to the American Negro. Something within has reminded him of his birthright of freedom; something without has reminded him that he can gain it. Consciously and unconsciously, he has been swept in by what the Germans call the *Zeitgeist*, and with his black brothers of Africa, and his brown and yellow brothers of Asia, South America, and the Caribbean, he is moving with a sense of cosmic urgency toward the promised land of racial justice. Recognizing this vital urge that has engulfed the Negro community, one should readily understand public demonstrations. The Negro has many pent-up resentments and latent frustrations. He has to get them out. So let him march sometime; let him have his prayer pilgrimages to the city hall; understand why he must have sit-ins and freedom rides. If his repressed emotions do not come out in these nonviolent ways, they will come out in ominous expressions of violence. This is not a threat; it is a fact of history. So I have not said to my people, "Get rid of your discontent." But I have tried to say that this normal and healthy discontent can be channeled through the creative outlet of nonviolent direct action. Now this approach is being dismissed as extremist. I must admit that I was initially disappointed in being so categorized.

But as I continued to think about the matter I gradually gained a bit of satisfaction from being considered an extremist. Was not Jesus an extremist in love? "Love your enemies, bless them that curse you, pray for them that despitefully use you." Was not Amos an extremist for justice— "Let justice roll down like waters and righteousness like a mighty stream." Was not Paul an extremist for the gospel of Jesus Christ— "I bear in my body the marks of the Lord Jesus." Was not Martin Luther an extremist— "Here I stand; I can do none other so help me God." Was not John Bunyan an extremist— "I will stay in jail to the end of my days before I make a butchery of my conscience." Was not Abraham Lincoln an extremist— "This nation cannot survive half slave and half free." Was not Thomas Jefferson an extremist— "We hold these truths to be self-evident, that all men are created equal." So the question is not whether we will be extremist but what kind of extremist will we be. Will we be extremists for hate or will we be extremists for love? Will we be extremists for the preservation of injustice—or will we be extremists for the cause of justice? In that dramatic scene on Calvary's hill three men were crucified. We must never forget that all three were crucified for the same crime—the crime of extremism. Two were extremists for immorality, and thus fell below their environment. The other, Jesus Christ, was an extremist for love, truth, and goodness, and thereby rose above His environment. So, after all, maybe the South, the nation, and the world are in dire need of creative extremists.

30   I had hoped that the white moderate would see this. Maybe I was too optimistic. Maybe I expected too much. I guess I should have realized that few members of a race that has oppressed another race can understand or appreciate the deep groans and passionate yearnings of those that have been oppressed, and still fewer have the vision to see that injustice must be rooted out by strong, persistent, and determined action. I am thankful, however, that some of our white brothers have grasped the meaning of this social revolution and committed themselves to it. They are still all too small in quantity, but they are big in quality. Some like Ralph McGill, Lillian Smith, Harry Golden, and James Dabbs have written about our struggle in eloquent, prophetic, and understanding terms. Others have marched with us down nameless streets of the South. They have languished in filthy, roach-infested jails, suffering the abuse and brutality of angry policemen who see them as "dirty nigger lovers." They, unlike so many of their moderate brothers and sisters, have recognized the urgency of the moment and sensed the need for powerful "action" antidotes to combat the disease of segregation.

Let me rush on to mention my other disappointment. I have been so greatly disappointed with the white Church and its leadership. Of course there are some notable exceptions. I am not unmindful of the fact that each of you has taken some significant stands on this issue. I commend you, Rev. Stallings, for your Christian stand on this past Sunday, in welcoming Negroes to your worship service on a non-segregated basis. I commend the Catholic leaders of this state for integrating Spring Hill College several years ago.

But despite these notable exceptions I must honestly reiterate that I have been disappointed with the Church. I do not say that as one of those negative critics who can always find something wrong with the Church. I say it as a minister of the gospel, who loves the Church; who was nurtured in its bosom; who has been sustained by its spiritual blessings and who will remain true to it as long as the cord of life shall lengthen.

I had the strange feeling when I was suddenly catapulted into the leadership of the bus protest in Montgomery several years ago that we would have the support of the white Church. I felt that the white ministers, priests, and rabbis of the South would be some of our strongest allies. Instead, some have been outright opponents, refusing to understand the freedom movement and misrepresenting its leaders; all too many others have been more cautious than courageous and have remained silent behind the anesthetizing security of the stained glass windows.

In spite of my shattered dreams of the past, I came to Birmingham with the hope that the white religious leadership of this community would see the justice of our cause and with deep moral concern, serve as the channel through which our just grievances could get to the power structure. I had hoped that each of you would understand. But again I have been disappointed.

I have heard numerous religious leaders of the South call upon their worshippers to comply with a desegregation decision because it is the law, but I have longed to hear white ministers say follow this decree because integration is morally right and the Negro is your brother. In the midst of blatant injustices inflicted upon the Negro, I have watched white churches stand on the sideline and merely mouth pious irrelevancies and sanctimonious trivialities. In the midst of a mighty struggle to rid our nation of racial and economic injustice, I have heard so many ministers say, "Those are social issues with which the gospel has no real concern," and I have watched so many churches commit themselves to a completely other-worldly religion which made a strange distinction between body and soul, the sacred and the secular.

So here we are moving toward the exit of the twentieth century with a religious community largely adjusted to the status quo, standing as a tail-light behind other community agencies rather than a headlight leading men to higher levels of justice.

I have travelled the length and breadth of Alabama, Mississippi and all the other southern states. On sweltering summer days and crisp autumn mornings I have looked at her beautiful churches with their spires pointing heavenward. I have beheld the impressive outlay of her massive religious education buildings. Over and over again I have found myself asking: "Who worships here? Who is their God?

Where were their voices when the lips of Governor Barnett dripped with words of interposition and nullification? Where were they when Governor Wallace gave the clarion call for defiance and hatred? Where were their voices of support when tired, bruised, and weary Negro men and women decided to rise from the dark dungeons of complacency to the bright hills of creative protest?"

Yes, these questions are still in my mind. In deep disappointment, I have wept over the laxity of the church. But be assured that my tears have been tears of love. There can be no deep disappointment where there is not deep love. Yes, I love the Church; I love her sacred walls. How could I do otherwise? I am in the rather unique position of being the son, the grandson, and the great-grandson of preachers. Yes, I see the Church as the body of Christ. But, oh! How we have blemished and scarred that body through social neglect and fear of being nonconformist.

There was a time when the Church was very powerful. It was during that period when the early Christians rejoiced when they were deemed worthy to suffer for what they believed. In those days the Church was not merely a thermometer that recorded the ideas and principles of popular opinion; it was a thermostat that transformed the mores of society. Wherever the early Christians entered a town the power structure got disturbed and immediately sought to convict them for being "disturbers of the peace" and "outside agitators." But they went on with the conviction that they were "a colony of heaven" and had to obey God rather than man. They were small in number but big in commitment. They were too God-intoxicated to be "astronomically intimidated." They brought an end to such ancient evils as infanticide and gladiatorial contest.

40   Things are different now. The contemporary Church is so often a weak, ineffectual voice with an uncertain sound. It is so often the arch-supporter of the status quo. Far from being disturbed by the presence of the Church, the power structure of the average community is consoled by the Church's silent and often vocal sanction of things as they are.

But the judgment of God is upon the Church as never before. If the Church of today does not recapture the sacrificial spirit of the early Church, it will lose its authentic ring, forfeit the loyalty of millions, and be dismissed as an irrelevant social club with no meaning for the twentieth century. I am meeting young people every day whose disappointment with the Church has risen to outright disgust.

Maybe again I have been too optimistic. Is organized religion too inextricably bound to the status quo to save our nation and the world? Maybe I must turn my faith to the inner spiritual Church, the church within the Church, as the true ecclesia and the hope of the world. But again I am thankful to God that some noble souls from the ranks of organized religion have broken loose from the paralyzing chains of conformity and joined us as active partners in the struggle for freedom. They have left their secure congregations and walked the streets of Albany, Georgia, with us. They have gone through the highways of the South on torturous rides for freedom. Yes, they have gone to jail with us. Some have been kicked out of their churches and lost the support of their bishops and fellow ministers. But they have gone with the faith that right defeated is stronger than evil triumphant. These men have been the leaven in the lump of the race. Their witness has been the spiritual salt that has preserved the true meaning of the Gospel in these troubled times. They have carved a tunnel of hope through the dark mountain of disappointment.

I hope the Church as a whole will meet the challenge of this decisive hour. But even if the Church does not come to the aid of justice, I have no despair about the future. I have no fear about the outcome of our struggle in Birmingham, even if our motives are presently misunderstood. We will reach the goal of freedom in Birmingham and all over the nation, because the goal of America is freedom. Abused and scorned though we may be, our destiny is tied up with the destiny of America. Before the pilgrims landed at Plymouth, we were here. Before the pen of Jefferson etched across the pages of history the majestic words of the Declaration of Independence, we were here. For more than two centuries our foreparents labored in this country without wages; they made cotton "king"; and they built the homes of their masters in the midst of brutal injustice and shameful humiliation—and yet out of a bottomless vitality they continued to thrive and develop. If the inexpressible cruelties of slavery could not stop us, the opposition we now face will surely fail. We will win our freedom because the sacred heritage of our nation and the eternal will of God are embodied in our echoing demands.

I must close now. But before closing I am impelled to mention one other point in your statement that troubled me profoundly. You warmly commend the Birmingham police force for keeping "order" and "preventing violence." I don't believe you would have so warmly commended the police force if you had seen its angry violent dogs literally biting six unarmed, nonviolent Negroes. I don't believe you would so quickly commend the policemen if you would observe their ugly and inhuman treatment of Negroes here in the city jail; if you would watch them push and curse old Negro women and young Negro girls; if you would see them slap and kick old Negro men and young Negro boys; if you will observe them, as they did on two occasions, refuse to give us food because we wanted to sing our grace together. I'm sorry that I can't join you in your praise for the police department.

45   It is true that they have been rather disciplined in their public handling of the demonstrators. In this sense they have been rather publicly "nonviolent." But for what purpose? To preserve the evil system of segregation. Over the last few years I have consistently preached that nonviolence demands the means we use must be as pure as the ends we seek. So I have tried to make it clear that it is wrong to use immoral means to attain moral ends. But now I must affirm that it is just as wrong or even more so to use moral means to preserve immoral ends. Maybe Mr. Connor and his policemen have been rather publicly nonviolent, as Chief Pritchett was in Albany, Georgia, but they have used the moral means of nonviolence to maintain the immoral end of flagrant injustice. T. S. Eliot has said that there is no greater treason than to do the right deed for the wrong reason.

I wish you had commended the Negro sit-inners and demonstrators of Birmingham for their sublime courage, their willingness to suffer, and their amazing discipline in the midst of the most inhuman provocation. One day the South will recognize its real heroes. They will be the James Merediths, courageously and with a majestic sense of purpose, facing jeering and hostile mobs and the agonizing loneliness that characterizes the life of the pioneer. They will be old, oppressed, battered Negro women, symbolized in a seventy-two year old woman of Montgomery, Alabama, who rose up with a sense of dignity and with her people decided not to ride the segregated buses, and responded to one who inquired about her tiredness with ungrammatical profundity: "My feets is tired, but my soul is rested." They will be the young high school and college students, young ministers of the gospel and a host of their elders courageously and nonviolently sitting-in at lunch counters and willingly going to jail for conscience sake. One day the South will know that when these disinherited children of God sat down at lunch counters they were in reality standing up for the best in the American dream and the most sacred values in our Judeo-Christian heritage, and thus carrying our whole nation back to great wells of democracy which were dug deep by the founding fathers in the formulation of the Constitution and the Declaration of Independence.

Never before have I written a letter this long (or should I say a book?). I'm afraid it is much too long to take your precious time. I can assure you that it would have been much shorter if I had been writing from a comfortable desk, but what else is there to do when you are alone for days in the dull monotony of a narrow jail cell other than write long letters, think strange thoughts, and pray long prayers?

If I have said anything in this letter that is an overstatement of the truth and is indicative of an unreasonable impatience, I beg you to forgive me. If I have said anything in this letter that is an understatement of the truth and is indicative of my having a patience that makes me patient with anything less than brotherhood, I beg God to forgive me.

I hope this letter finds you strong in the faith. I also hope that circumstances will soon make it possible for me to meet each of you, not as an integrationist or a civil rights leader, but as a fellow clergyman and a Christian brother. Let us all hope that the dark clouds of racial prejudice will soon pass away and the deep fog of misunderstanding will be lifted from our fear-drenched communities and in some not too distant tomorrow the radiant stars of love and brotherhood will shine over our great nation with all their scintillating beauty.

Yours for the cause of
Peace and Brotherhood,

MARTIN LUTHER KING, JR

SECOND INAUGURAL ADDRESS

March 4, 1865

Abraham Lincoln

◆

ABRAHAM LINCOLN (1809-1865)

The sixteenth President of the United States, Abraham Lincoln was born in Kentucky in 1809. After the death of his mother when Lincoln was nine, his family relocated, eventually settling in Illinois in 1830. In 1832, at 23, Lincoln began his political career with an unsuccessful campaign for the Illinois General Assembly; two years later he won election to the state senate as a Whig. Lincoln practiced law in Springfield for the next decade. He was elected to the U.S. House of Representatives in 1846, serving a single term, and returned to politics with a run for the U.S. Senate in 1854 as a reaction against the pro-slavery Kansas-Nebraska Act. While his campaign failed, it led to the formation of the Republican Party and raised his profile. While running for U.S. Senate as a Republican in 1858, he engaged in the famous Lincoln-Douglas debates with Democratic candidate and Senator Stephen A. Douglas of Illinois, focusing on the issue of slavery's extension. Douglas was re-elected, but Lincoln had gathered enough support to be nominated for and win the Presidency in 1860. The Civil War erupted partially as a consequence of his election, with Southern states seceding in reaction. Throughout the war, Lincoln's primary focus was to restore the unity of the nation, though his most notable acts came in support of abolitionism. The Emancipation Proclamation of 1863 ended slavery in Southern states, while the Thirteenth Amendment outlawed slavery throughout the United States. Though re-elected in 1864, Lincoln presided over a militarily and politically divided nation, and on April 15, 1865, soon after the surrender of the Confederacy, he was assassinated by Confederate supporter John Wilkes Booth. Lincoln's most lasting impact came not only in his political acts, but his oratory. While his most significant speech was 1863's *Gettysburg Address*, others, including his *House Divided* Speech of 1858 and *Second Inaugural Address*, are still remembered and referenced today.

Fellow Countrymen:

At this second appearing to take the oath of the Presidential office,   1
there is less occasion for an extended address than there was at the
first. Then a statement, somewhat in detail, of a course to be pursued
seemed fitting and proper. Now, at the expiration of four years, during
which public declarations have been constantly called forth on every
point and phase of the great contest which still absorbs the attention
and engrosses the energies [sic] of the nation, little that is new could
be presented. The progress of our arms, upon which all else chiefly
depends, is as well known to the public as to myself; and it is, I trust,
reasonably satisfactory and encouraging to all. With high hope for the
future, no prediction in regard to it is ventured.

On the occasion corresponding to this four years ago, all thoughts
were anxiously directed to an impending civil war. All dreaded it—all
sought to avert it. While the inaugural address was being delivered
from this place, devoted altogether to saving the Union without war,
insurgent agents were in the city seeking to destroy it without war—
seeking to dissolve the Union and divide effects by negotiation. Both
parties deprecated war; but one of them would make war rather than
let the nation survive; and the other would accept war rather than let
it perish. And the war came.

One-eighth of the whole population were colored slaves, not
distributed generally over the Union, but localized in the Southern
part of it. These slaves constituted a peculiar and powerful interest.
All knew that this interest was somehow the cause of the war. To
strengthen, perpetuate, and extend this interest was the object for
which the insurgents would rend the Union, even by war; while the
government claimed no right to do more than to restrict the territorial
enlargement of it. Neither party expected for the war, the magnitude,
or the duration, which it has already attained. Neither anticipated that
the cause of the conflict might cease with, or even before, the conflict
itself should cease. Each looked for an easier triumph, and a result
less fundamental and astounding. Both read the same Bible and pray
to the same God; and each invokes His aid against the other. It may
seem strange that any men should dare to ask a just God's assistance
in wringing their bread from the sweat of other men's faces; but let us
judge not, that we be not judged. The prayers of both could not be
answered; that of neither has been answered fully. The Almighty has
His own purposes. "Woe unto the world because of offenses! for it
must needs be that offenses come; but woe to that man by whom the

offense cometh." If we shall suppose that American Slavery is one of those offenses which, in the providence of God, must needs come, but which, having continued through His appointed time, He now wills to remove, and that He gives to both North and South, this terrible war as the woe due to those by whom the offense came, shall we discern therein any departure from those divine attributes which the believers in a living God always ascribe to Him? Fondly do we hope—fervently do we pray—that this mighty scourge of war may speedily pass away. Yet, if God wills that it continue until all the wealth piled by the bondsman's two hundred and fifty years of unrequited toil shall be sunk, and until every drop of blood drawn with the lash shall be paid by another drawn with the sword, as was said three thousand years ago, so still it must be said "the judgments of the Lord are true and righteous altogether."

With malice toward none, with charity for all, with firmness in the right as God gives us to see the right, let us strive on to finish the work we are in, to bind up the nation's wounds; to care for him who shall have borne the battle, and for his widow and his orphan—to do all which may achieve and cherish a just and lasting peace among ourselves and with all nations.

THE DECLARATION OF INDEPENDENCE

JULY 4, 1776

Thomas Jefferson

❖

THOMAS JEFFERSON (1743-1826)

Founding Father Thomas Jefferson was born in Virginia in 1743. The avid student entered the College of William & Mary at age 16 and completed his degree within two years. Thereafter he began law studies, and was admitted to the Virginia bar association in 1767. Jefferson's law career quickly became political in nature after the passage of the Coercive Acts in 1774, when he wrote a defense of the American colonists' right to self-governance. His central work came in the summer of 1776, when he drafted the Declaration of Independence, asserting the separation of the colonies from British rule and ushering in the American Revolution. After the war, Jefferson served several government positions, as minister to France in the 1780s, the first Secretary of State under George Washington, and Vice President to John Adams. Jefferson was elected to the presidency in 1800, serving two terms which saw the Louisiana Purchase and the Lewis and Clark Expedition. In addition to his political activities, Jefferson was also a farmer, architect, and philosopher, among other varied pursuits. He founded the University of Virginia in 1819, notable for its public funding and freedom from official church influence. Jefferson wrote a number of books, though 1785's *Notes on the State of Virginia* was the only one published in his lifetime. Additional works include the *Manual of Parliamentary Practice for the Use of the Senate of the United States* (1801), which established American parliamentary procedure, and his Autobiography, written in 1821.

When in the course of human events it becomes necessary for one people to dissolve the political bands which have connected them with another, and to assume among the powers of the earth, the separate and equal station to which the Laws of Nature and of Nature's God entitle them, a decent respect to the opinions of mankind requires that they should declare the causes which impel them to the separation.

We hold these truths to be self-evident, that all men are created equal, that they are endowed by their Creator with certain unalienable rights, that among these are life, liberty, and the pursuit of happiness. That to secure these rights, governments are instituted among men, deriving their just powers from the consent of the governed. That whenever any form of government becomes destructive of these ends, it is the right of the people to alter or to abolish it, and to institute new government, laying its foundation on such principles and organizing its powers in such form, as to them shall seem most likely to effect their safety and happiness. Prudence, indeed, will dictate that governments long established should not be changed for light and transient causes; and accordingly all experience hath shown that mankind are more disposed to suffer, while evils are sufferable, than to right themselves by abolishing the forms to which they are accustomed. But when a long train of abuses and usurpations, pursuing invariably the same object, evinces a design to reduce them under absolute despotism, it is their right, it is their duty, to throw off such government, and to provide new guards for their future security. Such has been the patient sufferance of these Colonies; and such is now the necessity which constrains them to alter their former systems of government. The history of the present King of Great Britain is a history of repeated injuries and usurpations, all having in direct object the establishment of an absolute tyranny over these States. To prove this, let facts be submitted to a candid world.

He has refused his assent to laws, the most wholesome and necessary for the public good.

He has forbidden his Governors to pass laws of immediate and pressing importance, unless suspended in their operation till his assent should be obtained; and when so suspended, he has utterly neglected to attend to them.

5   He has refused to pass other laws for the accommodation of large districts of people, unless those people would relinquish the right of representation in the legislature, a right inestimable to them and formidable to tyrants only.

He has called together legislative bodies at places unusual, uncomfortable, and distant from the depository of their public records, for the sole purpose of fatiguing them into compliance with his measures.

He has dissolved representative houses repeatedly, for opposing with manly firmness his invasions on the rights of the people.

He has refused for a long time, after such dissolutions, to cause others to be elected; whereby the legislative powers, incapable of annihilation, have returned to the people at large for their exercise; the State remaining in the meantime exposed to all the dangers of invasion from without and convulsions within.

He has endeavoured to prevent the population of these States; for that purpose obstructing the laws for naturalization of foreigners; refusing to pass others to encourage their migrations hither, and raising the conditions of new appropriations of lands.

He has obstructed the administration of justice, by refusing his   10 assent to laws for establishing judiciary powers.

He has made judges dependent on his will alone for the tenure of their offices, and the amount and payment of their salaries.

He has erected a multitude of new offices, and sent hither swarms of officers to harass our people and eat out their substance.

He has kept among us, in times of peace, standing armies without the consent of our legislatures.

He has affected to render the military independent of and superior to the civil power.

He has combined with others to subject us to a jurisdiction   15 foreign to our constitution, and unacknowledged by our laws; giving his assent to their acts of pretended legislation:

For quartering large bodies of armed troops among us:

For protecting them, by a mock trial from punishment for any murders which they should commit on the inhabitants of these States:

For cutting off our trade with all parts of the world:

For imposing taxes on us without our consent:

For depriving us in many cases, of the benefit of trial by jury: 20

For transporting us beyond seas to be tried for pretended offences:

For abolishing the free system of English laws in a neighbouring Province, establishing therein an arbitrary government, and enlarging its boundaries so as to render it at once an example and fit instrument for introducing the same absolute rule into these Colonies:

For taking away our Charters, abolishing our most valuable laws and altering fundamentally the forms of our governments:

For suspending our own legislatures, and declaring themselves invested with power to legislate for us in all cases whatsoever.

He has abdicated government here, by declaring us out of his   25 protection and waging war against us.

He has plundered our seas, ravaged our coasts, burnt our towns, and destroyed the lives of our people.

He is at this time transporting large armies of foreign mercenaries to complete the works of death, desolation, and tyranny, already begun with circumstances of cruelty and perfidy scarcely paralleled in the most barbarous ages, and totally unworthy the head of a civilized nation.

He has constrained our fellow citizens taken captive on the high seas to bear arms against their country, to become the executioners of their friends and brethren, or to fall themselves by their hands.

He has excited domestic insurrections amongst us, and has endeavoured to bring on the inhabitants of our frontiers, the merciless Indian savages whose known rule of warfare, is an undistinguished destruction of all ages, sexes and conditions.

30   In every stage of these oppressions we have petitioned for redress in the most humble terms: our repeated petitions have been answered only by repeated injury. A prince whose character is thus marked by every act which may define a tyrant, is unfit to be the ruler of a free people.

Nor have we been wanting in attentions to our British brethren. We have warned them from time to time of attempts by their legislature to extend an unwarrantable jurisdiction over us. We have reminded them of the circumstances of our emigration and settlement here. We have appealed to their native justice and magnanimity, and we have conjured them by the ties of our common kindred to disavow these usurpations, which would inevitably interrupt our connections and correspondence. They too have been deaf to the voice of justice and of consanguinity. We must, therefore, acquiesce in the necessity, which denounces our separation, and hold them, as we hold the rest of mankind, enemies in war, in peace friends.

We, therefore, the Representatives of the United States of America, in General Congress assembled, appealing to the Supreme Judge of the world for the rectitude of our intentions, do, in the name, and by authority of the good people of these Colonies, solemnly publish and declare, That these United Colonies are, and of right ought to be Free and Independent States; that they are absolved from all allegiance to the British Crown, and that all political connection between them and the state of Great Britain, is and ought to be totally dissolved; and that as Free and Independent States, they have full power to levy war, conclude peace, contract alliances, establish commerce, and to do all other acts and things which Independent States may of right do. And for the support of this declaration, with a firm reliance on the protection of Divine Providence, we mutually pledge to each other our lives, our fortunes, and our sacred honor.

TALKING BACK

bell hooks

---

bell hooks (1952-)

Born Gloria Jean Watkins in Kentucky, to a family that included five sisters and a brother, hooks adopted her pen name in tribute to sharp-tongued great-grandmother Bell Blair Hooks, using lowercase to distinguish herself from the original and to focus attention on the work itself. hooks received a B.A. in English from Stanford University in 1973, a M.A. from University of Wisconsin-Madison in 1976, and a Ph.D. from University of California, Santa Cruz in 1983. Prior to obtaining her doctorate, hooks taught English literature at the University of Southern California from 1976-1979, at which time her writing career also began, with poetry collection "*And There We Wept.*" 1981's *Ain't I a Woman?* black women and feminism is among her most significant works, focusing largely on the precarious position of black women throughout American history and social movements; in 1992, Publisher's Weekly named it to a list of the twenty most influential women's books of the past twenty years. hooks has written over thirty works, including *Yearning: Race, Gender, and Cultural Politics* (1990), which won the American Book Awards/Before Columbus Foundation Award in 1991, and most recently *Teaching Critical Thinking: Practical Wisdom* in 2010. hooks has taught at Yale, Oberlin College, and the City College of New York.

Since 2004, she has served as Distinguished Professor in Residence in Appalachian Studies at Berea College in Kentucky.

---

1   In the world of the southern black community I grew up in, "back talk" and "talking back" meant speaking as an equal to an authority figure. It meant daring to disagree and sometimes it just meant having an opinion. In the "old school," children were meant to be seen and not heard. My great-grandparents, grandparents, and parents were all from the old school. To make yourself heard if you were a child was to invite punishment, the back-hand lick, the slap across the face that would catch you unaware, or the feel of switches stinging your arms and legs.

296

To speak then when one was not spoken to was a courageous act—an act of risk and daring. And yet it was hard not to speak in warm rooms where heated discussions began at the crack of dawn, women's voices filling the air, giving orders, making threats, fussing. Black men may have excelled in the art of poetic preaching in the male-dominated church, but in the church of the home, where the everyday rules of how to live and how to act were established, it was black women who preached. There, black women spoke in a language so rich, so poetic, that it felt to me like being shut off from life, smothered to death if one were not allowed to participate.

It was in that world of woman talk (the men were often silent, often absent) that was born in me the craving to speak, to have a voice, and not just any voice but one that could be identified as belonging to me. To make my voice, I had to speak, to hear myself talk—and talk I did—darting in and out of grown folks' conversations and dialogues, answering questions that were not directed as me, endlessly asking questions, making speeches. Needless to say, the punishments for these acts of speech seemed endless. They were intended to silence me—the child—and more particularly the girl child. Had I been a boy, they might have encouraged me to speak believing that I might someday be called to preach. There was no "calling" for talking girls, no legitimized rewarded speech. The punishments I received for "talking back" were intended to suppress all possibility that I would create my own speech. That speech was to be suppressed so that the "right speech of womanhood" would emerge.

Within feminist circles, silence is often seen as the sexist "right speech of womanhood"—the sign of woman's submission to patriarchal authority. This emphasis on woman's silence may be an accurate remembering of what has taken place in the households of women from WASP backgrounds in the United States, but in black communities (and diverse ethnic communities), women have not been silent. Their voices can be heard. Certainly for black women, our struggle has not been to emerge from silence into speech but to change the nature and direction of our speech, to make a speech that compels listeners, one that is heard.

Our speech, "the right speech of womanhood," was often the soliloquy, the talking into thin air, the talking to ears that do not hear you—the talk that is simply not listened to. Unlike the black male preacher whose speech was to be heard, who was to be listened to, whose words were to be remembered, the voices of black women—giving orders, making threats, fussing—could be tuned out, could

5

become a kind of background music, audible but not acknowledged as significant speech. Dialogue—the sharing of speech and recognition—took place not between mother and child or mother and male authority figure but among black women. I can remember watching fascinated as our mother talked with her mother, sisters, and women friends. The intimacy and intensity of their speech—the satisfaction they received from talking to one another, the pleasure, the joy. It was in this world of woman speech, loud talk, angry words, women with tongues quick and sharp, tender sweet tongues, touching our world with their words, that I made speech my birthright—and the right to voice, to authorship, a privilege I would not be denied. It was in that world and because of it that I came to dream of writing, to write.

Writing was a way to capture speech, to hold onto it, keep it close. And so I wrote down bits and pieces of conversations, confessing in cheap diaries that soon fell apart from too much handling, expressing the intensity of my sorrow, the anguish of speech—for I was always saying the wrong thing, asking the wrong questions. I could not confine my speech to the necessary corners and concerns of life. I hid these writings under my bed, in pillow stuffings, among faded underwear. When my sisters found and read them, they ridiculed and mocked me—poking fun. I felt violated, ashamed, as if the secret parts of my self had been exposed, brought into the open, and hung like newly clean laundry, out in the air for everyone to see. The fear of exposure, the fear that one's deepest emotions and innermost thoughts will be dismissed as mere nonsense, felt by so many young girls keeping diaries, holding and hiding speech, seems to me now one of the barriers that women have always needed and still need to destroy so that we are no longer pushed into secrecy or silence.

Despite my feelings of violation, of exposure, I continued to speak and write, choosing my hiding places well, learning to destroy work when no safe place could be found. I was never taught absolute silence, I was taught that it was important to speak but to talk a talk that was in itself a silence. Taught to speak and yet beware of the betrayal of too much heard speech, I experienced intense confusion and deep anxiety in my efforts to speak and write. Reciting poems at Sunday afternoon church service might be rewarded. Writing a poem (when one's time could be "better" spent sweeping, ironing, learning to cook) was luxurious activity, indulged in at the expense of others. Questioning authority, raising issues that were not deemed appropriate subjects, brought pain, punishments—like telling mama I wanted to die before her because I could not live without her—that was crazy talk, crazy speech, the kind that would lead you to end up in a mental institution. "Little girl," I would be told, "if you don't stop all this crazy talk and crazy acting you are going to end up right out there at Western State."

Madness, not just physical abuse, was the punishment for too much talk if you were female. Yet even as this fear of madness haunted me, hanging over my writing like a monstrous shadow, I could not stop the words, making thought, writing speech. For this terrible madness which I feared, which I was sure was the destiny of daring women born to intense speech (after all, the authorities emphasized this point daily), was not as threatening as imposed silence, as suppressed speech.

Safety and sanity were to be sacrificed if I was to experience defiant speech. Though I risked them both, deep-seated fears and anxieties characterized my childhood days. I would speak but I would not ride a bike, play hardball, or hold the gray kitten. Writing about the ways we are traumatized in our growing-up years, psychoanalyst Alice Miller makes the point in *For Your Own Good* that it is not clear why childhood wounds become for some folk an opportunity to grow, to move forward rather than backward in the process of self-realization. Certainly, when I reflect on the trials of my growing-up years, the many punishments, I can see now that in resistance I learned to be vigilant in the nourishment of my spirit, to be tough, to courageously protect that spirit from forces that would break it.

While punishing me, my parents often spoke about the necessity   10 of breaking my spirit. Now when I ponder the silences, the voices that are not heard, the voices of those wounded and/or oppressed individuals who do not speak or write, I contemplate the acts of persecution, torture—the terrorism that breaks spirits, that makes creativity impossible. I write these words to bear witness to the primacy of resistance struggle in any situation of domination (even within family life); to the strength and power that emerges from sustained resistance and the profound conviction that these forces can be healing, can protect us from dehumanization and despair.

These early trials, wherein I learned to stand my ground, to keep my spirit intact, came vividly to mind after I published *Ain't I A Woman* and the book was sharply and harshly criticized. While I had expected a climate of critical dialogue, I was not expecting a critical avalanche that had the power in its intensity to crush the spirit, to push one into silence. Since that time, I have heard stories about black women, about women of color, who write and publish (even when the work is quite successful) having nervous breakdowns, being made mad because they cannot bear the harsh responses of family, friends, and unknown critics, or becoming silent, unproductive. Surely, the absence of a humane critical response has tremendous impact on the writer from any oppressed, colonized group who endeavors to speak. For us, true speaking is not solely an expression of creative power; it is an act of resistance, a political gesture that challenges politics of domination that would render us nameless and voiceless. As such, it is a courageous act—as such, it represents a threat. To those who wield oppressive power, that which is threatening must necessarily be wiped out, annihilated, silenced.

Recently, efforts by black women writers to call attention to our work serve to highlight both our presence and absence. Whenever I peruse women's bookstores, I am struck not by the rapidly growing body of feminist writing by black women, but by the paucity of available published material. Those of us who write and are published remain few in number. The context of silence is varied and multi-dimensional. Most obvious are the ways racism, sexism, and class exploitation act to suppress and silence. Less obvious are the inner struggles, the efforts made to gain the necessary confidence to write, to re-write, to fully develop craft and skill—and the extent to which such efforts fail.

Although I have wanted writing to be my life-work since childhood, it has been difficult for me to claim "writer" as part of that which identifies and shapes my everyday reality. Even after publishing books, I would often speak of wanting to be a writer as though these works did not exist. And though I would be told, "you are a writer," I was not yet ready to fully affirm this truth. Part of myself was still held captive by domineering forces of history, of familial life that had charted a map of silence, of right speech. I had not completely let go of the fear of saying the wrong thing, of being punished. Somewhere in the deep recesses of my mind, I believed I could avoid both responsibility and punishment if I did not declare myself a writer.

One of the many reasons I chose to write using the pseudonym bell hooks, a family name (mother to Sarah Oldham, grandmother to Rosa Bell Oldham, great-grandmother to me), was to construct a writer-identity that would challenge and subdue all impulses leading me away from speech into silence. I was a young girl buying bubble gum at the corner store when I first really heard the full name bell hooks. I had just "talked back" to a grown person. Even now I can recall the surprised look, the mocking tones that informed me I must be kin to bell hooks—a sharp-tongued woman, a woman who spoke her mind, a woman who was not afraid to talk back. I claimed this legacy of defiance, of will, of courage, affirming my link to female ancestors who were bold and daring in their speech. Unlike my bold and daring mother and grandmother, who were not supportive of talking back, even though they were assertive and powerful in their speech, bell hooks as I discovered, claimed, and invented her was my ally, my support.

That initial act of talking back outside the house was empowering.   15 It was the first of many acts of defiant speech that would make it possible for me to emerge as an independent thinker and writer. In retrospect, "talking back" became for me a rite of initiation, testing my courage, strengthening my commitment, preparing me for the days ahead—the days when writing, rejection notices, periods of silence, publication, ongoing development seem impossible but necessary.

Moving from silence into speech is for the oppressed, the colonized, the exploited, and those who stand and struggle side by side a gesture of defiance that heals, that makes new life and new growth possible. It is that act of speech, of "talking back," that is no mere gesture of empty words, that is the expression of our movement from object to subject—the liberated voice.

THE NEW COMMUNITY

Amitai Etzioni

AMITAI ETZIONI (1929-)

Amitai Etzioni was born in Germany shortly before the Nazis' rise to power, eventually settling in Palestine where he attended boarding school. Etzioni obtained his B.A. and M.A. in sociology from Hebrew University, subsequently earning a Ph.D. in sociology from the University of California, Berkeley, in 1958. He taught at Columbia University for two decades, there directing for the Center for Policy Research, and became University Professor of Sociology at George Washington University in 1980, where he remains today. He has also taught at Harvard Business School, and served as a Senior Advisor to the White House from 1979-1980. In 1989, he founded the International Society for the Advancement of Socio-Economics, and became its first president. Etzioni has authored several scholarly and more general works, including most recently *Law in a New Key: Essays on Law and Society* (2011).

1   It's hard to believe now, but for a long time the loss of community was considered to be liberating. Societies were believed to progress from closely knit, "primitive," or rural villages to unrestrictive, "modern," or urban societies. The former were depicted as based on kinship and loyalty in an age in which both were suspect; the latter, however, were seen as based on reason (or "rationality") in an era in which reason's power to illuminate was admired with little attention paid to the deep shadow it casts. The two types of social relations have often been labeled with the terms supplied by a German sociologist, Ferdinand Tönnies. One is *gemeinschaft*, the German term for community, and the other is *gesellschaft*, the German word for society, which he used to refer to people who have rather few bonds, like people in a crowd or a mass society (*Community and Society*).

    Far from decrying the loss of community, this sanguine approach to the rise of modernity depicted small towns and villages as backward places that confined behavior. American writers such as Sinclair Lewis and John O'Hara satirized small towns as insular, claustrophobic

302

places, inhabited by petty, mean-spirited people. They were depicted as the opposite of "big cities," whose atmosphere was said to set people free. Anonymity would allow each person to pursue what he or she wished rather than what the community dictated. It was further argued that relations in the *gesellschaft* would be based not on preexisting, "ascribed" social bonds, such as between cousins, but on contractual relations, freely negotiated among autonomous individuals.

Other major forms of progress were believed to accompany the movement from a world of villages to one of cities. Magic, superstition, alchemy, and religion—"backward beliefs"—would be replaced by bright, shining science and technology. There would be no more villagers willing to sell their wares only to their own kind and not to outsiders—a phenomenon anthropologists have often noted. Old-fashioned values and a sense of obligation were expected to yield to logic and calculation. Social bonds dominating all relations (you did not charge interest on a loan to members of your community because such a charge was considered indecent usury) were pushed aside to make room for a free market, with prices and interest rates set according to market logic. By the same token, the network of reciprocal obligations and care that is at the heart of communities would give way to individual rights protected by the state. The impersonal right to social services and welfare payments, for instance, would replace any reliance on members of one's family, tribe, or ethnic benevolent association.

The sun, moon, and stars of the new universe would be individuals, not the community. In a typical case, the U.S. Supreme Court ruled that the Sierra Club had no legal standing to argue for the preservation of parkland as a community resource (Glendon 112). Rather, if the Sierra Club wished to show standing, it would have to demonstrate that particular individuals were harmed.

Throughout twentieth-century America, as the transition to   5
gesellschaft evolved, even its champions realized that it was not the unmitigated blessing they had expected. Although it was true that those who moved from villages and small towns into urban centers often shed tight social relations and strong community bonds, the result for many was isolation, lack of caring for one another, and exposure to rowdiness and crime.

Criminologists report that young farmhands in rural America in the early nineteenth-century did not always work on their parents' land. However, when they were sent to work outside their home they usually lived with other farmers and were integrated into their family life. In this way they were placed in a community context that sustained the moral voice, reinforced the values of their upbringing, and promoted socially constructive behavior. It was only when these farmhands went to work in factories in cities—and were housed on their own in barracks without established social networks, elders, and values—that rowdy and criminal behavior, alcoholism, and prostitution became common. Even in those early days attempts to correct these proclivities were made not by returning these young people to their families and villages, but by trying to generate Communitarian elements in the cities. Among the best analysts of these developments is James Q. Wilson, a leading political scientist. He notes that associations such as the Young Men's Christian Association (YMCA), temperance societies, and the Children's Aid society sought to provide a socially appropriate, morality-sustaining context for young people ("Rediscovery" 13).

Other experiences paralleled those of the factory hands. The migration to the American West, for example, is usually thought of as a time when individuals were free to venture forth and carve out a life of their own in the Great Plains. Actually, many people traveled in caravans and settled as communities, although each family claimed its own plot of land. Mutual assistance in such rough terrain was an absolute requirement. Mining towns and trading posts, however, in which rampant individualism often did prevail, were places of much chicanery. People who had mined gold often lost their stakes to unscrupulous traders; those who owned land were driven off it with little compensation by railroad companies, among others. Fly-by-night banks frequently welshed on notes that they themselves had issued. An unfettered market, one without a community context, turned out to lack the essential moral underpinnings that trade requires, and not just by sound social relations.

In many ways these frontier settlements—with their washed-out social bonds, loose morals, and unbridled greed—were the forerunners of Wall Street in the 1980s. The Street became a "den of thieves," thick with knaves who held that anything went as long as you made millions more than the next guy. Moreover, the mood of self-centered "making it" of the me generation spilled over into large segments of society. It was celebrated by the White House and many in Congress, who saw in an unfettered pursuit of self-interest the social force that revitalizes economies and societies. By the end of the eighties even some of the proponents of me-ism felt that the pursuit of greed had run amok.

By the early nineties the waning of community, which had long concerned sociologists, became more pronounced and drew more attention. As writer Jonathan Rowe put it: "It was common to think about the community as we used to think about air and water. It is there. It takes care of itself, and it can and will absorb whatever we unleash into it" ("Left and Right"). Now it became evident that the social environment needed fostering just as nature did. Responding to the new cues, George Bush evoked the image of a "kinder, gentler" society as a central theme for his first presidential campaign in 1988. The time was right to return to community and the moral order it harbored. Bill Clinton made the spirit of community a theme of his 1992 campaign.

The prolonged recession of 1991-1992 and the generally low   10 and slowing growth of the American economy worked against this new concern with we-ness. Interracial and interethnic tensions rose considerably, not only between blacks and whites, but also between blacks and Hispanics and among various segments of the community and Asian-Americans. This is one more reason why the United States will have to work its way to a stronger, growing, more competitive economy: interracial and ethnic peace are much easier to maintain in a rising than in a stagnant economy. However, it does not mean that community rebuilding has to be deferred until the economy is shored up. It does indicate that enhancing we-ness will require greater commitment and effort from both the government and the people, if community rebuilding is to take place in a sluggish economy.

Does this mean that we all have to move back to live in small towns and villages in order to ensure the social foundations of morality, to rebuild and shore up we-ness? Can one not bring up decent young people in the city? Isn't it possible to have a modern society, which requires a high concentration of labor and a great deal of geographic mobility—and still sustain a web of social bonds, a Communitarian nexus? There is more than one sociological answer to these queries. First, many cities have sustained (or reclaimed) some elements of community. Herbert Gans, a Columbia University sociologist, observed that within cities there were what he called "urban villages." He found communities where, generally speaking, "neighbors were friendly and quick to say hello to each other," where the various ethnic groups, transients, and bohemians "could live together side by side without much difficulty." Gans further noted that "for most West Enders (in Boston)...life in the area resembled that found in the village or small town, and even in the suburb" (*The Urban Villagers*, 14-15). Even in large metropolises, such as New York City, there are neighborhoods in which many people know their neighbors, their shopkeepers, and their local leaders. They are likely to meet one another in neighborhood bars, bowling alleys, and places of worship. They watch out for each other's safety and children. They act in concert to protect their parks and bus stops. They form political clubs and are a force in local politics. (Jim Sleeper's *Closest of Strangers* provides a fine description of these New York City communities.)

In some instances members of one ethnic group live comfortably next to one another, as in New York City's Chinatown and Miami's Little Havana. In other cities ethnic groups are more geographically dispersed but sustain ethnic-community bonds around such institutions as churches and synagogues, social clubs, and private schools. In recent decades a measure of return to community has benefited from the revival of loyalty to ethnic groups. While the sons and daughters of immigrants, the so-called second generation, often sought to assimilate, to become Americanized to the point that their distinct backgrounds were lost in a new identity, *their* children, the third generation and onward, often seek to reestablish their ethnic identity and bonds.

How does one reconcile the two sociological pictures—the James Q. Wilson concept of the city as *gesellschaft*, with little community or moral base, and the Herbert Gans image of *gemeinschaft*, of urban villages? The answer, first of all, is that both exist side by side. Between the urban villages, in row houses and high rises, you find large pockets of people who do not know their next-door neighbors, with whom they may have shared a floor, corridors, and elevators for a generation. Elderly people especially, who have no social bonds at work and are largely abandoned by their families, often lead rather isolated lives. In 1950 14.4 percent of those sixty-five years of age and older lived alone (Monk 534); by 1990 the percentage stood at nearly 31 percent (U.S. Bureau of the Census, table L, 12).

Also, to some extent a welcome return to small-town life of sorts has been occurring in modern America. Although not all suburbs, which attracted millions of city dwellers, make for viable communities, as a rule the movement to the suburbs has enhanced the Communitarian nexus.

15   In addition, postmodern technology helps. More people are again able to work at home or nearby, and a high concentration of labor is less and less necessary, in contrast with the industrial age. People can use their computers and modems at home to do a good part of their office work, from processing insurance claims to trading worldwide

commodities, stocks, and bonds. Architects can design buildings and engineers monitor faraway power networks from their places of residence.

It used to be widely observed that Americans, unlike Europeans, move around so much that they are hard-pressed to put down real community roots. On average, it is said, the whole country moves about once every five years. These figures, however, may be a bit obsolete. For various reasons, in recent years Americans seem to move somewhat less often (Barringer A16). One explanation is a growing desire to maintain the bonds of friendship and local social roots of their children, spouses, and themselves. In effect there is little reason to believe that the economy will suffer if this trend continues, and it may actually benefit from less shuttling around of people. Surely the Communitarian nexus will benefit.

Finally, there are new, nongeographic, communities made up of people who do not live near one another. Their foundations may not be as stable and deep-rooted as residential communities, but they fulfill many of the social and moral functions of traditional communities. Work-based and professional communities are among the most common of these. That is, people who work together in a steel mill or a high-tech firm such as Lotus or Microsoft often develop work-related friendships and community webs; groups of co-workers hang around together, help one another, play and party together, and go on joint outings. As they learn to know and care for one another, they also form and reinforce moral expectations.

Other communities are found in some law firms, on many campuses (although one community may not encompass everyone on campus), among physicians at the same hospital or with the same specialty in a town, and among some labor union members.
Some critics have attacked these communities as being artificially constructed, because they lack geographical definition or because they are merely social networks, without a residential concentration. Ray Oldenburg, author of *The Great Good Place*, decries the new definitions of community that encompass co-workers and even radio call-in show audiences. "Can we really create a satisfactory community apart from geography?" he asks (Baldwin 17). "My answer is 'no.'" But people who work every day in the same place spend more hours together and in closer proximity than people who live on the same village street. Most important, these nongeographic communities often provide at least some elements of the Communitarian nexus, and hence they

tend to have the moral infrastructure we consider essential for a civil and humane society.

In short, our society is neither without community nor sufficiently Communitarian; it is neither *gemeinschaft* nor *gesellschaft*, but a mixture of the two sociological conditions. America does not need a simple return to *gemeinschaft*, to the traditional community. Modern economic prerequisites preclude such a shift, but even if it were possible, such backpedaling would be undesirable because traditional communities have been too constraining and authoritarian. Such traditional communities were usually homogeneous. What we need now are communities that balance both diversity and unity. As John W. Gardner has noted: "To prevent the wholeness from smothering diversity, there must be a philosophy of pluralism, an open climate for dissent, and an opportunity for subcommunities to retain their identity and share in the setting of larger group goals" (*Building Community* 11). Thus, we need to strengthen the communitarian elements in the urban and suburban centers, to provide the social bonds that sustain the moral voice, but at the same time avoid tight networks that suppress pluralism and dissent. James Pinkerton, who served in the Bush White House, speaks eloquently about a new paradigm focused around what he calls a "new *gemeinschaft*." It would be, he says, neither oppressive nor hierarchical. In short, we need new communities in which people have choices and readily accommodate divergent *sub*communities but still maintain common bonds.

Notes

Deborah Baldwin, "Creating Community," *Common Cause Magazine*, July/August 1990, 17.

Felicity Barringer, "18 Percent of Households in U.S. Moved in '89," *New York Times*, December 20, 1991, A16.

Herbert Gans, *The Urban Villagers: Group and Class in the Life of Italian-Americans* (New York: The Free Press, 1962, 1982), 14-15.

John W. Gardner, *Building Community* (Washington, D.C.: Independent Sector, 1991), 11.

Mary Ann Glendon, *Rights Talk* (New York: The Free Press, 1991), 112.

Abraham Monk, "Aging, Loneliness, and Communications," *American Behavioral Scientist* 31 (5): 534.

Jonathan Rowe, "Left and Right: The Emergence of a New Politics in the 1990s?" sponsored by the Heritage Foundation and the Progressive Foundation, October 30, 1991, Washington, D.C.

Jim Sleeper, *Closest of Strangers: Liberalism and the Politics of Race in New York* (New York: W.W. Norton & Company, 1990).

Ferdinand Tönnies, *Community and Society*, translated and edited by Charles P. Loomis (East Lansing: Michigan State University Press, 1957).

HOW SOCIAL
MOVEMENTS MATTER

David S. Meyer

◇

DAVID S. MEYER

David S. Meyer received a B.A. in literature from Hampshire College in 1980 and a M.A. (1984) and Ph.D. (1988) in political science from Boston University. He has taught at institutions including Tufts University, the City College of New York, and the University of Michigan. His works include *A Winter of Discontent: The Nuclear Freeze and American Politics* (1990), his first book, and *The Politics of Protest: Social Movements in America* (2006). He currently teaches sociology at the University of California, Irvine.

1   In January 2003, tens if not hundreds of thousands of people assembled in Washington, D.C. to try to stop the impending invasion of Iraq. It did not look good for the demonstrators. Months earlier, Congress authorized President Bush to use force to disarm Iraq, and Bush repeatedly said that he would not let the lack of international support influence his decision about when—or whether—to use military force. Opposition to military action grew in the intervening months; the Washington demonstration coincided with sister events in San Francisco, Portland, Tampa, Tokyo, Paris, Cairo and Moscow. Protests, albeit smaller and less frequent, continued after the war began. Did any of them change anything? Could they have? How? And how would we know if they did?

Such questions are not specific to this latest peace mobilization, but are endemic to protest movements more generally. Social movements are organized challenges to authorities that use a broad range of tactics, both inside and outside of conventional politics, in an effort to promote social and political change. Opponents of the Iraq War wrote letters to elected officials and editors of newspapers, called talk radio shows and contributed money to antiwar groups.

Many also invited arrest by civil disobedience; some protesters, for example, blocked entrances to government offices and military bases. A group of 50 "Unreasonable Women of West Marin" lay naked on a northern California beach, spelling out "Peace" with their bodies for a photographer flying overhead. Besides using diverse methods of protest, opponents of the war also held diverse political views. Some opposed all war, some opposed all U.S. military intervention, while others were skeptical only about this particular military intervention. This is a familiar social movement story: broad coalitions stage social movements, and differences within a movement coalition are often nearly as broad as those between the movement and the authorities it challenges.

Political activists and their targets act as if social movements matter, and sociologists have been trying, for the better part of at least four decades, to figure out why, when and how. It is too easy—and not very helpful—to paint activists as heroes or, alternatively, as cranks. It is similarly too easy to credit them for social change or, alternatively, to dismiss their efforts by saying that changes, such as advances in civil rights or environmental protections, would have happened anyway. What we have learned is that social movements are less a departure from conventional institutional politics than an extension of them—a "politics by other means." In the end, we find that movements crest and wane, often failing to attain their immediate goals, but they can lastingly change political debates, governmental institutions and the wider culture.

It is often difficult to tell whether activism makes a difference because the forces that propel people to mobilize are often the same forces responsible for social change. For example, it is difficult to decide whether the feminist movement opened new opportunities to women or whether economic changes fostered both the jobs and feminism. Also, authorities challenged by movements deny that activism influenced their decisions. What politicians want to admit that their judgments can be affected by "mobs"? Why risk encouraging protesters in the future? Finally, movements virtually never achieve all that their partisans demand, and so activists are quick to question their own influence. As a result, proving that movements influence politics and policy involves difficult detective work.

But research shows that social movements can affect government 5 policy, as well as how it is made. And movement influence extends further. Activism often profoundly changes the activists, and through them, the organizations in which they participate, as well as the broader culture. The ways that movements make a difference are complex, veiled, and take far longer to manifest themselves than the news cycle that covers a single demonstration, or even a whole protest campaign.

When Movements Emerge

Activists protest when they think it might help them achieve their goals—goals they might not accomplish otherwise. Organizers successfully mobilize movements when they convince people that the issue at hand is urgent, that positive outcomes are possible and that their efforts could make a difference. In the case of the war on Iraq, for example, President Bush set the agenda for a broad range of activists by explicitly committing the country to military intervention. More conventional politics—elections, campaign contributions and letter-writing—had already played out and it became clear that none of these activities were sufficient, in and of themselves, to stop the war. In addition, the President's failure to build broad international or domestic support led activists to believe that direct pressure might prevent war. The rapid worldwide growth of the movement itself encouraged activism, assuring participants that they were part of something larger than themselves, something that might matter. In effect, President Bush's actions encouraged anti-war activism to spread beyond a small group of perpetual peace activists to a broader public.

With peace movements, it is clear that threat of war helps organizers mobilize people. Threats generally help political opposition grow beyond conventional politics. Movements against nuclear armaments, for example, emerge strongly when governments announce they are building more weapons. Similarly, environmental movements expand when government policies toward forests, pesticides, or toxic wastes become visibly negligent. In the case of abortion politics, each side has kept the other mobilized for more than 30 years by periodically threatening to take control of the issue. In each of these cases, those who lose in traditional political contests such as elections or lobbying campaigns often take to the streets.

Other sorts of movements grow when the promise of success arises. American civil rights activists, for example, were able to mobilize most broadly when they saw signals that substantial change was possible. Rosa Parks knew about Jackie Robinson and *Brown v. Board of Education*—as well as Gandhian civil disobedience—before deciding not to move to the back of the bus in Montgomery, Alabama. Government responsiveness to earlier activism—such as President Truman's desegregation of the armed forces and calling for an antilynching law—though limited, fitful, and often strategic, for a time encouraged others in their efforts. And the success of African-American activists encouraged other ethnic groups, as well as women, to pursue social change through movement politics.

As social movements grow, they incorporate more groups with a broader range of goals and more diverse tactics. Absent a focus like an imminent war, activists inside and political figures outside compete with one another to define movement goals and objectives. Political authorities often respond with policy concessions designed to diminish the breadth and depth of a movement. While such tactics can divide a movement, they are also one way of measuring a movement's success.

How Movements Matter: Public Policy

By uniting, however loosely, a broad range of groups and individuals,   10
and taking action, social movements can influence public policy, at least by bringing attention to their issues. Newspaper stories about a demonstration pique political, journalistic and public interest in the demonstrators' concerns. By bringing scrutiny to a contested policy, activists can promote alternative thinking. By displaying a large and engaged constituency, social movements provide political support for leaders sympathetic to their concerns. Large demonstrations show that there are passionate citizens who might also donate money, work in campaigns, and vote for candidates who will speak for them. Citizen mobilization against abortion, taxes, and immigration, for example, has encouraged ambitious politicians to cater to those constituencies. In these ways, social movement activism spurs and supports more conventional political action.

Activism outside of government can also strengthen advocates of minority positions within government. Social movements—just like presidential administrations and congressional majorities—are coalitions. Anti-war activists in the streets may have strengthened the bargaining position of the more internationalist factions in the Bush administration, most notably Colin Powell, and led, at least temporarily, to diplomatic action in the United Nations. Mobilized opposition also, for a time, seemed to embolden Congressional critics, and encouraged lesser-known candidates for the Democratic presidential nomination to vocally oppose the war.

Social movements, by the popularity of their arguments, or more frequently, the strength of their support, can convince authorities to re-examine and possibly change their policy preferences. Movements can demand a litmus test for their support. Thus, George H.W. Bush, seeking the Republican nomination for president in 1980, revised his prior support for abortion rights. A few years later, Jesse Jackson likewise reconsidered his opposition to abortion. Movements raised the profile of the issue, forcing politicians not only to address their concerns, but to accede to their demands.

Although movement activists promote specific policies—a nuclear freeze, an equal rights amendment, an end to legal abortion, or, more recently, a cap on malpractice awards—their demands are usually so absolute that they do not translate well into policy. (Placards and bumper stickers offer little space for nuanced debate.) Indeed, the clearest message that activists can generally send is absolute rejection: no to nuclear weapons, abortion, pesticides or taxes. These admonitions rarely become policy, but by promoting their programs in stark moral terms, activists place the onus on others to offer alternative policies that are, depending on one's perspective, more moderate or complex. At the same time, politicians often use such alternatives to capture, or at least defuse, social movements. The anti-nuclear weapons movement of the late 1950s and early 1960s did not end the arms race or all nuclear testing. It did, however, lead to the Limited Test Ban Treaty, which ended atmospheric testing. First Eisenhower, then Kennedy, offered arms control proposals and talks with the Soviet Union, at least in part as a response to the movement. This peace movement established the framework for arms control in superpower relations, which subsequently spread to the entire international community.

In these ways, activists shape events—even if they do not necessarily get credit for their efforts or achieve everything they want. The movement against the Vietnam War, for instance, generated a great deal of attention which, in turn, changed the conduct of that war and much else in domestic politics. President Johnson chose bombing targets with attention to minimizing political opposition; President Nixon, elected at least partly as a result of the backlash against the anti-war movement nonetheless tailored his military strategy to respond to some of its concerns. In later years, he suggested that the anti-war movement made it unthinkable for him to threaten nuclear escalation in Vietnam—even as a bluff. In addition, the movement helped end the draft, institutionalizing all-volunteer armed forces. And, according to Colin Powell, the Vietnam dissenters provoked a new military approach for the United States, one that emphasized the use of overwhelming force to minimize American casualties. Thus, the military execution of the 1991 Persian Gulf War was influenced by an anti-war movement that peaked more than three decades earlier. This is significant, if not the effect most anti-war activists envisioned.

Political Institutions

Social movements can alter not only the substance of policy, but also how policy is made. It is not uncommon for governments to create new institutions, such as departments and agencies, in response to activists' demands. For example, President Kennedy responded to the nuclear freeze movement by establishing the Arms Control and Disarmament Agency, which became a permanent voice and venue in the federal bureaucracy for arms control. A glance at any organizational chart of federal offices turns up numerous departments, boards, and commissions that trace their origins to popular mobilization. These include the Department of Labor, the Department of Housing and Urban Development, the National Labor Relations Board, the Environmental Protection Agency, the National Council on Disability, the Consumer Product Safety Commission and the Equal Employment Opportunity Commission. Although these offices do not always support activist goals, their very existence represents a permanent institutional concern and a venue for making demands. If, as environmentalists argue, the current Environmental Protection Agency is often more interested in facilitating exploitation of the environment than in preventing it, this does not negate the fact that the environmental movement established a set of procedures through which environmental concerns can be addressed.

Government responses to movement demands also include ensuring that diverse voices are heard in decision-making. In local zoning decisions, for example, environmental impact statements are now a routine part of getting a permit for construction. Congress passed legislation establishing this requirement in 1970 in response to the growing environmental movement. Indeed, movement groups, including Greenpeace and the Sierra Club, negotiated directly with congressional sponsors. Similarly, juries and judges now routinely hear victim impact statements before pronouncing sentences in criminal cases, the product of the victims' rights movement. Both public and private organizations have created new departments to manage and, perhaps more importantly, document personnel practices, such as hiring and firing, to avoid being sued for discrimination on the basis of gender, ethnicity or disability. Workshops on diversity, tolerance, and sexual harassment are commonplace in American universities and corporations, a change over just two decades that would have been impossible to imagine without the activism of the 1960s and 1970s. In such now well-established bureaucratic routines, we can see how social movements change practices, and through them, beliefs.

Social movements also spawn dedicated organizations that generally survive long after a movement's moment has passed. The environmental movement, for example, firmly established a "big ten" group of national organizations, such as the Wildlife Defense Fund, which survives primarily by raising money from self-defined environmentalists. It cultivates donors by monitoring and publicizing government actions and environmental conditions, lobbying elected officials and administrators, and occasionally mobilizing supporters to do something more than mail in their annual membership renewals. Here, too, the seemingly permanent establishment of "movement organizations" in Washington, D.C. and in state capitals across the United States has—even if these groups often lose—fundamentally changed policymaking. Salaried officers of the organizations routinely screen high-level appointees to the judiciary and government bureaucracy and testify before legislatures. Mindful of this process, policymakers seek to preempt their arguments by modifying policy— or at least their rhetoric.

Political Activists

Social movements also change the people who participate in them, educating as well as mobilizing activists, and thereby promoting ongoing awareness and action that extends beyond the boundaries of one movement or campaign. Those who turn out at anti-war demonstrations today have often cut their activist teeth mobilizing against globalization, on behalf of labor, for animal rights or against welfare reform. By politicizing communities, connecting people, and promoting personal loyalties, social movements build the infrastructure not only of subsequent movements, but of a democratic society more generally.

Importantly, these consequences are often indirect and difficult to document. When hundreds of thousands of activists march to the Supreme Court to demonstrate their support for legal abortion, their efforts might persuade a justice. More likely, the march signals commitment and passion to other activists and inspires them to return home and advocate for abortion rights in their communities across the country, thereby affecting the shape of politics and culture more broadly.

The 2003 anti-Iraq War movement mobilized faster, with better 20
organizational ties in the United States and transnationally, than, for
example, the movement against the 1991 Persian Gulf War. But how
are we to assess its influence? Many activists no doubt see their efforts as
having been wasted, or at least as unsuccessful. Moreover, supporters
of the war point to the rapid seizure of Baghdad and ouster of Saddam
Hussein's regime as evidence of the peace movement's naïveté. But a
movement's legacy extends through a range of outcomes beyond a
government's decision of the moment. It includes consequences for
process, institutional practices, organizations and individuals. This
anti-war movement changed the rhetoric and international politics of
the United States' preparation for war, leading to a detour through the
United Nations that delayed the start of the war. The activists who
marched in Washington, San Francisco and Los Angeles may retreat for
awhile, but they are likely to be engaged in politics more intensively in
the future. This may not be much consolation to people who marched
to stop a war, but it is true. To paraphrase a famous scholar: activists
make history, but they do not make it just as they please. In fighting
one political battle, they shape the conditions of the next one.

Reprinted from *Contexts 2, no. 4*, by permission of the University of
California Press.

◈

Called Home

Barbara Kingsolver

Barbara Kingsolver (1955-)

Barbara Kingsolver was born in Maryland and raised in Kentucky, but at age seven was taken by her family for two years to the Congo, where her parents worked in public health service. Kingsolver pursued undergraduate study at DePauw University, entering with a music scholarship but graduating in 1977 with a Bachelor of Science degree in biology. She followed that with a master's degree in ecology from the University of Arizona, after which she began a writing career, working initially for the university but expanding into work for outside publications. Kingsolver's first book, 1988's novel *The Bean Trees*, was quickly followed by several critically acclaimed works of both fiction and non-fiction, including *The Poisonwood Bible* (1998), inspired by that childhood excursion to the Congo, which was a Pulitzer Prize finalist. Other notable works include 1993's *Pigs in Heaven*, winner of the Los Angeles Times Book Prize, and most recently *The Lacuna* (2009), which won the United Kingdom's Orange Prize for Fiction. *Animal, Vegetable, Miracle*, recounting her family's year spent consuming locally-grown food, was named one of Time's Top 10 Non-Fiction Books of 2007. In 2011, Kingsolver became the first recipient of the Dayton Literary Peace Prize Richard C. Holbrooke Distinguished Achievement Award, celebrating written works which promote peace.

1 This story about good food begins in a quick-stop convenience market. It was our family's last day in Arizona, where I'd lived half my life and raised two kids for the whole of theirs. Now we were moving away forever, taking our nostalgic inventory of the things we would never see again: the bush where the roadrunner built a nest and fed lizards to her weird-looking babies; the tree Camille crashed into learning to ride a bike; the exact spot where Lily touched a dead snake. Our driveway was just the first tributary on a memory river sweeping us out.

One person's picture postcard is someone else's normal. This was the landscape whose every face we knew: giant saguaro cacti, coyotes, mountains, the wicked sun reflecting off bare gravel. We were leaving it now in one of its uglier moments, which made good-bye easier, but also seemed like a cheap shot—like ending a romance right when your partner has really bad bed hair. The desert that day looked like a nasty case of prickly heat caught in a long, naked wince.

This was the end of May. Our rainfall since Thanksgiving had measured less than *one inch*. The cacti, denizens of deprivation, looked ready to pull up roots and hitch a ride out if they could. The prickly pears waved good-bye with puckered, grayish pads. The tall, dehydrated saguaros stood around all teetery and sucked-in like very prickly supermodels. Even in the best of times desert creatures live on the edge of survival, getting by mostly on vapor and their own life savings. Now, as the southern tier of U.S. states came into a third consecutive year of drought, people elsewhere debated how seriously they should take global warming. We were staring it in the face.

Away went our little family, like rats leaping off the burning ship. It hurt to think about everything at once: our friends, our desert, old home, new home. We felt giddy and tragic as we pulled up at a little gas-and-go market on the outside edge of Tucson. Before we set off to seek our fortunes we had to gas up, of course, and buy snacks for the road. We did have a cooler in the back seat packed with respectable lunch fare. But we had more than two thousand miles to go. Before we crossed a few state lines we'd need to give our car a salt treatment and indulge in some things that go crunch.

This was the trip of our lives. We were ending our existence outside   5 the city limits of Tucson, Arizona, to begin a rural one in southern Appalachia. We'd sold our house and stuffed the car with the most crucial things: birth certificates, books-on-tape, and a dog on drugs. (Just for the trip, I swear.) All other stuff would come in the moving van. For better or worse, we would soon be living on a farm.

For twenty years Steven had owned a piece of land in the southern Appalachians with a farmhouse, barn, orchards and fields, and a tax zoning known as "farm use." He was living there when I met him, teaching college and fixing up his old house one salvaged window at a time. I'd come as a visiting writer, recently divorced, with something of a fixer-upper life. We proceeded to wreck our agendas in the predictable fashion by falling in love. My young daughter and I were attached to our community in Tucson; Steven was just as attached to his own green pastures and the birdsong chorus of deciduous eastern woodlands. My father-in-law to be, upon hearing the exciting news about us, asked Steven, "Couldn't you find one closer?"

Apparently not. We held on to the farm by renting the farmhouse to another family, and maintained marital happiness by migrating like birds: for the school year we lived in Tucson, but every summer headed back to our rich foraging grounds, the farm. For three months a year we lived in a tiny, extremely crooked log cabin in the woods behind the farmhouse, listening to wood thrushes, growing our own food. The girls (for another child came along shortly) loved playing in the creek, catching turtles, experiencing real mud. I liked working the land, and increasingly came to think of this place as my home too. When all of us were ready, we decided, we'd go there for keeps.

We had many conventional reasons for relocation, including extended family. My Kingsolver ancestors came from that county in Virginia; I'd grown up only a few hours away, over the Kentucky line. Returning now would allow my kids more than just a hit-and-run, holiday acquaintance with grandparents and cousins. In my adult life I'd hardly shared a phone book with anyone else using my last name. Now I could spend Memorial Day decorating my ancestors' graves with peonies from my backyard. Tucson had opened my eyes to the world and given me a writing career, legions of friends, and a taste for the sensory extravagance of red hot chiles and five-alarm sunsets. But after twenty-five years in the desert, I'd been called home.

There is another reason the move felt right to us, and it's the purview of this book. We wanted to live in a place that could feed us: where rain falls, crops grow, and drinking water bubbles right up out of the ground. This might seem an abstract reason for leaving beloved friends and one of the most idyllic destination cities in the United States. But it was real to us. As it closes in on the million-souls mark, Tucson's charms have made it one of this country's fastest-growing cities. It keeps its people serviced across the wide, wide spectrum of daily human wants, with its banks, shops, symphonies, colleges, art galleries, city parks, and more golf courses than you can shake a stick at. By all accounts it's a bountiful source of everything on the human-need checklist, save for just the one thing—the stuff we put in our mouths every few hours to keep us alive. Like many other modern U.S. cities, it might as well be a space station where human sustenance is concerned. Virtually every unit of food consumed there moves into town in a refrigerated module from somewhere far away. Every ounce of the city's drinking, washing, and goldfish-bowl-filling water is pumped from a nonrenewable source—a fossil aquifer that is dropping so fast, sometimes the ground crumbles. In a more recent development, some city water now arrives via a three-hundred-mile-long open canal across the desert from the Colorado River, which—owing to our thirsts—is a river that no longer reaches the ocean, but peters out in a sand flat near the Mexican border.

If it crosses your mind that water running through hundreds   10
of miles of open ditch in a desert will evaporate and end up full of concentrated salts and muck, then let me just tell you, that kind of negative thinking will never get you elected to public office in the state of Arizona. When this giant new tap turned on, developers drew up plans to roll pink stucco subdivisions across the desert in all directions. The rest of us were supposed to rejoice as the new flow rushed into our pipes, even as the city warned us this water was kind of special. They said it was okay to drink, but don't put it in an aquarium because it would *kill the fish*.

Drink it we did, then, filled our coffee makers too, and mixed our children's juice concentrate with fluid that would gag a guppy. Oh, America the Beautiful, where are our standards? How did Europeans, ancestral cultures to most of us, whose average crowded country would fit inside one of our national parks, somehow hoard the market share of Beautiful? They'll run over a McDonald's with a bulldozer because it threatens the way of life of their fine cheeses. They have international trade hissy fits when we try to slip modified genes into their bread. They get their favorite ham from Parma, Italy, along with a favorite cheese, knowing these foods are linked in an ancient connection the farmers have crafted between the milk and the hogs. Oh. We were thinking *Parmesan* meant, not "coming from Parma," but "coming from a green shaker can." Did they kick us out for bad taste?

No, it was mostly for vagrancy, poverty, or being too religious. We came here for the freedom to make a *Leaves of Grass* kind of culture and hear America singing to a good beat, pierce our navels as needed, and eat whatever we want without some drudge scolding: "You don't know where that's been!" And boy howdy, we do not.

The average food item on a U.S. grocery shelf has traveled farther than most families go on their annual vacations. True fact. Fossil fuels were consumed for the food's transport, refrigeration, and processing, with the obvious environmental consequences. The option of getting our household's food closer to home, in Tucson, seemed no better to us. The Sonoran desert historically offered to humans baked dirt as a construction material, and for eats, a corn-and-beans diet organized around late summer monsoons, garnished in spring with cactus fruits and wild tubers. The Hohokam and Pima were the last people to live on that land without creating an environmental overdraft. When the Spaniards arrived, they didn't rush to take up the Hohokam diet craze. Instead they set about working up a monumental debt: planting orange trees and alfalfa, digging wells for irrigation, withdrawing millions more gallons from the water table each year than a dozen inches of annual rainfall could ever restore. Arizona is still an agricultural state. Even after the population boom of the mid-nineties, 85 percent of the state's water still went to thirsty crops like cotton, alfalfa, citrus, and pecan trees. Mild winters offer the opportunity to create an artificial endless summer, as long as we can conjure up water and sustain a chemically induced illusion of topsoil.

Living in Arizona on borrowed water made me nervous. We belonged to a far-flung little community of erstwhile Tucson homesteaders, raising chickens in our yards and patches of vegetables for our own use, frequenting farmers markets to buy from Arizona farmers, trying to reduce the miles-per-gallon quotient of our diets in a gasoholic world. But these gardens of ours had a drinking problem. So did Arizona farms. That's a devil of a choice: Rob Mexico's water or guzzle Saudi Arabia's gas?

15   Traditionally, employment and family dictate choices about where to live. It's also legitimate to consider weather, schools, and other quality-of-life indices. We added one more wish to our list: more than one out of three of the basic elements necessary for human life. (*Oxygen* Arizona has got.) If we'd had family ties, maybe we'd have felt more entitled to claim a seat at Tucson's lean dining table. But I moved there as a young adult, then added through birth and marriage three more mouths to feed. As a guest, I'd probably overstayed my welcome. So, as the U.S. population made an unprecedented dash for the Sun Belt, one carload of us dog-paddled against the tide, heading for the Promised Land where water falls from the sky and green stuff grows all around. We were about to begin the adventure of realigning our lives with our food chain.

Oily Food

Americans put almost as much fossil fuel into our refrigerators as our cars. We're consuming about 400 gallons of oil a year per citizen—about 17 percent of our nation's energy use—for agriculture, a close second to our vehicular use. Tractors, combines, harvesters, irrigation, sprayers, tillers, balers, and other equipment all use petroleum. Even bigger gas guzzlers on the farm are not the machines, but so-called inputs. Synthetic fertilizers, pesticides, and herbicides use oil and natural gas as their starting materials, and in their manufacturing. More than a quarter of all farming energy goes into synthetic fertilizers.

But getting the crop from seed to harvest takes only one-fifth of the total oil used for our food. The lion's share is consumed during the trip from the farm to your plate. Each food item in a typical U.S. meal has traveled an average of 1,500 miles. In addition to direct transport, other fuel-thirsty steps include processing (drying, milling, cutting, sorting, baking), packaging, warehousing, and refrigeration. Energy calories consumed by production, packaging, and shipping far outweigh the energy calories we receive from the food.

A quick way to improve food-related fuel economy would be to buy a quart of motor oil and drink it. More palatable options are available. If every U.S. citizen ate just one meal a week (any meal) composed of locally and organically raised meats and produce, we would reduce our country's oil consumption by over 1.1 million barrels of oil every week. That's not gallons, but barrels. Small changes in buying habits can make big differences. Becoming a less energy-dependent nation may just need to start with a good breakfast.

—Steven L. Hopp

Naturally, our first stop was to buy junk food and fossil fuel.

In the cinder-block convenience mart we foraged the aisles for blue corn chips and Craisins. Our family's natural-foods teenager scooped up a pile of energy bars big enough to pass as a retirement plan for a hamster. Our family's congenitally frugal Mom shelled out two bucks for a fancy green bottle of about a nickel's worth of iced tea. As long as we were all going crazy here, we threw in some 99-cent bottles of what comes free out of drinking fountains in places like Perrier, France. In our present location, 99 cents for good water seemed like a bargain. The goldfish should be so lucky.

As we gathered our loot onto the counter the sky darkened suddenly. After two hundred consecutive cloudless days, you forget what it looks like when a cloud crosses the sun. We all blinked. The cashier frowned toward the plate-glass window.

"*Dang*," she said, "it's going to rain."

20   "I hope so," Steven said.

She turned her scowl from the window to Steven. This bleached-blond guardian of gas pumps and snack food was not amused. "It better not, is all I can say."

"But we need it," I pointed out. I am not one to argue with cashiers, but the desert was dying, and this was my very last minute as a Tucsonian. I hated to jinx it with bad precipitation-karma.

"I know that's what they're saying, but I don't care. Tomorrow's my first day off in two weeks, and I want to wash my car."

For three hundred miles we drove that day through desperately parched Sonoran badlands, chewing our salty cashews with a peculiar guilt. We had all shared this wish, in some way or another: that it wouldn't rain on our day off. Thunderheads dissolved ahead of us, as if honoring our compatriot's desire to wash her car as the final benediction pronounced on a dying land. In our desert, we would not see rain again.

25   It took us five days to reach the farm. On our first full day there we spent ten hours mowing, clearing brush, and working on the farmhouse. Too tired to cook, we headed into town for supper, opting for a dinner of the southern type that puts grits on your plate until noon and biscuits after, whether you ask for them or not. Our waitress was young and chatty, a student at the junior college nearby studying to be a nurse or else, if she doesn't pass the chemistry, a television broadcaster. She said she was looking forward to the weekend, but smiled broadly nevertheless at the clouds gathering over the hills outside. The wooded mountainsides and velvet pastures of southwestern Virginia looked remarkably green to our desert-scorched eyes, but the forests and fields were suffering here too. Drought had plagued most of the southern United States that spring.

A good crack of thunder boomed, and the rain let loose just as the waitress came back to clear our plates. "Listen at that," she clucked. "Don't we need it!"

We do, we agreed. The hayfields aren't half what they should be.

"Let's hope it's a good long one," she said, pausing with our plates balanced on her arm, continuing to watch out the window for a good long minute. "And that it's not so hard that it washes everything out."

It is not my intention here to lionize country wisdom over city ambition. I only submit that the children of farmers are likely to know where food comes from, and that the rest of us might do well to pay attention. For our family, something turned over that evening in the diner: a gas-pump cashier's curse of drought was lifted by a waitress's simple, agricultural craving for rain. I thought to myself: There is hope for us.

Who is *us*, exactly? I live now in a county whose economic base is farming. A disastrous summer will mean some of our neighbors will lose their farms. Others will have to keep farming *and* go looking for a job at the end of a long commute. We'll feel the effects in school enrollments, local businesses, shifts in land use and tax structure. The health of our streams, soils, and forests is also at stake, as lost farms get sold to developers whose business it is to rearrange (drastically) the topsoil and everything on it. When I recognize good agricultural sense, though, I'm not just thinking of my town but also my species. It's not a trivial difference: praying for or against rainfall during a drought. You can argue that wishes don't count, but humans are good at making our dreams manifest and we do, historically speaking, get what we wish for. What are the just deserts for a species too selfish or preoccupied to hope for rain when the land outside is dying? Should we be buried under the topsoil in our own clean cars, to make room for wiser creatures?

We'd surely do better, if only we *knew* any better. In two generations we've transformed ourselves from a rural to an urban nation. North American children begin their school year around Labor Day and finish at the beginning of June with no idea that this arrangement was devised to free up children's labor when it was needed on the farm. Most people of my grandparents' generation had an intuitive sense of agricultural basics: when various fruits and vegetables come into season, which ones keep through the winter, how to preserve the others. On which day autumn's first frost will likely fall on their county, and when to expect the last one in spring. Which crops can be planted before the last frost, and which must wait. Which grains are autumn-planted. What an asparagus patch looks like in August. Most importantly: what animals and vegetables thrive in one's immediate region and how to live well on those, with little else thrown into the

30

mix beyond a bag of flour, a pinch of salt, and a handful of coffee. Few people of my generation, and approximately none of our children, could answer any of those questions, let alone all. This knowledge has vanished from our culture.

We also have largely convinced ourselves it wasn't too important. Consider how Americans might respond to a proposal that agriculture was to become a mandatory subject in all schools, alongside reading and mathematics. A fair number of parents would get hot under the collar to see their kids' attention being pulled away from the essentials of grammar, the all-important trigonometry, to make room for down-on-the-farm stuff. The baby boom psyche embraces a powerful presumption that education is a key to moving *away* from manual labor, and dirt—two undeniable ingredients of farming. It's good enough for us that somebody, somewhere, knows food production well enough to serve the rest of us with all we need to eat, each day of our lives.

If that is true, why isn't it good enough for someone else to know multiplication and the contents of the Bill of Rights? Is the story of bread, from tilled ground to our table, less relevant to our lives than the history of the thirteen colonies? Couldn't one make a case for the relevance of a subject that informs choices we make *daily*—as in, What's for dinner? Isn't ignorance of our food sources causing problems as diverse as overdependence on petroleum, and an epidemic of diet-related diseases?

If this book is not exactly an argument for reinstating food production classes in schools (and it might be), it does contain a lot of what you might learn there. From our family's gas-station beginnings we have traveled far enough to discover ways of taking charge of one's food, and even knowing where it has been. This is the story of a year in which we made every attempt to feed ourselves animals and vegetables whose provenance we really knew. We tried to wring most of the petroleum out of our food chain, even if that meant giving up some things. Our highest shopping goal was to get our food from so close to home, we'd know the person who grew it. Often that turned out to be *us*, as we learned to produce more of what we needed, starting with dirt, seeds, and enough knowledge to muddle though. Or starting with baby animals and enough sense to refrain from naming them.

35   This is not a how-to book aimed at getting you cranking out your own food. We ourselves live in a region where every other house has a garden out back, but to many urban people the idea of growing your food must seem as plausible as writing and conducting your own

symphonies for your personal listening pleasure. If that is your case, think of the agricultural parts of the story as a music appreciation course for food—acquainting yourself with the composers and conductors can improve the quality of your experience. Knowing the secret natural history of potatoes, melons, or asparagus gives you a leg up on detecting whether those in your market are wholesome kids from a nearby farm, or vagrants who idled away their precious youth in a boxcar. Knowing how foods grow is to know how and when to look for them; such expertise is useful for certain kinds of people, namely, the ones who eat, no matter where they live or grocery shop.

Absence of that knowledge has rendered us a nation of wary label-readers, oddly uneasy in our obligate relationship with the things we eat. We call our food animals by different names after they're dead, presumably sparing ourselves any vision of the beefs and the porks running around on actual hooves. Our words for unhealthy contamination—"soiled" or "dirty"—suggest that if we really knew the number-one ingredient of a garden, we'd all head straight into therapy. I used to take my children's friends out to the garden to warm them up to the idea of eating vegetables, but this strategy sometimes backfired: they'd back away slowly saying, "Oh *man*, those things touched *dirt!*" Adults do the same by pretending it all comes from the clean, well-lighted grocery store. We're like petulant teenagers rejecting our mother. We *know* we came out of her, but *ee-ew*.

We don't know beans about beans. Asparagus, potatoes, turkey drumsticks—you name it, we don't have a clue how the world makes it. I usually think I'm exaggerating the scope of the problem, and then I'll encounter an editor (at a well-known nature magazine) who's nixing the part of my story that refers to pineapples growing from the ground. She insisted they grew on trees. Or, I'll have a conversation like this one:

"What's new on the farm?" asks my friend, a lifelong city dweller who likes for me to keep her posted by phone. She's a gourmet cook, she cares about the world, and has been around a lot longer than I have. This particular conversation was in early spring, so I told her what was up in the garden: peas, potatoes, spinach.

"Wait a minute," she said. "When you say, 'The potatoes are up,' what do you mean?" She paused, formulating her question: "What part of a potato comes *up*?"

"Um, the plant part," I said. "The stems and leaves."   40

"Wow," she said. "I never knew a potato *had* a plant part."

Many bright people are really in the dark about vegetable life. Biology teachers face kids in classrooms who may not even believe in the metamorphosis of bud to flower to fruit and seed, but rather, some continuum of pansies becoming petunias becoming chrysanthemums; that's the only reality they witness as landscapers come to campuses and city parks and surreptitiously yank out one flower before it fades from its prime, replacing it with another. (My biology-professor brother pointed this out to me.) The same disconnection from natural processes may be at the heart of our country's shift away from believing in evolution. In the past, principles of natural selection and change over time made sense to kids who'd watched it all unfold. Whether or not they knew the terms, farm families understood the processes well enough to imitate them: culling, selecting, and improving their herds and crops. For modern kids who intuitively believe in the spontaneous generation of fruits and vegetables in the produce section, trying to get their minds around the slow speciation of the plant kingdom may be a stretch.

Steven, also a biology professor, grew up in the corn belt of Iowa but has encountered his share of agricultural agnostics in the world. As a graduate student he lived in an urban neighborhood where his little backyard vegetable garden was a howling curiosity for the boys who ran wild in the alley. He befriended these kids, especially Malcolm, known throughout the neighborhood as "Malcolm-get-your-backside-in-here-now-or-you-won't-be-*having*-no-dinner!" Malcolm liked hanging around when Steven was working in the garden, but predictably enough, had a love-hate thing with the idea of the vegetables touching the dirt. The first time he watched Steven pull long, orange carrots out of the ground, he demanded: "How'd you get them *in* there?"

Steven held forth with condensed Intro Botany. Starts with a seed, grows into a plant. Water, sunlight, leaves, roots. "A carrot," Steven concluded, "is actually a root."

45   "Uh-huh..." said Malcolm doubtfully.

A crowd had gathered now. Steven engaged his audience by asking, "Can you guys think of other foods that might be root vegetables?"

Malcolm checked with his pals, using a lifeline before confidently submitting his final answer: "Spaghetti?"

We can't know what we haven't been taught. Steven couldn't recognize tobacco in vivo before moving in his twenties to southwestern Virginia, where the tobacco leaf might as well be the state flag. One Saturday morning soon after he'd moved, he was standing on a farmer's porch at a country yard sale when a field of giant, pale leaves and tall pink flower spikes caught his eye. He asked the farmer the name of this gorgeous plant. The man grinned hugely and asked, "You're not *from* here, are you, son?"

That farmer is probably still telling this story; Steven is his Malcolm. Every one of us is somebody's Malcolm. Country folks can be as food-chain-challenged as the city mice, in our own ways. Rural southern cooking is famous for processed-ingredient recipes like Coca-Cola cake, and plenty of rural kids harbor a potent dread of compost and earthworms. What we all don't know about farming could keep the farmers laughing until the cows come home. Except that they are barely making a living, while the rest of us play make-believe about the important part being the grocery store.

When we walked as a nation away from the land, our knowledge   50
of food production fell away from us like dirt in a laundry-soap commercial. Now it's fair to say, the majority of us don't want to be farmers, see farmers, pay farmers, or hear their complaints. Except as straw-chewing figures in children's books, we don't quite believe in them anymore. When we give it a thought, we mostly consider the food industry to be a *thing* rather than a person. We obligingly give 85 cents of our every food dollar to that thing, too—the processors, marketers, and transporters. And we complain about the high price of organic meats and vegetables that might send back more than three nickels per buck to the farmers: those actual humans putting seeds in the ground, harvesting, attending livestock births, standing in the fields at dawn casting their shadows upon our sustenance. There seems to be some reason we don't want to compensate or think about these hardworking people. In the grocery store checkout corral, we're more likely to learn which TV stars are secretly fornicating than to inquire as to the whereabouts of the people who grew the cucumbers and melons in our carts.

This drift away from our agricultural roots is a natural consequence of migration from the land to the factory, which is as old as the Industrial Revolution. But we got ourselves uprooted entirely by a drastic reconfiguration of U.S. farming, beginning just after World War II. Our munitions plants, challenged to beat their swords into plowshares, retooled to make ammonium nitrate surpluses into chemical fertilizers instead of explosives. The next explosions were yields on Midwestern corn and soybean fields. It seemed like a good thing, but some officials saw these new surpluses as reason to dismantle New Deal policies that had helped farmers weather the economic uncertainties notorious to their vocation. Over the next decades, nudged by industry, the government rewrote the rules on commodity subsidies so these funds did not safeguard farmers, but instead guaranteed a supply of cheap corn and soybeans.

These two crops, formerly food for people and animals, became something entirely new: a standardized raw material for a new extractive industry, not so different from logging or mining. Mills and factories were designed for a multibranched production line as complex as the one that turns iron and aluminum ores into the likes of automobiles, paper clips, and antiperspirants. But instead, this new industry made piles of corn and soybeans into high-fructose corn syrup, hydrogenated oils, and thousands of other starch- or oil-based chemicals. Cattle and chickens were brought in off the pasture into intensely crowded and mechanized CAFOs (concentrated animal feeding operations) where corn—which is no part of a cow's natural diet, by the way—could be turned cheaply and quickly into animal flesh. All these different products, in turn, rolled on down the new industrial food pipeline to be processed into the soft drinks, burgers, and other cheap foods on which our nation now largely runs—or sits on its bottom, as the case may be.

This is how 70 percent of all our Midwestern agricultural land shifted gradually into single-crop corn or soybean farms, each one of them now, on average, the size of Manhattan. Owing to synthetic fertilizers and pesticides, genetic modification, and a conversion of farming from a naturally based to a highly mechanized production system, U.S. farmers now produce 3,900 calories per U.S. citizen, per day. That is twice what we need, and 700 calories a day more than they grew in 1980. Commodity farmers can only survive by producing their maximum yields, so they do. And here is the shocking plot twist: as the farmers produced those extra calories, the food industry figured out how to get them into the bodies of people who didn't really *want* to eat 700 more calories a day. That is the well-oiled machine we call Late Capitalism.

Most of those calories enter our mouths in forms hardly recognizable as corn and soybeans, or even vegetable in origin: high-fructose corn syrup (HFCS) owns up to its parentage, but lecithin, citric acid, maltodextrin, sorbitol, and xanthan gum, for example, are also manufactured from corn. So are beef, eggs, and poultry, in a different but no less artificial process. Soybeans also become animal flesh, or else a category of ingredient known as "added fats." If every product containing corn or soybeans were removed from your grocery store, it would look more like a hardware store. Alarmingly, the lightbulbs might be naked, since many packaging materials also now contain cornstarch.

With so many extra calories to deliver, the packages have gotten   55 bigger. The shapely eight-ounce Coke bottle of yesteryear became twenty ounces of carbonated high-fructose corn syrup and water; the accompanying meal morphed similarly. So did the American waistline. U.S. consumption of "added fats" has increased by one-third since 1975, and our HFCS is up by 1000 percent. About a third of all our calories now come from what is known, by community consent, as junk food.

No cashier held a gun to our heads and made us supersize it, true enough. But humans have a built-in weakness for fats and sugar. We evolved in lean environments where it was a big plus for survival to gorge on calorie-dense foods whenever we found them. Whether or not they understand the biology, food marketers know the weakness and have exploited it without mercy. Obesity is generally viewed as a failure of personal resolve, with no acknowledgment of the genuine conspiracy in this historical scheme. People actually did sit in strategy meetings discussing ways to get all those surplus calories into people who neither needed nor wished to consume them. Children have been targeted especially; food companies spend over $10 billion a year selling food brands to kids, and it isn't broccoli they're pushing. Overweight children are a demographic in many ways similar to minors addicted to cigarettes, with one notable exception: their parents are usually their suppliers. We all subsidize the cheap calories with our tax dollars, the strategists make fortunes, and the overweight consumers get blamed for the violation. The perfect crime.

All industrialized countries have experienced some commodification of agriculture and increased consumption of processed foods. But nowhere else on earth has it become normal to layer on the love handles as we do. (Nude beaches are still popular in Europe.) Other well-fed populations have had better luck controlling caloric excess through culture and custom: Italians eat Italian food, the Japanese eat Japanese, and so on, honoring ancient synergies between what their land can give and what their bodies need. Strong food cultures are both aesthetic and functional, keeping the quality and quantity of foods consumed relatively consistent from one generation to the next. And so, while the economies of many Western countries expanded massively in the late twentieth century, their citizens did not.

Here in the U.S. we seem puzzled by these people who refrain from gluttony in the presence of a glut. We've even named a thing we call the French Paradox: How can people have such a grand time eating cheese and fattened goose livers and still stay slim? Having logged some years in France, I have some hunches: they don't suck down giant sodas; they consume many courses in a meal but the portions of the fatty ones tend to be tiny; they smoke like chimneys (though that's changing); and they draw out meals sociably, so it's not just about shoveling it in. The all-you-can-eat buffet is an alien concern to the French, to put it mildly. Owing to certain rules about taste and civility in their heads, their bodies seem to know when enough is enough. When asked, my French friends have confided with varying degrees of tact that the real paradox is how people manage to consume, so very much, the scary food of America.

Why do we? Where are our ingrained rules of taste and civility, our ancient treaties between our human cravings and the particular fat of our land? Did they perhaps fly out the window while we were eating in a speeding car?

60   Food culture in the United States has long been cast as the property of a privileged class. It is nothing of the kind. Culture is the property of a species. Humans don't do everything we crave to do— that is arguably what makes us human. We're genetically predisposed toward certain behaviors that we've collectively decided are unhelpful; adultery and racism are possible examples. With reasonable success, we mitigate those impulses through civil codes, religious rituals, maternal warnings—the whole bag of tricks we call culture. Food cultures concentrate a population's collective wisdom about the plants and animals that grow in a place, and the complex ways of rendering them tasty. These are mores of survival, good health, and control of excess. Living without such a culture would seem dangerous.

And here we are, sure enough in trouble. North America's native cuisine met the same unfortunate fate as its native people, save for a few relics like the Thanksgiving turkey. Certainly, we still have regional specialties, but the Carolina barbecue will almost certainly have California tomatoes in its sauce (maybe also Nebraska-fattened feedlot hogs), and the Louisiana gumbo is just as likely to contain Indonesian farmed shrimp. If either of these shows up on a fast-food menu with lots of added fats or HFCS, we seem unable either to discern or resist the corruption. We have yet to come up with a strong set of generalized norms, passed down through families, for savoring and sensibly consuming what our land and climate give us. We have, instead, a string of fad diets convulsing our bookstores and bellies, one after another, at the scale of the national best seller. Nine out of ten nutritionists (unofficial survey) view this as evidence that we have entirely lost our marbles. A more optimistic view might be this: these sets of mandates captivate us because we're looking hard for a food culture of our own. A profit-driven food industry has exploded and nutritionally bankrupted our caloric supply, and we long for a Food Leviticus to save us from the sinful roil of cheap fats and carbs.

What the fad diets don't offer, though, is any sense of national and biological integrity. A food culture is not something that gets sold to people. It arises out of a place, a soil, a climate, a history, a temperament, a collective sense of belonging. Every set of fad-diet rules is essentially framed in the negative, dictating what you must give up. Together they've helped us form powerfully negative associations with the very act of eating. Our most celebrated models of beauty are starved people. But we're still an animal that must eat to live. To paraphrase a famous campaign slogan: it's the biology, stupid. A food culture of anti-eating is worse than useless.

People hold to their food customs because of the positives: comfort, nourishment, heavenly aromas. A sturdy food tradition even calls to outsiders; plenty of red-blooded Americans will happily eat Italian, French, Thai, Chinese, you name it. But try the reverse: hand the Atkins menu to a French person, and run for your life.

Will North Americans ever have a food culture to call our own? Can we find or make up a set of rituals, recipes, ethics, and buying habits that will let us love our food and eat it too? Some signs point to "yes." Better food—more local, more healthy, more sensible—is a powerful new topic of the American conversation. It reaches from the epicurean quarters of Slow Food convivial to the matter-of-fact Surgeon General's Office; from Farm Aid concerts to school lunch programs. From the rural routes to the inner cities, we are staring at our plates and wondering where that's been. For the first time since our nation's food was ubiquitously local, the point of origin now matters again to some consumers. We're increasingly wary of an industry that puts stuff in our dinner we can't identify as animal, vegetable, mineral, or what. The halcyon postwar promise of "better living through chemistry" has fallen from grace. "No additives" is now often considered a plus rather than the minus that, technically, it is.

We're a nation with an eating disorder, and we know it. The multiple maladies caused by bad eating are taking a dire toll on our health—most tragically for our kids, who are predicted to be this country's first generation to have a shorter life expectancy than their parents. That alone is a stunning enough fact to give us pause. So is a government policy that advises us to eat more fruits and vegetables, while doling out subsidies not to fruit and vegetable farmers, but to commodity crops destined to become soda pop and cheap burgers. The farm bill, as of this writing, could aptly be called the Farm Kill, both for its effects on small farmers and for what it does to us, the consumers who are financing it. The Green Revolution of the 1970s promised that industrial agriculture would make food cheaper and available to more people. Instead, it has helped more of us become less healthy.

A majority of North Americans do understand, at some level, that our food choices are politically charged, affecting arenas from rural culture to international oil cartels and global climate change. Plenty of consumers are trying to get off the petroleum-driven industrial food wagon: banning fast food from their homes and schools, avoiding the unpronounceable ingredient lists. However, banning is negative and therefore fails as a food culture per se.

Something positive is also happening under the surface of our nation's food preference paradigm. It could be called a movement. It includes gardeners who grow some of their own produce—one-quarter of all U.S. households, according to the U.S. Census Bureau. Just as importantly, it's the city dwellers who roll their kids out of bed on Saturday mornings and head down to the farmers' markets to pinch the tomatoes and inhale the spicy-sweet melons—New York, alone, has about a quarter million such shoppers. It involves the farmers' markets themselves, along with a new breed of restaurant owner (and customer) dedicated to buying locally produced food. It has been embraced by farmers who manage to keep family farms by thinking outside the box, learning to grow organic peppers or gourmet mushrooms. It engages schoolchildren and teachers who are bringing food-growing curricula into classrooms and lunchrooms from Berkeley, California, to my own county in southern Appalachia. It includes the kids who get dirty in those outdoors classrooms planting tomatoes and peppers at the end of third grade, then harvesting and cooking their own pizza when they start back into fourth. And it owes a debt to parents who can watch those kids getting dirty, and not make a fuss.

Hungry World

All these heirloom eggplants and artisan cheeses from the farmers' market are great for weekend dinner parties, but don't we still need industrial farming to feed the hungry?

In fact, all the world's farms currently produce enough food to make every person on the globe fat. Even though 800 million people are chronically underfed (6 will die of hunger-related causes while you read this article), it's because they lack money and opportunity, not because food is unavailable in their countries. The UN Food and Agriculture Organization (FAO) reports that current food production can sustain world food needs even for the 8 billion people who are projected to inhabit the planet in 2030. This will hold even with anticipated increases in meat consumption, and without adding genetically modified crops.

Is all this the reliable bounty of industrial production? Yes and no—with the "no" being more of a problem in the near future. Industrial farming methods, wherever they are practiced, promote soil erosion, salinization, desertification, and loss of soil fertility. The FAO estimates that over 25 percent of arable land in the world is already compromised by one or more of these problems. The worst-affected areas are those with more arid climates or sloped terrain. Numerous field trials in both the United States and the United Kingdom have shown that organic practices can produce commodity crop yields (corn, soybeans, wheat) comparable to those of industrial farms. By using cover crops or animal manures for fertilizer, these practices improve soil fertility and moisture-holding capacity over seasons, with cumulative benefits. These techniques are particularly advantageous in regions that lack the money and technology for industrial approaches.

(continued on the next page)

At its heart, a genuine food culture is an affinity between people and the land that feeds them. Step one, probably, is to live on the land that feeds them, or at least on the same continent, ideally the same region. Step two is to be able to countenance the ideas of "food" and "dirt" in the same sentence, and three is to start poking into one's supply chain to learn where things are coming from. In the spirit of this adventure, our family set out to find ourselves a real American culture of food, or at least the piece of it that worked for us, and to describe it for anyone who might be looking for something similar.

Conventional methods are definitely producing huge quantities of corn, wheat, and soybeans, but not to feed the poor. Most of it becomes animal feed for meat production, or the ingredients of processed foods for wealthier consumers who are already getting plenty of calories. Food sellers prefer to market more food to people who have money, rather than those who have little. World food trade policies most often favor developed countries at the expense of developing countries; distributors, processors, and shippers reap most of the benefits. Even direct food aid for disasters (a small percentage of all the world's hunger) is most profitable for grain companies and shippers. By law, 75 percent of such aid sent from the United States to other nations must be grown, packaged, and shipped by U.S. companies. This practice, called "tied aid," delays shipments of food by as much as six months, increases the costs of the food by over 50 percent, and directs over two-thirds of the aid money to the distributors.

If efficiency is the issue, resources go furthest when people produce their own food, near to where it is consumed. Many hunger-relief organizations provide assistance not in the form of bags of food, but in programs that teach and provide support technology for locally appropriate, sustainable farming. These programs do more than alleviate hunger for a day and send a paycheck to a multinational. They provide a livelihood to the person in need, addressing the real root of hunger, which is not about food production, but about poverty.

For more information, visit www.wn.org, www.journeytoforever.org, or www.heifer.org.

—Steve L. Hopp

This book tells the story of what we learned, or didn't; what we ate, or couldn't; and how our family was changed by one year of deliberately eating food produced in the same place where we worked, loved our neighbors, drank the water, and breathed the air. It's not at all necessary to live on a food-producing farm to participate in this culture. But it is necessary to know such farms exist, understand something about what they do, and consider oneself basically in their court. This book is about those things.

70   The story is pegged, as we were, to a one-year cycle of how and when foods become available in a temperate climate. Because food cultures affect everyone living under the same roof, we undertook this project—both the eating and the writing—as a family. Steven's

sidebars are, in his words, "fifty-cent buckets of a dollar's worth of goods" on various topics I've mentioned in the narrative. Camille's essays offer a nineteen-year-old's perspective on the local-food project, plus nutritional information, recipes, and meal plans for every season. Lily's contributions were many, including more than fifty dozen eggs and a willingness to swear off Pop-Tarts for the duration, but she was too young to sign a book contract.

Will our single-family decision to step off the nonsustainable food grid give a big black eye to that petroleum-hungry behemoth? Keep reading, but don't hold your breath. We only knew, when we started, that similar choices made by many families at once were already making a difference: organic growers, farmers' markets, and small exurban food producers now comprise the fastest-growing sector of the U.S. food economy. A lot of people at once are waking up to a troublesome truth about cheap fossil fuels: we are going to run out of them. Our jet-age dependence on petroleum to feed our faces is a limited-time-only proposition. Every food calorie we presently eat has used dozens or even hundreds of fossil-fuel calories in its making: grain milling, for example, which turns corn into the ingredients of packaged foods, costs ten calories for every one food calorie produced. That's *before* it gets shipped anywhere. By the time my children are my age, that version of dinnertime will surely be an unthinkable extravagance.

I enjoy denial as much as the next person, but this isn't rocket science: our kids will eventually have to make food differently. They could be assisted by some familiarity with how vegetables grow from seeds, how animals grow on pasture, and how whole ingredients can be made into meals, gee whiz, right in the kitchen. My husband and I decided our children would not grow up without knowing a potato has a plant part. We would take a food sabbatical, getting our hands dirty in some of the actual dying arts of food production. We hoped to prove—at least to ourselves—that a family living on or near green land need not depend for its life on industrial food. We were writing our Dear John letter to a roomie that smells like exhaust fumes and the feedlot.

But sticking it to the Man (whoever he is) may not be the most inspired principle around which to organize one's life. We were also after tangible, healthy pleasures, in the same way that boycotting tobacco, for example, brings other benefits besides the satisfaction of withholding your money from Philip Morris. We hoped a year away from industrial foods would taste so good, we might actually enjoy it. The positives, rather than the negatives, ultimately nudged us to step away from the agribusiness supply line and explore the local food landscape. Doing the right thing, in this case, is not about abstinence-only, throwing out bread, tightening your belt, wearing a fake leather belt, or dragging around feeling righteous and gloomy. Food is the rare moral arena in which the ethical choice is generally the one more likely to make you groan with pleasure. Why resist that?

In Nikos Kazantzakis's novel *Zorba the Greek*, the pallid narrator frets a lot about his weaknesses of the flesh. He lies awake at night worrying about the infinite varieties of lust that call to him from this world; for example, cherries. He's way too fond of cherries. Zorba tells him, Well then, I'm afraid what you must do is stand under the tree, collect a big bowl full, and stuff yourself. Eat cherries like they're going out of season.

75   This was approximately the basis of our plan: the Zorba diet.

Reprinted from *Animal, Vegetable, Miracle: A Year of Food Life* (2007), by permission of HarperCollins, Inc.